OM GANESHA NAMAH

Ganesh is regarded as the deity for astrology. It is through him our minds become more aware and able to move onto higher levels of understanding.

THE

ESSENTIALS

OF

VEDIC

ASTROLOGY

Komilla Sutton

First Published in 1999 by
The Wessex Astrologer Ltd.
PO Box 2751
Bournemouth
BH6 3ZJ
England
Tel/Fax (0)1202 424695
www.wessexastrologer.com

2nd printing 2001

Cover design by Arbuckle and Company, Swindon

Printed and bound by in Great Britain by
Biddles Ltd., Guildford and King's Lynn

A catalogue record for this book is available from The British Library

ISBN 1902405064

FOR

NANIJI

AND

MUM

ABOUT THE AUTHOR

Komilla Sutton started her astrological studies in Bombay, India, with Dr. Ajit Sinha in 1979. She moved to England in 1982 and in the last few years has reached the point where she can devote all her time to astrology. In December 1996 Komilla and Andrew Foss founded The British Association for Vedic Astrology (BAVA), which holds regular meetings and an annual conference attracting speakers from all over the world. As well as running a busy practice numbering hundreds of clients, Komilla teaches Vedic astrology to students in London and Romsey and helps many more students via her correspondence course. She also lectures and holds workshops on Vedic astrology throughout the UK.

Komilla would love to hear from you. Write to her at:

1, Greenwood Close
Romsey
Hants
SO51 7QT
England

Website at www.komilla.com

Other books published by The Wessex Astrologer:

Astrolocality Astrology   - Martin Davis
The Consulation Chart - Wanda Sellar
Karmic Connections - Judy Hall
Patterns of the Past - Judy Hall
You're not a person - just a birthchart - Paul F. Newman

The No Nonsense Guides to Astrology:
Elements and Modes
Progressions
Aspects
Transits

ACKNOWLEDGEMENTS

I'd like to thank the following people for their help and support :

Sally Davis, for her incredible patience in transcribing my tapes and integrating them with my notes to form the structure of this book.

Paul F. Newman, for his beautiful and sensitive artwork, including the Nakshatra Wheel, the picture of Ganesh inside the front cover, and the 27 images of the nakshatras.

My students - wherever they are! Their enthusiasm and challenging questions forced me to look at things from their point of view. Without them this book would probably not have been written.

Margaret Cahill, for editing this book so wonderfully, and for her help and encouragement in bringing out the best in me - and the book.

Jim Cahill, for his support and computer wizardry.

Marjie Neal - for being there.

My brother Kuldip for his continued encouragement and faith in me.

Komilla Sutton   January 1999

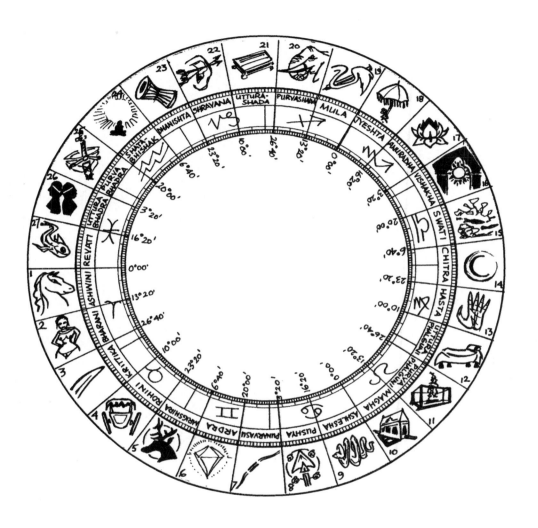

The Nakshatra Wheel

FOREWORD

It has always struck me as odd that, although most astrologers in the world are Indian, so little is known about Indian astrology in the West. That's especially inexplicable in the case of Britain, given this country's long love affair with the Indian subcontinent, and the fact that a substantial group of British visitors to India, such as the theosophists, broke with the stuffy conventions of the Raj and actively studied Hindu philosophy with priests and gurus. We see a few of the early 19th century British astrological magazines flirting with Hindu astrology, but for some reason, although Indian philosophy proved particularly seductive to the western mind, the technical complexities of the sub-continent's astrology were ignored. In fact the impact of Hindu teachings was, through the work of Alan Leo, to take Western astrology in a loose and non-technical direction, widening the gulf between Western and Eastern practices still further. So, while Western astrologers have long had a simple understanding of karma and a familiarity with reincarnation, they have had almost no concept of, for example, planetary periods.

Of course, we in the West have always known that Indian astrology existed. When I joined the Astrological Lodge in the '70s there was always a book by B.V. Raman on the bookstall, and in 1985 the AA asked Jeyar Sekhar to give a day workshop at its Nottingham conference. It was a the rediscovery of the complex practices of Medieval and Classical astrologers after 1985 which awoke astrologers in the English speaking world to a whole new approach to astrology, preparing receptive ground for the first Council for Vedic Astrology in the USA and, since 1997, the British Association for Vedic Astrology.

In India astrology is known as Jyotish, a term whose meaning Komilla explains in her introduction. The word doesn't easily translate into English and writers such as B.V. Raman preferred the simple term Hindu astrology. The name Vedic astrology has been adopted by the West as a label which is at once more recognisable than Jyotish, while avoiding any preconceptions Westerners may have about Hinduism and maintaining the connection between Indian astrology and its spiritual foundations. Although there is little sign of astrology in the Vedas themselves, the sacred texts lay great emphasis on the election of auspicious moments to perform significant rituals, providing the rationale for all subsequent Indian astrology.

Indeed, we might argue that the primary focus of Vedic astrology remains electional: it is estimated that ninety-five percent of Indian marriages are arranged with at least a partial reliance on astrological considerations, an astonishing figure which means that, in view of India's immense population, a substantial proportion of the world's marriages are astrologically elected. True, prediction is central to Vedic astrology, but to what end, we might ask? To arrange the future and to live harmoniously with the cosmos might be the answer. Vedic astrology is essentially a guide for living within a cosmic framework.

Vedic and Western astrology are cousins. They share origins in the third millennium BCE, in the river valleys of Mesopotamia and, we increasingly suspect, in those of Northern India. Two thousand years ago, astrologers in Athens and Rome would have practised a very similar sort of art to those in Varanasi, but since then we have grown apart. Yet, while Westerners have rediscovered the technical astrology of the classical world, it is shorn of its ancient philosophy. Vedic astrology, on the other hand, is still deeply embedded in an extraordinarily rich vision of the human spirit, arises out of an ancient cosmology and is intimately linked to spiritual practices. For all these reasons I welcome Komilla's efforts to educate Westerners in its techniques, traditions and wisdom. Some may wish to become practitioners of Vedic astrology, others merely to familiarise themselves with its basic tenets. Many will be fascinated by a divinatory discipline which is of immense importance simply by virtue of the extent of its use in one of the world's greatest countries.

Nicholas Campion December 1998

Contents

Introduction to the Philosophy of Vedic Astrology

The subject of this book is 'Vedic astrology', but the name itself implies a very Western concept. In India the full name of the science we are about to study is **Jyotish**. The word **jyoti** has several meanings. On a practical level, it means a candle-flame. Symbolically, it means light as the divine principle of life, because when there is no light there is no life - it also means the light that shines down on us from the heavens. The suffix 'sh' means 'best, wisest'. In full then, Jyotish can be translated as 'the science of light' or 'the wisdom of the heavens'. Light banishes darkness, the light of knowledge dispels ignorance.

The majority of people in the West tend to think of astrology in terms of a daily sun-sign column in the newspaper - something quite trivial, not worth exploring further. The ancient sages of India, however, understood the importance of the celestial bodies. It is the study of the planets, the stars and the horizon which is Jyotish; through this we are able to understand more about life and why we were born. In India even today, parents of a new baby will visit an astrologer to see how they can best guide their child in the future. Understanding its destiny means they can encourage the child to develop to its fullest potential and correct purpose in life. The more material questions of wealth and marriage are not usually considered at this point.

The Four Pillars or Purposes

These form the cornerstones of Vedic astrology. They are reflected through the houses of the natal charts:

Dharma is correct action; our duty to others and to ourselves. It is a very spiritual concept and the main thing each person should recognise as the purpose of their life. We should take the right action in life, regardless of the consequences to ourselves. The first, fifth and ninth are the 'dharma' houses.

Artha is the practical purpose of life, action taken with a particular, earthly purpose in mind: your work, your career, financial matters. Artha is goal-orientated. The second, sixth and tenth are 'artha' houses.

Kama represents our desires and needs on a very practical level. When we are born we have desires to motivate us towards progress. Kama is passion - sexual, religious, for life - for a cause. The third, seventh and eleventh are 'kama' houses.

Moksha is enlightenment. It means 'nirvana', giving up the physical life to attain higher consciousness. When we attain moksha we break away from the cycle of birth and death. Moksha is the final purpose of every incarnating soul. The fourth, eighth and twelfth are the 'moksha' houses.

The birth-chart indicates which purposes are to be (or may not be) fulfilled in this lifetime. Some people's lives only have the purpose of kama - of fulfilling desires, whilst others are only concerned with moksha - they don't want to experience passion or the practical things of life; their goal is to find true enlightenment.

The Journey of the Soul

The birth-chart in Vedic astrology is only a small part of the whole, because this lifetime is only one of a multitude of lives - as in a pearl necklace, which is only complete when all the pearls are strung together. Each time the soul reincarnates it brings consciousness into this life. Right from birth the child knows what he or she wants.

How does he know? How does she learn? The answer is inborn. As the child grows he or she becomes more and more aware.

In Vedic literature, the Earth is called **mrityusthana** or 'the place of death' because everything on Earth eventually dies. But with every death there is a rebirth - there is renewal. We see this cycle of life and death in plants every year, every season. In human terms this cycle of life and death and our individual place within it is the most important concept in Vedic astrology. We are part of a greater destiny that we must act out. We fear death because from our perspective life is the only reality, but life is just another experience along the way; understanding this principle is the key to using Vedic astrology with all its insights in your life.

The soul is born into a physical body to enjoy life - but not to become attached to it. The rays of the Sun fall everywhere - on a rubbish heap or in a beautiful garden - but their purity is always intact. It is important to understand right from birth that we will die; this understanding gives us the courage to become detached from our surroundings, to break through the entanglements of earthly life and regain the purity we are in danger of losing when we reincarnate. But the breaking-through can only happen when we become aware that changes need to be made.

The Soul's Progression Through Pain

The soul undergoes all sorts of experiences but it still has to retain its purity. We start to believe that what is actually an illusion is, in fact, reality; the illusion and the reality become confused in our minds and the soul gradually becomes attached to the material world As we move towards a higher consciousness we start to understand that all earthly attachments will be shed when we die. It is a difficult and painful process and the people who have reached a higher level of consciousness are likely to experience more pain than those who haven't. The people who are less aware and don't agonise over the meaning of life tend not to suffer so; this 'live for today' approach is also present in the animal kingdom. We need to stay calm during the periods of pain and realise it is just the shedding of a skin that will lead us to purity within. After all, we have to experience something before we can consciously give it up: the soul has to experience life so that it can finally be given up. Through multiple lives we rid ourselves of desires and attachments until our souls see the light. Vedic astrology is the science of this light.

I feel that many people in the West are moving towards higher consciousness because they've had everything they could, materially. Unfortunately, in India and the East, where poverty is so prevalent, people used to be extremely spiritual but they are now going backwards; in a sense they need to experience the money and material wealth, so they can then choose to give them up.

At every important stage of life, the chart is studied again. Hindus are meant to carry out 'shodasa karmas' (sixteen important functions) in their lives between birth and death: education, marriage, children and so on. We use our understanding of the birth chart and the transiting planets to ensure that each of these is completed at the best time to fulfil our karmic potential. Vedic astrology is not man being controlled by the stars, but man using the stars to enhance his life.

Karma

The law of karma is about choice, not retribution. The word 'karma' literally means 'action'. Every action we take in any lifetime - past, present or future - is our karma. If we can address the issues created by actions in past lives, we give our souls the chance to mature and move towards the ultimate goal of enlightenment. We deal with karma on three levels:

Sanchita karma is the storehouse of actions taken in our previous lives. Every action becomes part of our 'sanchita karma'. It is the karma we are born with and it is the sum total of both the good and bad actions in previous incarnations. Just as we can't change the colour of our eyes, neither can we do anything about sanchita karma. This can be a difficult concept for the Westerner to understand; in the East we accept that some things happen to us because of our actions in past lives. Whether we are robbed or have fantastically good luck, we accept that it has come from past actions. If money comes to you suddenly, maybe someone had an account to settle with you in a past life and it has now been settled. I look at karma as something the person did. Sanchita karma is something that is part of you and which cannot change: actions which, once carried out, cannot be undone.

Prarabdha karma is the karma that we face in this life - the good and the bad together and it is another karma you cannot change. In India we feel we are born to a destiny and we can't change the type of experiences we are going to have. The amount of control we have over our lives is really very small and personal, as can be shown by the impact of natural disasters and accidents. The only way to work with this is to accept that we are part of a cosmic Great Plan. That in itself is very humbling; just like the effects of a 100mph wind, you realise that you can't do anything about it. Prarabdha karma is both negative and positive. Although this chapter may sound somewhat doom-laden to the Westerner everyone has cycles of good and bad experiences; there are always moments to treasure and enjoy that balance out the more difficult times.

Kriyamana karma is the most important of the three. This is the karma that we actually make of our own choice and free will. It is the karma of choosing what to do - if we're angry, how will we react? If we feel victimised, will we change? Kriyamana karma is about how we intend to improve the quality of our lives. You are experiencing kriyamana karma now by reading this book. What you are reading is becoming part of your sanchita karma - your own book of life - and in a future life you will experience it as prarabdha karma. A great deal in Vedic astrology is concerned with understanding this particular karma and the choices we face. By deliberately making the right choices we're not only improving things in this lifetime, but also preventing negative karma from being carried forward; we're raising our consciousness that bit higher.

The Three Gunas or Qualities

Vedic philosophy teaches that creation is the product of a meeting between **Purusha** and **Prakriti** - the male and the female - the soul and the forces of regeneration. The purpose of purusha is to enjoy what prakriti has to offer, while prakriti has to fulfil purusha's desires. When this happens cosmic birth takes place and ahankara comes into being, which is the individual ego, the mind and all the senses.

The pure consciousness of purusha and prakriti is a balance of the three gunas or qualities. With the birth of ahankara that balance is disturbed: the birth of an individual has upset the balance of the universal and we each reflect that disturbed quality in our birth-chart. It is important to understand the impulses (gunas) of the planets, their signs and their nakshatras (lunar mansions), which give us our unique behaviour patterns. The three gunas are:

Sattva: Sattvic qualities are of truth and purity of purpose, of being good and looking for good in others. The path towards enlightenment and higher consciousness is important to sattvic people. They are fearless, generous, tranquil and self-controlled. They have an open mind and find it hard to hurt others. They rise above worldly matters. Vegetarians are sattvic by nature, choosing to eat what is provided by nature rather than kill to satisfy their appetites.
Anything can have these qualities - for example, sattvic food is pure and plain, without spices, whilst tamasic food is fatty and rajasic food is spicy. Water is pure sattva.

Rajas: the quality of taking action, of searching and trying to find new meanings. The ego has rajasic tendencies; it is passionate and ambitious, and has great inner thirst. It is restless, and insecure, and wants to achieve. Rajas is also the quality of dissatisfaction, because rajasic qualities are never satisfied. People with strong rajasic qualities tend to avoid difficult situations - they want worldly success and they want it now! They can be fickle, unreliable, and easily distracted.

Tamas: Tamasic qualities are of darkness and ignorance. People with tamasic qualities embrace the darkness. Maya, the illusory world of self-gratification, ties them to their desires. They are materialistic, sensuous and generally in love with the good things of life. Tamasic people must try very hard to escape the ignorance that surrounds them. Yoga and meditation are needed to strengthen their inner being if they want to move towards higher consciousness.

We each have a combination of the gunas but one will be pre-eminent, and this will be reflected in the natal chart. Each planet, sign and nakshatra represents a quality. I have a lot of tamasic qualities in my chart and I have a tendency to put on weight and be sluggish. I know that I need to follow a plan of action in order to achieve anything. The balance we see in the chart it not an excuse for the way we are, rather, it is a prompt to understand ourselves better. I can look at my birth chart and excuse myself, but that's not always a wise thing to do!

The Principles of Vedic Astrology

Why is it known as 'Vedic' astrology? The Vedas are scriptures that were written in Sanskrit almost 5000 years ago, and are known as **shrutti** because they are revealed to the student by the teacher. They are mantras in the form of poetry, prose and song. They are **samhitas**, compilations.

There are nine **Brahmana granathas**, which are a part of the Vedas. **Brahman** means 'supreme, the ultimate reality'; granatha are books. The four Vedas are always written in this order:

Rig Veda teaches **gyana** - knowledge. A group of forty chapters in the Rig Veda are called the **Aitereya** (which is a brahman, i.e. universal knowledge), written by Mahidas, who was an outcast or foreigner, not a brahman, indicating that new interpretations of the Vedas were welcome.

Yajur Veda deals with karma - action.

Sama Veda teaches **upasana** - meditation or worship

Atharva Veda teaches on a variety of subjects. It is divided into two parts called **shukla** (waxing) and **krishna** (waning); the shukla yajur Veda contains hymns, and the krishna contains their explanations.

The Vedas are at the root of Vedic astrology and any other Vedic science. They were written to sow the seed of a thought which would lead to deeper understanding and a guru (teacher) was needed to explain them. In the Vedas knowledge was, on purpose, only imparted with a great deal of difficulty - anyone seeking knowledge had to be prepared to study very hard. For this reason the gurus - those with knowledge - were respected above everybody else, even above warriors, kings and millionaires. One of the principles emphasised by the teachings is that everyone has his own rate of progression, his own abilities. The student must be allowed to follow the path he thinks is correct and come to an individual conclusion - however much you might want to help, you must not force your thoughts and beliefs on others.

Do try to study the Vedas as they will enhance your understanding of Vedic astrology. All the planets appear as gods or demigods (represented in human form with human weaknesses), and each has his or her own myth. We will be looking at the myths in more detail later, but you also need to explore the Vedas for yourself. But don't feel you need to be in a hurry! As students of Vedic astrology, after all, what we are studying is time. You will absorb many things as you go along; understanding will come as you are ready to receive it. More haste less speed!

The Upanishads

Upanishad means 'to sit near'. Shad also means 'destruction' - the destruction of ignorance. The Upanishads were tales told in the mountains, around the fire at night; great sages used them to teach their listeners about the mysteries of life. The tales aren't based on mythology like the Vedas: they are instead more spiritual and are concerned with the development of higher consciousness. The Vedas are rooted in the everyday world, so that people can identify with the stories of the demigods and put them into the context of their own lives.

There are 108 Upanishads and they are part of the Brahmans and therefore the Vedas. Eleven are considered particularly important: isha, kena, katha, prashna, mundaka, mandukya, taitiriya, aiteriya, chadogya, brihadaranyaka and shvetashvatara. The Vedas and the Upanishads are the main literary sources for Vedic astrology. The three that I would particularly recommend are the Bhagavad Gita, the Rig Veda and the Upanishads. They are not absolutely necessary to begin with but they do help Western students to understand the philosophy behind Vedic astrology. Some people in the West have more knowledge of them than many middle-class Indians. Indeed many of their concepts are now familiar terms in the west - karma, yoga, OM etc.

Vedic Astrology as Vedanga

Veda means 'scripture', 'anga' means 'limb'. Vedic astrology is called vedanga, the limbs that are designed to help the body operate and to help in the interpretation of the Vedas. Vedic astrology is the knowledge of time and its inter-relationship with human life. There are six vedangas:

- **Shiksha** - proper pronunciation and interpretation

- **Chanda** - contemplation

- **Vyakarna** - grammar

- **Nirukta** - ethical explanations of difficult vedic words

- **Jyotisha** - the science of light; astronomy and astrology

- **Sutra** - explanation of rituals, the duties of individuals and institutions. These are further divided into three:

  The **Shrauta** sutras explain the rituals of the Brahmana granthas.

  The **Grihya** sutras are the 16 sacred Sansakars or rituals the Hindu should perform between birth and death (the Shodasa karmas). Knowledge of Vedic astrology is essential for these as the dates for the rituals are 'elected' by looking at the placements of the planets, most especially the Moon and Sun.

  The Dharma sutras explain social responsibilities.

Why Study Vedic Astrology?

The basis of Vedic astrology is the birth-chart - the point at which the soul comes into life and an ego is formed: I, me, myself. The ego takes on a combination of the gunas and is then tied to the five senses; at this point we start relating to ourselves. The whole aim of Vedic astrology, and of life, is to find out how to release ourselves from these ties and reach towards the state of vishnu or brahma, the universal manifestation. We break the connection with this universal energy when we are born and, although the physical body will be different each time, there is a continuity of consciousness. When we die we go back into the universal energy to be reborn. Think of it in terms of the way water changes at different stages in its cycle: it falls to earth as rain, evaporates back into the atmosphere to take on the form of a cloud, and then at some point returns to earth as water. For the cycle of life and death to be completed we have to decide what our life-direction is: whether it is to have our desires satisfied, be a business person, or aim for a more spiritual existence, it will be indicated in the birth chart.

Vedic astrology recognises that as human beings we have a difficult task assigned to us. We have to live our present life and try to relate it to both the past and the future. **Karma phal** - the fruits of our actions - is what we study when we draw up a birth-chart. It can help us answer the difficult questions of existence: how will we reconcile the actions necessary for a successful life in this incarnation, considering the subtle influence exerted by the eternal aspects of life, and again how has the past conditioned our present; can we improve the quality of our future lives by our actions today?

Jyotish works on very deep levels. In this book we will be attempting to understand not only the material and physical side of our lives, but also the subtle, eternal aspects. Your growing knowledge of the fundamental principles will reveal layers of yourself that may previously have been hidden or misunderstood; things that either may delight you, or that maybe you are not ready to deal with yet. Take time. Astrology is a long journey of self-discovery.

Converting your Chart

Understanding the Tropical and Sidereal Zodiacs

The greatest difference between Western and Vedic astrology is that they use different zodiac systems. Western astrology uses the tropical zodiac, which shows the earth's relationship to the Sun, whilst Vedic astrology uses the sidereal zodiac which is concerned with the planets' relationship against a backdrop of the stars. 'Sidereal' actually means stars.

The tropical zodiac uses the vernal (spring) equinox as the beginning of the zodiac - the first point of Aries - and is fixed thus every year. However, this point in the zodiac is not in fact unmoving. Due to the tilt of the earth, when it returns to the same position each year there is approximately 50.3" difference. This is known as the precession of the equinoxes. The Vedic astrologer feels that this difference needs to be taken into account for the equinox point in relation to the stars moves gradually backwards from East to West.

Both tropical and sidereal zodiacs overlapped in 285 AD. Since then the difference between the two has reached 23° 53'. The longitudinal difference between them is known as **ayanamsha**. There are many ayanamshas used by astrologers, the most acceptable one being Lahiri at present running about the same amount behind the tropical zodiac. Thus, according to Vedic astrology, the first degree of Aries in Western astrology is calculated regarded as about 7°0' Pisces.

To construct your Vedic chart you will need to move all the planets on the Western chart backwards by the amount of ayanamsha applicable when you were born. The table on the next page will enable you to convert the planets to their Vedic positions; then you are ready to put them on the chart and get started!

There are two forms of chart in use, so it is really a matter of choice. In the North Indian chart the houses stay where they are and the signs move anti-clockwise, starting at the ascendant in the first house. In the South Indian chart the signs are fixed and are laid out in a clockwise direction. The ascendant sign is often marked with a diagonal line.

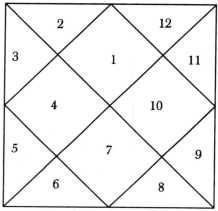

North Indian Style

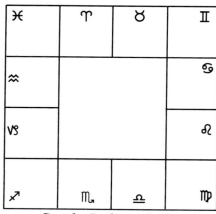

South Indian Style

What both styles of chart have in common is that very little detail is entered on the chart itself; all the planetary data is listed by the side. It is left to the astrologer to work out the aspects!

The easiest way to work out your Vedic chart is by subtracting the degrees of ayanamsha, shown in the year closest to your birth date, from the tropical position of the planets in your Western birth chart; many western computer programmes can work it out exactly for you. As a practical example of absolute precision though, the method of calculating the measurement of ayanamsha for a birth date is shown after the table, using Prince William's chart as an example. Note also that Vedic astrology does not use the outer planets, Uranus, Neptune and Pluto.

Ayanamsha Table

The Lahiri values through the years are :

1st January 1900	22° 27' 55"
1910	22° 35' 45"
1920	22° 44' 37"
1930	22° 52' 35"
1940	23° 01' 16"
1950	23° 09' 28"
1960	23° 17' 53"
1970	23° 26' 21"
1980	23° 34' 31"
1990	23° 43' 14"
2000	23° 51' 11"

Prince William
21st June 1982 21:03 BST (-1:00) London 51N30 00W10

Step one

Referring to the table of ayanamsha we see that Prince William's birth date falls between 1980 and 1990. The ayanamsha in 1980 was 23° 34' 31" and in 1990 was 23° 43' 14" - a difference of 8' 43".

To get the exact difference for the birth date we convert the 8' 43" into seconds:

$$8 \times 60 + 43 = 523 \text{ seconds.}$$

Step two

The difference of ayanamsha over a 10 year period is 523 seconds, so each year would be 52.3 seconds. Prince William was born in 1982, so we need to add two years of ayanamsha to the 1980 ayanamsha :

$$52.3 \times 2 = 104.6 \text{ seconds (divide into minutes and rounded up} = 1 \text{ minute } 45 \text{ seconds)}$$

Step three

The ayanamsha reduction every year is 52.3 seconds. So to find the monthly ayanamsha we divide 52.3 by $12 = 4.358$. Prince William was born in June, so we calculate 5 full months of 1982:

$$4.358 \times 5 = 21.79 \text{ (round up to 22)}$$

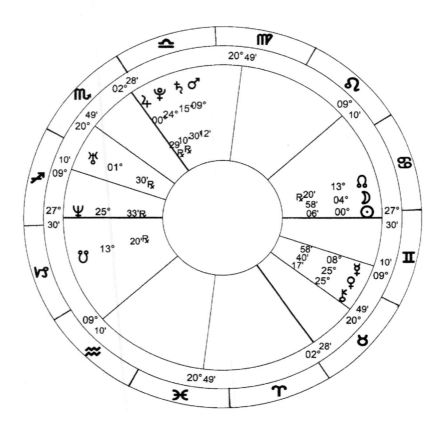

Step four

The ayanamsha of 1 month is 4.358 so to find one day we divide by 30 (as June has 30 days):

4.358 divided by 30 = 0.145

(Another way of doing the ayanamsha calculation for the day is to divide the yearly figure of 52.3 seconds by 365 days - which is 0.143 seconds per day.) Prince William was born on the 21st of June so we need to calculate the ayanamsha of 21 days :

0.145 x 21= 3.045 (rounded down to 3 seconds)

Step five

The amount to be added to the 1980 ayanamsha is:

1 minute 45 seconds for the 2 years

plus 22 seconds for the 5 months

and 3 seconds for the 21 days

.......which equals 2 minutes 10 seconds

Prince William's calculations are :
   1980 plus 2 years, 5 months and 21 days
so his ayanamsha is : 23° 34' 31" + 2' 10" = **23° 36' 41"**

The final stage is to convert William's Western chart to its Vedic equivalent using the amount of ayanamsha calculated:

	Tropical		**Vedic**		
Asc	27° 30'	Sag	03° 53' 19"	Sag	
Sun	00° 06'	Can	06° 29' 19"	Gem	
Moon	04°58'	Can	11° 21' 19"	Gem	
Mars	09°12'	Li	15° 35' 19"	Vir	
Mercury	08°58'	Gem	15° 21' 19"	Tau	
Jupiter (R)	00°29'	Sco	06° 52' 19"	Li	
Venus	25°40'	Tau	02° 03' 19"	Tau	
Saturn	15°00'	Li	21° 53' 19"	Vir	
Rahu (N. Node)	13°20'	Can	20° 28' 19"	Gem	
Ketu (S. Node)	13°20'	Cap	20° 28' 19"	Sag	

Now all that remains is to draw up the Vedic chart in whichever form you prefer. Prince William's is shown in both styles.

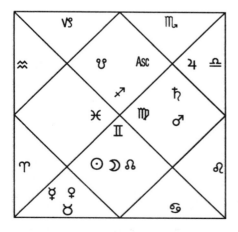

How the Planets Work in Vedic Astrology

Looking at the bigger picture......
In natal astrology we realise that Man has a sphere of activity and a special place in the cosmic law. His individual fortune, his negative and positive karma, the flowering of this life rests on universal law which encompasses past, present and future lives, the mental, spiritual and material realms of existence, the known and the unknown. These mysteries of life are revealed by the celestial bodies in the sky: the planets, which are moving, and the stars (Nakshatras), which are fixed (apparently stationary).

The planets correspond to every aspect of life on earth - the atmosphere, the nature of the seasons, plant and animal life and an individual's destiny. At birth they show which resources will be available to us in this life. Their daily motions and their changing influences through the story of people's lives subtly alter the energies that surround us, thereby changing **our** perception, life direction and focus.

The Sun, Moon and five planets each represent one of the seven levels of consciousness that encase the evolving soul. As they move they express the universal law of time, where nothing is without purpose. They influence Man consciously or unconsciously into recognising this law. They can hinder (malefic) or help (benefic). When malefic they cause problems, damming the flow of natural energies. When benefic they promote higher thought and facilitate progress in life.

To study the influence of the planets is to know your own strengths and weaknesses. By accepting restrictions, you can learn to act in harmony with the universal law as it is uniquely laid down for each individual in the birth-chart; you will thus be able to enhance your quality of life.

Vedic astrology uses the Sun and the Moon (known together as the luminaries), five planets - Mars, Mercury, Jupiter, Venus and Saturn, and the nodes of the Moon (known as Rahu Ketu). The heavenly bodies are called **grahas** in Sanskrit while Rahu Ketu are known as **Chayya grahas** (shadow planets) as they are the points on the ecliptic where the path of the Moon crosses that of the Sun and at which eclipses therefore take place.

Unlike modern Western astrology, we don't use the more recently discovered outer planets Uranus, Neptune and Pluto. We **do** however use what western astrology calls 'the fixed stars' or nakshatras.

The Basics

First I want to cover some basics about the planets as their energies are regarded somewhat differently in Vedic astrology. The planets have four roles to fulfil in a natal chart:

•   Their own energies.

•   Their role as the rulers of houses. The Sun and Moon rule one sign each, therefore they will rule one house of the chart. Mars, Mercury, Jupiter, Venus and Saturn rule two signs each, so they also rule two houses each. Rahu Ketu do not rule any houses.

•   Their role as karakas or significators. Each planet signifies certain things; for example, the Sun signifies the father, government, monarchy, people in authority and Jupiter signifies husband, sons, teacher or gurus. If you wanted to know more about your father you would look at the Sun in the chart as well.

•   Their rulership of periods of our lives (called dashas). The dashas run consecutively, vary in length and are each ruled by one planet:

The Sun	6 years
The Moon	10 years
Mars	7 years
Rahu	18 years
Jupiter	16 years
Saturn	19 years
Mercury	17 years
Ketu	7 years
Venus	20 years

We may not experience all the dashas during the one lifetime, but most of us experience at least five. If we are born during Rahu or Jupiter dashas the consecutive dasha covers long periods of our life whereas if you are born in the Sun dasha, the following ones are of a shorter duration.

The planets will also affect various times of our life due totheir rulership of the bhukti or antar dasha (sub-dasha) and prayantara dasha (sub-sub dasha). At any given time there are usually three planets affecting the quality of our life. Their position by sign, house and aspect will determine the focus of your life during that particular planetary period.

Planetary Characteristics

It really is important to have a thorough knowledge of planetary dispositions when you are embarking on chart interpretation. The way the planets work with each other reflects human relationships: in the same way that we have different feelings for people in our lives the planets also work in harmony or enmity with each other. If planets have a naturally difficult relationship with each other it is called an enemy relationship. Others relate to each other very well so they are considered to be friends. There are some planets which can be friends at times and enemies at others, and also those that have neutral relationships with each other. There is a duality in the way that the planets relate to each other and the manner in which they do this at different times reflects how they are going to influence life. In chart interpretation we need to consider their natural disposition and their 'temporary' one. Just as in real life we sometimes have to befriend those we may dislike or distrust, in Vedic astrology the planets may adapt their relationship to suit the circumstances - and it is vital for the student to master this basic principle. **There are always dual principles at work.** You do not interpret just what you see on the surface. Here are some aspects of duality you need to be aware of :

The exaltation and debilitation

Increasing and decreasing cycles

Permanent and temporary relationships

Malefics and benefics- natural and functional

Dik Bala or Directional Strength

The aspects the planets make with each other

These relationships are shown in the physical characteristics of the chart but are also concerned with the time dimension of Vedic charts, the dasha system. How these planets integrate in the chart and their relative strengths and weaknesses will show how you will be affected by the dashas.

Exaltation and Debilitation
In certain signs of the zodiac the planets are considered to be in their optimum position. This is known as being in 'exaltation'. Opposite this is the sign of debilitation, where the planet is at its weakest. In Vedic astrology there are degrees of exaltation and debilitation and these are used to determine the strength of the planet - where it gives its best or worst effects. The strength of the planet reduces as it moves from exaltation to debilitation and increases from the debilitated point to its exaltation point. This is like a waxing and waning of the planetary energies. Exaltation and debilitation

are not nasty or even necessarily difficult. In its sign of exaltation the planet gives of its best - its natural good qualities are especially strong. It behaves well. In its sign of debilitation the planet's natural good qualities are especially weak and cannot assert themselves. It struggles. However, a planet which seems debilitated at first glance in your chart may have achieved a 'cancellation from debilitation'. For more on this refer to the Neechabangha Raja section in the Yogas chapter.

There is another important position which is called **Mooltrikona**. This is a range of degrees where the planet functions well and is strong but not so much as at its point of exaltation. Any planet placed in the sign it rules is also considered to be strong.

The strength of the planets through exaltation, rulership and mooltrikona tells us a lot about our insight into the mysteries of life, and our quest for higher knowledge. As the soul passes through various lifetimes, it acquires strengths and weaknesses which then become the pivot of the current life and this is shown in the birth chart. If planets are in exaltation, mooltrikona or their own signs it indicates a great maturity of the soul. Debilitated planets indicate the areas where maturity has to be gained and obstacles faced so that latent faculties can come to the fore.

Rahu Ketu are exalted in Taurus/ Scorpio and debilitated in Scorpio/ Taurus respectively. They are also exalted in Gemini and Virgo.

Increasing and decreasing cycle
The increasing or decreasing cycle of the planets can be compared to the waxing and waning of the Moon. Planets are on the **increasing** stage of the cycle when they are located somewhere between their debilitation and exaltation points. They are on a **decreasing** cycle between their exaltation and debilitation points. This process highlights the gradual strengthening or weakening of the planetary energies and is very important when you study the divisional charts where no degrees are involved.

Planets in Exaltation and Debilitation

Planet	Exaltation	Mooltrikona	Debilitation	Sign r/ship
Sun	10° Aries	4°-20° Leo	10° Libra	Leo
Moon	3° Taurus	4°-20° Taurus	3° Scorpio	Cancer
Mars	28° Cap.	0°-12° Aries	28° Cancer	Aries Scorpio
Mercury	15° Virgo	16°-20°Virgo	15° Pisces	Gemini Virgo
Jupiter	5° Cancer	0°-10° Sag.	5° Cap.	Sag. Pisces
Venus	27° Pisces	0°-15° Libra	27° Virgo	Taurus Libra
Saturn	20° Libra	0°-20° Aq.	20° Aries	Cap. Aq.

Natural Planetary Relationships

Each planet has friendship, enmity or a neutral relationship with the other six planets. The rulers of the signs which are second, fourth, fifth, eighth, ninth, and twelfth from the mooltrikona sign of the planets will be friendly. Rulers of the signs other than the above are enemies. In the case of planets ruling more than one sign, if they have a friendly as well as an inimical relationship, they become neutral.

Planetary Relationships

Planet	Friends	Neutral	Enemies
Sun	Moon, Mars Jupiter	Mercury	Venus, Saturn
Moon	Sun, Mercury	Mars, Jupiter, Venus, Saturn	No enemies
Mars	Sun, Moon, Jupiter	Venus, Saturn	Mercury
Mercury	Sun, Venus	Mars, Jupiter, Saturn	Moon
Jupiter	Sun, Moon, Mars	Saturn	Mercury, Venus
Venus	Mercury, Saturn	Mars, Jupiter	Sun, Moon
Saturn	Venus, Mercury	Jupiter	Sun, Moon, Mars
Rahu Ketu	Mercury, Venus, Saturn	Mars	Sun, Moon, Jupiter

Temporary Relationships

These relationships are subject to change because of the positioning of planets in the natal chart. The planets situated in the second, third, fourth, tenth, eleventh, and twelfth houses from each other become temporary friends. The others become enemies. Temporary relationships reflect the changes which take place in the temperament of the planets in each individual chart. Each planet will modify its behaviour according to its relationship with the others at time of birth; for example a malefic planet like Saturn may become a benevolent influence, in which case its energies will help rather than hinder. On the other hand a benefic planet like Jupiter can be placed negatively and would lose some of its good qualities and create problems.

The main area where these relationships are useful is the position of planets in signs. If the sign they are placed in becomes temporary friends or enemies then the planet placed within the sign will react accordingly. This influence will further reflect how the planets discharge their responsibility as rulers of signs and karakas. For example: if the Sun is placed in an enemy sign of Saturn (Capricorn or Aquarius), the Sun's significations - Atmakaraka (self), father, authority etc. will be affected. This indicates you may have problems understanding your inner self, and dealing with your father and authority figures in general. If the Sun rules the fifth house, the significations of the fifth house, children and creativity will also be adversely affected. But if in the natal chart the Sun and Saturn are positively placed in relation to each other and become temporary friends, then the quality of the Sun's behaviour will improve. The Sun in Capricorn or Aquarius will still give problems but in this instance, due to its temporary relationship with Saturn, you will able to deal with the problems.

Compound Relationships
This relationship is formed by combining the natural and temporary relationships. There are five relationships which are formed thus: very friendly, neutral, inimical, very inimical.

Natural		Temporary		Aggregate
Friendship	+	Friendship	=	Great friendship
Neutral	+	Friendship	=	Friendship
Enmity	+	Enmity	=	Great enmity
Neutral	+	Enmity	=	Enmity
Enmity	+	Friendship	=	Neutral

Planetary Strengths from Relationships
Exaltation, debilitation and the range from friendship to enmity add up to nine possible statuses for one planet in any natal chart. Planets

give the best results when located in their exaltation signs. They are at their weakest in a debilitated sign so have the capacity to give extremely negative results. There are two percentage scales to show how this works:

Positive Strength the planets

Exaltation 100%
Mooltrikona 75%
Own sign 50%
Great Friends 37.5%
Friends 25%
Neutrals 12.5%
Enemy 6.25%
Great enemy 3.25%
Debilitation 0%

Negative Strength of the planets

Debilitation 100%
Great enemy 75%
Enemy 50%
Neutral 37.5%
Friends 25%
Great friends 12.5%
Own sign 6.25%
Mooltrikona 3.25%
Exaltation 0%

Natural Malefics and Benefics

Malefic planets are the planets that cause problems and create obstacles. Benefics enhance the quality of life. They improve the qualities of the house they are located in. However, malefic planets usually operate well when located in malefic houses because the house restricts their energies:

Malefic Planets: Sun, Waning Moon, Mars, Saturn , Rahu Ketu
Benefic Planets: Waxing Moon, Jupiter and Venus
Neutral: Mercury - Mercury takes on the disposition of the planet it is placed with.

Functional Benefics and Malefics

So far we've only looked at the natural tendencies of planets, but obviously their characteristics change according to the time of birth. Planets change their nature depending on the ascendant and the houses they rule. The basic rules regarding functional malefics and benefics are :

• Planets that rule trine houses (1, 5, 9,) are always benefic.

- Planets that rule the kendra houses (4, 7, 10) are benefic if they are natural malefics. Natural benefics ruling kendra houses become malefic.

- Planets that rules malefic houses (3, 6, 11,) are always malefic.

- Rulers of the 2nd, 8th and 12th houses are functionally neutral.

The planet that rules the ascendant is always benefic even if it rules a malefic house, as in the case of Libra and Taurus rising. For Libra, its ruler also rules Taurus (which will be in the eighth house). For Taurus, Venus rules the malefic sixth house (Libra). Venus would be considered benefic for both these ascendants. In case of dual rulership of a sign, the planet acts like its mooltrikona sign - so for instance Mercury, which rules both Gemini and Virgo, would act more as if it was in Virgo. (Refer to the table further back if you're not sure about this.) Another example: Saturn rules the eighth and ninth house in the case of a Gemini ascendant. The eighth house is the most difficult house and the ninth is the best house in the zodiac. Saturn's mooltrikona is situated in Aquarius, which rules the ninth house. So Saturn, the greatest malefic will give very good results for Gemini rising.

Dik bala or directional strength
Planets gain strength when they are placed in certain houses of the chart. This is known as Dik bala or directional strength. The planets are strong in certain directions so if at time of birth they are in the same direction they get added strength. Again if they are placed in opposition to the point where they are strong, they can become weak. Note that all the planets get their directional strength in the **cardinal** houses and directions. If you have a planet placed in its directional strength you could use that energy positively by re-locating your home in that direction. Front doors facing East and North, the powerful directions for Jupiter and Venus, are considered auspicious.

The Directional Strength of the planets :

Planet	Direction	House
The Sun	South	10th house
The Moon	North	4th house
Mars	South	10th house
Mercury	East	1st house
Jupiter	East	1st house
Venus	North	4th house
Saturn	West	7th house

Planetary Aspects

We recognise that the position of any planet in a chart causes it to have particular influence on other parts of the chart. There are two main rules for aspects:

• The aspect is to the whole sign, not just to one part of it (totally unlike western astrology). So Saturn at 14° Aries is opposite and aspecting the whole of the sign of Libra; it will aspect any planets anywhere in the house occupied by Libra.

• Planets only cast forward aspects: that is, on around the zodiac from the sign they are in (like Saturn in Aries to Libra; if Mars were in Virgo, the aspect would be from Mars to Saturn by the eighth house aspect of Mars, not Saturn to Mars). Some authorities have suggested that planets moving retrograde must cast their aspects backwards through the signs. I have occasionally found this to be true of Mars and Saturn, but you might like to draw your own conclusions as you study more charts.

All planets cast a 100% aspect on the seventh sign away from themselves - the percentages here are taken from the planetary strengths table shown earlier.

This list shows the other aspects:

Sun	7th house
Moon	7th house
Mars	4th, 7th, 8th houses
Mercury	7th house
Jupiter	5th, 7th, 9th houses (these will be in the same element)
Saturn	3rd, 7th, 10th houses
Rahu	5th, 7th, 9th houses
Ketu	5th, 7th, 9th houses

Note: we always count the house where the planet is located as the first house. Some minor aspects are also used. (That is, taking those above as representing 100%, aspects from 75% to as little as 25%.) I would only use minor aspects when looking into a particular chart very deeply indeed. For all normal purposes use only the 100% aspects.

Some special aspects:

Conjunction
This occurs when any two or more planets are in the same sign of the zodiac. Planets which are conjunct always influence each other, but the exact nature of that exchange depends on their individual nature and whether they are friends or enemies. Mercury always takes on the characteristics of the other planet when it is in a conjunction.

Yudh bala: warlike conjunction
This state of war occurs when two planets are within one whole degree of each other and the planet at the lower degree will win: that is, it will take over the energy of the other planet for its own aims. If Saturn is at 7° 10' Capricorn and Mercury is at 7° 18' Capricorn, they are less than one degree apart and are in yudh bala. Saturn is at the lower degree so it will take Mercury's energy and as a result Mercury, and whatever it represents in the chart, will lack energy and be weak. The Moon is not considered in this aspect.

Retrograde Motion

When viewed from the Earth, all the planets except the Sun and the Moon go through periods when, to the observer, they seem to slow down and thus move backwards, before eventually speeding up and returning to their normal direction around the zodiac. These periods of 'retrograde' motion are just taken from the Earth's perspective - they are not a physical phenomenon. However, in Jyotish retrograde planets are seen as having symbolic importance: they are interpreted as strong; and their normal exaltations and debilitations are reversed so that a planet in its sign of debilitation is exalted if retrograde and one in its sign of exaltation is debilitated if retrograde. Some authorities say that the retrograde planets cast a 'hind sight'. A planet is shown to be retrograde on a vedic chart by 'R' after its symbol. The Rahu Ketu axis always moves retrograde.

The Navgraha, or the nine planets in daily life

The planets and Rahu Ketu are known collectively as **Nav Graha** and are part of the daily rituals of Indian life. There are temples in India for the various planets where prayers are performed. A special prayer for the Nav graha (the Nav graha puja) is performed to keep their energies happy. People in India wear rings or pendants studded with jewels of the Nav graha to balance their energies. Each planet has an important practical and spiritual role to play in life. Stories in the Vedas and the Upanishads describe their characteristics. Becoming familiar with these myths leads to a better understanding of their powers and how they can affect us individually. We have used the **Navgraha Yantra,** a mandala symbolising the planets, on our cover. Each planet has a special combination of numbers and when combined they represent the energy of all the planets. This yantra would be used in Navgraha puja.

Each day in the week is ruled by a different planet with its name affixed to **Vaar,** the word for 'day':

Ravivaar	Sun's day	Brihaspativaar	Jupiter's day
Somvaar	Moon's day	Shukravaar	Venus' day
Mangalvaar	Mars' day	Shanivaar	Saturn's day
Budhvaar	Mercury's day		

The days of the week are also combined with the lunar phases and the nakshatras to harness the planetary energy to its optimum. The Sun, Moon and planets are traditionally referred to in this order. The list also shows that on specific days particular planetary energies are more dominant; you would strengthen a weak planet by fasting or performing the relevant rituals on its special day. As Mars and Saturn are considered malefic planets, auspicious activities are never performed on those days. The word 'auspicious' is used frequently in Vedic astrology; it means that you would plan activities (marriage, festivals and travelling, for example) for a time when they are most likely to succeed. There are a couple of exceptions in that you **can** move house on a Saturday, and Tuesday is considered fine for surgical operations even though it has the Mars connection.

The Sun and Moon

The Sun: Surya

The Sun is vital to our existence. Without its energy to warm us, we would not be here; the Sun exerts the gravitational pull that holds the planets of the solar system together. It is pivotal to our life here. Surya represents the eternal soul. The Sun is **purusha**, the male polarity of the life force.

  The Sun is sattvic in quality which gives it a purity but it is considered malefic - that is, it brings difficulties. Because it is fiery, it has to stand alone. According to the Vedic myths, although the Sun was desperate to be married his wife left him. He had to have some of his brightness reduced by the Creator before she would return and even then he was too hot to enjoy a proper marital relationship!

The Facts
The Sun rules **Leo**
It rules nakshatras **Krittika** **Uttara Phalguni** **Uttara Ashadha**
It is a **malefic** and is **male**
Guna: **sattvic**
Karakas: **your father, government, royalty, ruling powers, places of worship, prana, self, soul.**

As we know, the Sun signifies the father, authority and vitality. If you have a strong Sun you are likely to be an authoritative person, and feel happy and harmonious within. Your inner and outer selves would be in harmony. You would have a good relationship with your father (here you also have to look at planetary conjunctions which, with Saturn and/or Rahu, would mean issues to be worked out with your father). A very strong Sun can lead to you being too authoritarian and unable to change your way of life, expecting everyone else to revolve around you. Others might find it hard to get close to you.

A strong Sun in the natal chart suggests a mature soul and a highly developed consciousness.

An average strength of Sun indicates that you are learning to deal with your soul lessons; you may feel at times that your inner self is not always in harmony with your outer self and that might create problems for you. You would be working towards your goals even though doubt and indecision sometimes might make it difficult for you.

A weak Sun shows the lack of paternal influence in your life. You may not be separated from your father but there could be an emotional distance between you. There might be a lack of vitality and inner power. This lifetime will be about learning solar lessons. You will always feel there is more to life than you are experiencing and that you are missing out in some way, but don't allow yourself to be negative about this. Enhance your solar energy by using appropriate colours - yellow or red are good - and by positive

Strengths

Strong in **Leo**

Exaltation
10° Aries

Mooltrikona
4 - 20° Leo

Friends' Houses
Cancer
Scorpio
Sagittarius
Pisces

Strong in these houses:
3rd, 6th, 11th but strongest in the **10th**

Neutral

In **Gemini** and **Virgo**

Will have strengths and weaknesses in the **1st, 2nd, 5th, 7th, 9th** and **12th** houses

Weaknesses

Debilitation
10° Libra

Enemies are:
Taurus
Capricorn
Aquarius

Weak in the **4th** house

thinking. Living in warm climates, activating your vitality with herbs or vitamins will help, as will doing Surya Namashkar (which is the yoga salutation to the Sun) every morning. Practise pranayama or breathing exercises. This life will bring karma from past lives which reflects the need to work on your Solar karma. By being conscious of it, you will be able to deal successfully with this difficult energy. Because the Sun brings light into our life it signifies the right eye; thus a weak Sun might lead to problems with the eyes. It rules the East and moves only in a forward motion.

Dina - the Solar Day
The Indian solar day lasts from sunrise to sunrise, so that Sunday lasts from sunrise on Sunday morning to sunrise on Monday morning. The solar day is divided into hora: twelve divisions of day and twelve divisions of night which vary in length according to the seasons. Hora shastra is another word for Jyotish, the study of astrology. Each hora has a planetary ruler, beginning with the planet whose day of the week it is.

Masa - the Solar Month: lasts 30 solar days, or the Sun's transit from 0 - 30° of one sign.

Varsha - the Solar Year
A solar year represents the Sun's transit around the 360° of the ecliptic through the 12 signs of the zodiac. It begins at 0° Capricorn and is divided into two parts, known as **ayanas**. At 0° Capricorn the Sun begins its northerly course (as witnessed also in the solstice in the Northern hemisphere) and is known as **Uttaryana**: this continues until the last degree of Gemini. From 0° Cancer to the last degree of Sagittarius, the Sun now in the Northern hemisphere takes a southerly course, known as **Dakshinayana**. During the Sun's transit through Uttarayana its light is bright, its energies pristine and strong. This period is always selected when choosing a suitable time for auspicious activities. Dakshinayana is also known as **Yamaayana**- the period ruled by Yama, the god of death. Solar energy is considered depleted and the Sun's rays defective. Dakshinayana is not a good time to begin new ventures.

Combustion

Planets in conjunction with the Sun are described as 'combust' - burning with solar fire. Of course, Mercury and Venus orbit close to the Sun all the time so they are thought better able to survive being combust than the other planets. The energy of the other planets is burnt out by close contact with the Sun. The degrees within which a particular planet is considered combust are:

Moon	12
Mars	17
Mercury	13
Jupiter	11
Venus	9
Saturn	15

Among other things the Sun represents courage, power, fame, health, healing, fame, success, politicians, heads of state, leaders and commanders.

The Moon: Chandrama or Soma

The Moon is the agent of the Sun; it does not act independently. It reflects the Sun's life-giving force onto the Earth. The Sun gives life to the whole universe but the Moon gives life on earth. The Moon is **prakriti** - the female regenerative principle, compared to the Sun's purusha. Both polarities are needed to create life. In Vedic literature one of the personas of the Moon is Soma who is a **god** not a goddess, but it has a feminine energy. The Moon is the cosmic Mother. With water it nurtures and encourages growth in all living creatures, regardless of their nature. It controls nature, life and death, birth and rebirth. Thus it has the capacity to destroy life as well as sustain it.

In Vedic astrology the Moon reflects the total mind - the intellect too is considered an integral part of it. When the Moon is strongly placed, it lends a potency to the horoscope. A strong mind can override many of life's difficulties. The Moon waxes and wanes and its many shades are reflected in our psyche; it can take us to the highest pinnacles of thought and give us the ability to conquer our worldly desires, but it can also deprive us of light, leaving us to live in ignorance, governed by the desires and passions of animal instinct. Purity of mind is essential in the pursuit of spiritual realisation.

The Moon is the most important planet in Jyotish. It is used as an ascendant in its own right and all transits are calculated from the position of the Moon. To use it in this way we rotate the chart until the Moon is in the first house - then all the other planets can be seen in relation to it. (Refer to the chapter on Sudharshana for more information on this). The Moon's natal position decides your planetary periods and the major influences you will face.

As a reflection of the Sun (the soul) it represents the physical embodiment of our lives - the ebb and flow of our feelings, our

The Facts
The Moon rules **Cancer**
It rules nakshatras: **Rohini** **Hasta** **Shravana**
In its waxing phase the Moon is **benefic** and in waning is **malefic.**
It is **female**
Guna: **sattvic**
Karakas: **Mother** and the **mind**

34

emotions and our needs which change on a daily basis. The Moon's position within the nakshatras determines the life cycles we are to experience, and in representing the womb, it shows what our past life was about and the specific issues we will bring into this life. Its main work, however, is on the material level. In the Vedas the Moon god likes to enjoy life. He has 27 wives (the nakshatras)! Enjoyment of the material world is not seen as bad in itself; the problem is becoming too attached to material things.

The Lunar Cycle

When the Moon is conjunct the Sun it is called a new moon. Travelling 13° 20' a day it takes 2¼ days to transit one house or zodiac sign (30°). It circles the whole ecliptic and returns to its original position in 27 days. Of course, the Sun has been moving too, so the Moon then needs another 2½ days to catch up with it for another new Moon. Thus the period from one new Moon to the next is 29½ days - a lunar month. It is divided into two fortnights known as **pakshas**:

The waxing phase of **Shukla paksha** - the bright half of the Moon from new Moon to the full - is a more outgoing expression of energy and is thought of as easier. When the Moon is 180° away from the Sun we have a full Moon - a good time with the mind in full bloom, a period which continues for five days into the second phase.

Strengths
Strong in **Cancer**

Exaltation
3° Taurus

Mooltrikona
0 - 20° Taurus

Friends' Houses
Gemini
Leo
Virgo

Strong in **5th, 9th** and **11th** houses, but strongest in the **4th**

The Moon is **strong** when it is 72° away from the Sun.

Neutral
In **Aries, Sagittarius** and **Pisces**

Will have strengths and weaknesses in:
1st, 2nd and 3rd houses

Weaknesses
Debilitation
3° Scorpio

The Moon is **weak** when it is less than 72° away from the Sun.

Enemies: **Capricorn** and **Aquarius**

Shows emotional turmoil in **6th, 8th** and **12th**; weak in the **10th** house

---

The waning phase of **Krishna paksha** - the dark half of the Moon, from the full moon to the new moon, produces inward-looking and difficult attributes which continue for the first five days of the waxing phase when the Moon has not yet found its own light.

Tithi - the Lunar Day

The Sun and the Moon separate by 12° every day. This interval is known as a lunar day or a **Tithi**. A lunar month of 30 days has 30 tithis. In the Indian almanac these are always represented by numbers from 1 (the first day) to 15 (the full moon), then from number 1 again to 14. The darkest night of the lunar month is known as **Amavasya** - it is represented by number 30, when the Sun and Moon are at the same longitude again.

Tithis have different meanings as well as different ruling deities. Prayers to a personal god would always be offered on the appropriate day; tithis are also taken into account when casting a chart for a particular event, but as it's a fairly advanced technique I am leaving it for my next book!

The Moon in the Horoscope

The waxing Moon is considered benefic and the waning Moon malefic in the natal chart, so it is important to know the phase of your Moon at birth. It indicates your emotional make-up and how you will react to its changing energies - the waxing Moon is more outgoing, while the waning Moon is introspective.

The Moon representation of the mother also shows the relationship she will have with her offspring - her natural instinct is to nurture her child and this relationship inevitably has a powerful influence in later life.

A strong Moon would give you the ability to deal with the practical issues of life at the same time as allowing for spiritual growth. It is likely that your mother was able to help you through the traumas and dramas of childhood by providing security and a sense of well-being, but again any conjunctions to Saturn and/or Rahu must be considered here.

An average Moon shows the usual struggles both internally, mentally, and with one's mother. You might have a relationship with her that is both strong and difficult. Your mind too could swing between a positive then a negative outlook.

A weak Moon usually shows disenchantment with life. The inability to come to terms with circumstances can lead to negativity and depression. It can also show disenchantment with the material side of life. The Moon, as controller of life, is very important and its weakness can lead to difficult relationships as well - usually a weak Moon is connected to a difficult relationship with your mother.

A weak Moon can be strengthened through meditation or contemplation. Emotionally you are very vulnerable and should try never to over-stress yourself. A weak Moon reflects agitation and little peace of mind. Try to live in calm surroundings with peaceful music. White is the colour for the Moon, so clothes and rooms which reflect this would work well - a yearly retreat in peaceful surroundings would also help.

Among other things the Moon represents travel, water, blood, emotions, liquids, gardening, nurturing, changes, milk, farming and fisheries, anything to do with the sea, and any business trading in alcohol.

Grahas - The Planets

Mars: Kartika - also known as Mangala or Kuja

The first myth regarding Mars is suitably warlike and dramatic and concerns **Lord Shiva**. The demon **Taraka** was terrorising the world and consequently subjugating the gods, who knew that he could only be destroyed by the seven day-old son of Lord Shiva. As Lord Shiva had no intention of fathering a child, **Kamadeva,** the god of love, shot an arrow from his quiver towards the meditating Lord Shiva with the hope of arousing him and collecting his semen. When he realised what was happening Shiva became angry; opening his third he eye burnt Kamadeva to a cinder, but the gods had succeeded in their mission. The resulting semen was so hot that it had to be cooled in the river Ganges. The Krittikas (the six stars making up Krittikas nakshatra) were bathing in the Ganges at the time and became collectively impregnated with Shiva's seed - this led directly

> **The Facts**
>
> Mars rules **Aries** and **Scorpio**
>
> It rules nakshatras:
> **Mrigsira**
> **Chitra**
> **Dhanishta**
>
> It is a **malefic** and is **male**
>
> Guna: **tamasic**
>
> Karakas: **brothers, courage**

to the birth of Kartika, who killed the demon when he was just seven days old. This myth shows the strength of Mars.

The second story features Kartika and his brother Ganesh; in it they both vie for the chance to get married. Ganesh used his mind to win over both the brides chosen for the sons by their parents **Shiva** and **Parvati** - Kartika was left alone and never did get married. He went into the Himalayas to meditate and live a life of austerity. This story shows another side of the Martian nature: it is passionate, it thirsts for relationships but is always being disappointed in love.

Mars is a male planet and the only one of the Vedic planets to be concerned with action. War is his dharma - it is what he was born to do. He does not recognise danger. His duty is to defend, and he is the commander-in-chief of the planetary cabinet. Mars always represents prowess, courage, valour, immense strength and physical stamina. He has the capacity to achieve whatever goals he is set. Mars has the capacity to control nature's forces.

Mars is strong in the tenth house. He is the significator of brothers in a natal chart. Recently it has been suggested that Mars represents sexual relationships in Vedic astrology, but traditionally he has not signified the men in a woman's chart. However Mars is considered malefic - that is, he creates difficulties in life. Mars indicates accidents, injury and violence. Because he strives towards the unattainable, Mars has a strong connection with spiritual realisation and the search for

Strengths

Strong in **Aries** and **Scorpio**

Exaltation
28° Capricorn

Mooltrikona
0 - 12° Aries

Friends' Houses:
Leo
Sagittarius
Pisces

Strong in these houses:
3rd, 6th and 11th but strongest in the **10th**

Neutral

In **Aquarius, Taurus** and **Libra**

Will have strengths and weaknesses in:
1st, 2nd, 5th, 7th, 8th 9th and **12th** houses

Weaknesses

Debilitation
28° Cancer

Enemies are:
Gemini
Virgo

Weak in the **4th** house, but also considered weak for relationships in **7th**, **8th** and **12th** houses

truth. Martian courage is required in plenty if we are to move towards a path of self-realisation. This is always a difficult path to choose, and many obstacles and restrictions have to be faced for which courage is a prerequisite.

Not surprisingly Mars is the planet of energy, courage and action. A strong Mars will make you very action-orientated and can enable you to pursue a goal with great single-mindedness - it is important to use this power in a positive way as you can easily dominate others. Mars as the karaka of brothers would indicate a good relationship with them. You are also likely to have courage and strength in abundance. Here it is important to note that a strong Mars placed in the seventh house can result in you becoming very fiery, militant and dominating in a relationship. This particular planet can cause many problems if it is too strong - try using white and other cool colours and soothing music to calm it down.

A weak Mars shows the existence of issues about strength and is likely to dissipate its energy in too many directions. It shows a latent energy seeking expression in the outer world. I have Mars in debilitation and too close to the Sun in my chart and I have always found difficulty expressing this energy. If I don't plan an exercise programme or find positive ways of stimulating my trapped energy it causes me problems; it also renders me passive and too calm. Additionally, if a debilitated Mars is placed in the seventh house it could bring up issues within relationships.

A weak Mars can be activated through planned exercise - preferably outside the home so you can't get out of it too easily! Learn to focus on the task at hand without becoming diverted by distractions. The colour red also helps to energise Mars, as will taking certain tonics and vitamins.

Mars is associated with muscles, action, passion, science, anger, passions, blood pressure, cruelty, confidence, the police, dictators, surgeons, mining and geology; maths and computing; estate agents and property dealers; athletics and other sports.

Mercury: Buddha

Mercury represents pure intellect. With the Sun and Moon it forms the basis of life, the essential requisites of consciousness:

> **atma** - Sun - soul
> **manas** - Moon - mind
> **buddhi** - Mercury - intellect

Their combination makes **Ahankar**, the individual ego.

Mercury is the child of the Moon and Jupiter's wife **Tara** (star). The Moon, as the god **Soma**, seduced Tara away from Jupiter. She was no longer interested in Jupiter's rituals and purity and became attracted to Soma's worldliness. When Jupiter heard about his wife's elopement he wanted her back, but Tara refused to return so he threatened war. The war that ensued had the gods siding with Jupiter and the demons siding with Soma. Immense destruction resulted and Brahma, the creator, realising that the end of the world was near, forced Tara to go back to her husband; not before the damage was done however, as Tara had already conceived Mercury during her relationship with the Moon. Jupiter rejected the child at the beginning, but Mercury's charm soon won him over!

> **The Facts**
>
> Mercury rules **Gemini** and **Virgo**
>
> It rules nakshatras
> **Ashlesha**
> **Jyeshtha**
> **Revati**
>
> It can be a **benefic** or **malefic** depending on its position in the chart and is **androgynous**
>
> Guna: **rajasic**
>
> Karakas: **intellect, childhood, speech**

The story of Mercury's birth reflects the need for purity and godliness (the wife is considered the greatest symbol of purity in India) to experience both sides of human nature. However spiritual you are, you still need to experience different aspects of life; in the story Tara's purity is defiled by her contact with the Moon, comparable to the soul's entanglement in the web of material desires and illusion. However, from the contact of the pure soul with the world of matter and the emotional mind, intellect is born.

Mercury is the son of the Moon, the rational and intellectual part of consciousness. The Moon is the sub-conscious mind. Mercury is the rational, practical, conscious mind but it is still only a fragment of total consciousness. What Mercury perceives as reality is only a small part of outer manifestation.

Mercury orbits close to the Sun. Whenever it moves away, the Sun's gravity pulls it back, therefore Mercury goes retrograde periodically, usually three times in a year. It is regarded as the Messenger of the Gods because it conjoins with the Sun three times a year to receive and pass on the celestial messages. It has a powerful connection with the all-pervading entity of the Sun.

Mercury is charming and adaptable and moves fast - not surprisingly it represents childhood, youth, and the need to learn what and why.

People with Mercury strong in their horoscope are constantly striving to attain knowledge. They can also be dualistic in character and changeable in nature - they are easily bored.

Mercury is androgynous and asexual. Vedic literature calls it a eunuch! It is also impotent. It has connections with homosexuality. In medical astrology, Mercury represents the skin. It can indicate skin allergies and diseases and respiratory problems. It is benefic on its own, but changes its personality if placed with other planets, for example with a malefic like Mars it could demonstrate anger or become involved in powerplay.

A strong Mercury usually indicates sharp intelligence, piercing insight and the ability to understand life and its complexities. It can be overly dispassionate, only understanding what can be explained in-

Strengths

Strong in **Gemini** and **Virgo**

Exaltation
15° Virgo

Mooltrikona
16 - 20° Virgo

Friends' Houses:
Taurus
Leo
Libra

Strong in **2nd, 4th, 5th, 9th, 10th** and **11th** houses but strongest in the **1st**

Neutral

In:
Aries
Scorpio
Sagittarius
Capricorn
Aquarius

It is neutral in the **3rd** house

Weaknesses

Debilitation
15° Pisces

Enemy is **Cancer**

It is weak in the **6th, 8th** and **12th** houses but is weakest in the **7th**

tellectually. A person with a strong Mercury can be insensitive and may be accused of being unable to feel emotion. It also shows critical facilities. In this case Mercury as the karaka of speech would indicate the ability to express oneself very well and impress others with superb communication skills.

A weak Mercury is changeable. It shows someone who relies on emotion rather than intellect as a rule, which can be wonderful if you can learn to trust your intuition. The combination of a weak Moon with a weak Mercury can lead to mental problems, as both are significators of the mind and intellect; they would also indicate someone who finds it hard to deal with their mind and emotions, and has a struggle to retain knowledge.

The best way to deal with a weak Mercury is to try to balance the mind; yoga or meditation helps to bring inner peace. Perseverance will be needed here as the Mercurial energy will not make it easy! It is better to avoid instant decisions as you will most certainly be reacting at an emotional level rather than thinking logically through the situation. Major issues require detachment as a weak Mercury can result in wrong choices.

Among other things Mercury represents speech, the pursuit of knowledge, astrology, transport, diplomacy, proficiency in languages, writers, entertainers, multiple careers, trading, accountancy and teaching.

Jupiter: Brihaspati or Guru

For insight into Jupiter's character, refer back to the myth of Mercury!

In the Vedas, Brihaspati is the teacher of the gods, the beings whose motivation is towards the good of humanity. Jupiter is a **brahmin**; one of those who have knowledge of **Brahman**, the creator of the universe. Their knowledge and highly developed consciousness gives them a duty to guide people from the illusions of the outer world to the inner light.

Jupiter is a teacher in the true sense. Jupiter in a natal chart represents expansion, happiness and higher knowledge. Jupiter is the most benefic planet in the zodiac, therefore it always gives a lot. In India, astrologers feel that a strong Jupiter gives the capacity to face any problems life throws at you. Despite being a spiritual planet, Jupiter gives material benefits to his devotees. The fruits of past karma are brought forth in this life as affluence, comfort and happiness. Jupiter makes conditions easier for those on a righteous path by removing obstacles and giving unexpected help towards their life purpose. Those with strong Jupiterian charts are seeking a better quality of life. Jupiter's main concern is to give them a soundly based material life so they can concentrate on essential spiritual development. Financial problems make it difficult to put oneself in the proper frame of mind for observing spiritual ritual and enhancing the inner light!

Jupiter enhances whatever it touches. It rules fat! Jupiterians have a tendency to be overweight. Its position also answers the two questions most frequently asked of astrologers in India: Will I marry? Will I have a son? In a woman's horoscope, Jupiter represents her relationships: whether they will work, what type of person her husband will be, and how long he will live. Jupiter is also the significator of the son. Even placed in a difficult house like the sixth, eighth or twelfth, Jupiter will still give you a son (if it is retrograde).

The Facts

Jupiter rules **Sagittarius** and **Pisces**

It rules nakshatras
Punarvasu
Vishakha
Purvabhadrapada

It is a **benefic** and is **male**

Guna: **sattvic**

In a woman's chart - **her husband or partner; sons, guru, teacher**

Although a strong Jupiter is supposed to alleviate all your problems, it's not wise to rely totally on this statement! In the case of Taurus and Libra ascendants the Jupiter energy can be difficult to handle. A strong Jupiter suggests inherent wisdom and the ability to express this wisdom for the benefit of others. This strength should enhance your partnerships or marriage. Its significations of wealth, learning, knowledge and religion will all thus be enhanced.

A weak Jupiter will cause problems with relationships. I find that having a weak Jupiter in the chart sometimes leads us into relationships where we have something to learn - partners who are not on the same spiritual path, or maybe someone we love but are unable to respect. A weak Jupiter can create a conflict between your ideals and real life. You may be forced to work in a foreign country or in a different culture where the path to knowledge may not be smooth; you may not be able to find the guru or teacher you seek.

A weak Jupiter can be strengthened by wearing yellow to enhance spiritual energies. You may not be able to find the right teacher so try to learn to study on your own. A weak Jupiter suggests that you are more materially inclined and not particularly interested in religion or spirituality; expressing your material karma is part of your life. This is likely to leave you feeling unfulfilled, but by consciously enhancing Jupiterian aims through charity and selfless work you will

Strengths
Strong in **Sagittarius** and **Pisces**

Exaltation
5° Cancer

Mooltrikona
0 - 10° Sagittarius

Friends' Houses
Aries
Cancer
Leo
Scorpio

It is strong in the **5th, 9th, 10th** and **11th** houses, but strongest in the **1st**

Neutral
In:
Taurus
Gemini
Virgo
Libra

Will have strengths and weaknesses in the **2nd, 3rd, 4th, 6th, 8th** and **12th** houses

Weaknesses
Debilitation
5° Capricorn

Enemy is **Aquarius**

It is weak in the **7th house,** giving multiple relationships intead of a steady one

45

become more satisfied.

Some of the words associated with Jupiter are wisdom, justice, knowledge, the legal profession, astrology, asceticism, religion, belief, benevolence, fat, and philosophy.

Venus: Shukra

As Jupiter was teacher of the gods, Venus was teacher of the demons, highly evolved souls who have lost their spiritual purpose in life and whose actions therefore tend towards personal enhancement and glory. We, as humans, are mostly demonic in nature. Venus as the advisor of the demons is a spiritual teacher par excellence. He is the only planet who has the secret of immortality: he guides the demons so they may regain their lost souls. It should be noted here that although Venus is a **male** entity, he has a **feminine** energy.

Venus stands for refinement and the desires of man, procreation and life on earth. It will give you pleasures and fulfil your desires, however outrageous they may be. The one thing Venus cannot do

The Facts
Venus rules **Taurus** and **Libra**
It rules nakshatras **Bharani** **Purva Phalguni** **Purva ashadha**
It is a **benefic** and is **female**
Guna: **rajasic**
Karakas: **in a man's chart - his wife; marriage, sex and semen**

is avert your karma or make you happy. In some ways the excessive materialism of Venus makes you realise that any amount of earthly trappings cannot bring true happiness. If you want money, Venus will give it to you; if you desire success it will be granted, but if your chart indicates that you are not actually going to enjoy this wealth, Venus cannot change that. The story of Venus's daughter is a very good illustration of this. She was in love with a particular king and in accordance with his daughter's wishes, her father arranged for them to be married - sadly the king was already in love with another woman and although he went through with the marriage he never showed any love or affection for his wife. Venus could arrange for his daughter to marry the man of her dreams but he could not give her happiness. Happiness in marriage and the love of a good man was not part of his daughter's karma.

A strong Venus will draw the opposite sex towards you even if you are not considered physically attractive. Venus represents the marriage but not the happiness; if Venus is not well-placed in your natal chart you might have problems in your marriage and other partnerships.

Venus reflects the good things in life, so a strong Venus will give you a love of luxury, arts, beauty and wealth. Because of its connection with material goods it can make you overly attached to the commercial aspects of life; you will have to be careful not to make money your god. A strong Venus is essential for fame and popularity, and it may suggest you can achieve your heart's desire, but you had better look elsewhere for happiness and peace of mind!

A weak Venus may make you too critical of relationships. Maybe you set unachievable standards that partners cannot measure up to, or perhaps you have such a poor self-image that you think nobody would want to be with you anyway. Your inner beauty is not allowed expression.

To strengthen your Venus, learn to love your inner self. I find people with a weak Venus don't care about their physical appearance and deliberately play themselves down - which of course reinforces the feeling that nobody will find them attractive. Looking at this aspect of yourself is very important. Learn to make the best of yourself and

Strengths

Strong in **Taurus** and **Libra**

Exaltation
27° Pisces

Mooltrikona
0 - 15° Libra

Friends' Houses:
Gemini
Capricorn
Aquarius

Strong in **1st, 5th, 9th 11th** and **12th houses** but strongest in the **4th**

Neutral

In **Aries, Scorpio** and **Sagittarius**

Will have strengths and weaknesses in the **2nd, 3rd,** and **7th** houses

Weaknesses

Debilitation
27° Virgo

Enemies are:
Cancer
Leo

Weak in the **6th, 8th** and **10th houses**

be more realistic about relationships. Colour, jewellery, good clothes and a well-groomed appearance will do wonders for your self-image and strengthen your Venus.

Some of the words associated with Venus are wealth, vehicles, clothes, jewellery, semen, music, dance, luxury goods, prosperity, fame, fashion, acting and design. In a male chart, Venus represents the wife. In all charts Venus represents marriage.

Saturn: Shani

Saturn is the great teacher of cosmic truths; it works through restrictions, obstructions, frustrations, unhappiness, disillusionment, setbacks and even death. Saturn is considered malefic. It is the significator of misery in a natal chart but there is a definite purpose to Saturnian suffering. Through restriction and limitation, Saturn forces the soul to recognise inner truth obscured by veils of matter.

Saturn is the planet of karmic retribution. It keeps an account of all the past acts and releases this karma unexpectedly in this life. Faced with such powerful karmic forces, we have to dig deep into our inner resources, enduring immense misery and frustration. But once we start to understand the dark forces of Saturn, we can slowly move along the path towards self realisation.

The Facts
Saturn rules **Capricorn** and **Aquarius**
It rules nakshatras: **Pushya** **Anuradha** **Uttarabhadrapada**
It is a **malefic** and is **androgynous**
Guna: **tamasic**
Karakas: **landed property, longevity and old age, disease, work**

Saturn detaches us from the pleasures of life by making us consider the true reason for our birth. This stripping away of illusions brings about immense psychological transformation.

Moving more slowly than the other planets Saturn has plenty of time to teach its lessons and change the course of our lives. Its unrelenting progress through a chart by transit brings up the karmic issues we have to deal with - things we cannot avoid in this life, the unpleasant tasks we each have to face. Saturn is very evenhanded. It teaches everyone, whether friend or enemy.

In the Vedas, Saturn is the son of the Sun and his shadow wife, **Chayya**. According to the myth, the Sun's wife went to visit her parents' home one day and deliberately left her shadow behind. The Sun mistook the shadow for his real wife and had sex with her; Saturn is the product of this union. Once the Sun realised his mistake he immediately rejected both Chayya and Saturn. The relationship between the Sun and Saturn is a very difficult one as Saturn always blames the Sun for rejecting him as a child.

Saturn is the most dreaded planet in India, but its malefic forces are very often misunderstood. Saturn helps us to mature through everyday life experiences and the resultant growth brings with it detachment from both the pleasures and the miseries of life. With this knowledge comes strength.

Saturn is at its strongest in the seventh house, the house of sensuous relationships and the area where for most of us, the key action takes place. Saturn separates the individual from whatever it touches; it is also a **Brahmachari** - a bachelor at heart. In the seventh house its strength makes relationships very difficult. In the end it forces you to recognise that marriage and sensual happiness are an illusion; you are led towards the non-materialistic path. Saturn is the servant in the planetary cabinet. In modern terms, that means it represents workers or people with menial jobs. Saturn's tendency to cause separation means that if it is associated with the Sun or the ninth house (both representing

Strengths

Saturn is strong in
Capricorn and **Aquarius**

Exaltation
20° Libra

Mooltrikona
0 - 20° Aquarius

Friends' Houses
Taurus
Gemini
Virgo

Strong in the **3rd, 6th, 10th** and **11th houses** but strongest in the **7th**

Neutral

In **Sagittarius** and **Pisces**

Will have strengths and weaknesses in the **2nd, 4th, 5th, 9th** and **12th** houses

Weaknesses

Debilitation
20° Aries

Enemies are:
Cancer
Leo
Scorpio

Weak in the **1st house**

Father) you will face separation from your father.

The most difficult planetary relationship Saturn has is with the Moon. Saturn conjunct the Moon or placed in the twelfth or second house from the Moon makes life especially difficult for a person because Saturn casts a large shadow over the mind, causing depression, loneliness and melancholia. This combination can bring about the right circumstances for **sanyas** - which means the giving up of worldly goods and relationships for the pursuit of spiritual realisation. It is very obvious in natal charts of the great yogis and spiritual masters.

Anything to do with Saturn takes a long time; it usually represents delay, long-lasting or prolonged influences. It is the most difficult energy we have to face, as the karaka of unhappiness, difficulty and struggle. It is however a democratic planet - it gives you difficulty regardless of whether it is weak or strong; its lessons have to be learnt. Some of us can deal with this easier than others; Libra, Taurus and Gemini find Saturn an easier taskmaster but only after a struggle. It represents the karmic issues we have to face and if we deal with them we will emerge stronger and more in control than before, having cleared away some difficult karma.

A weak Saturn is more difficult to handle than a strong one; it suggests that we fight against the energy, but in fact the only way to deal with Saturn is **not** to fight. It can be helped by fasting and meditation. Most remedial measures for Saturn are difficult undertakings as they only work at some personal cost.

Some of the words associated with Saturn are disease (in general), paralysis, arthritis, depression, dishonour, debts, delays, renunciation, buildings, land and property, any work requiring great effort, teaching and research.

Rahu Ketu

Rahu and Ketu are always powerful and their placement in the houses indicates certain lessons we have to learn. They are covered in depth elsewhere - but their strengths and weaknesses are given here.

Rahu	Ketu
Strengths Strong in **Virgo** Exalted in **Taurus** and **Gemini** Friend's house - **Libra** Strong in **3rd**, **6th** and **10th** houses but strongest in the **11th** **Weaknesses** Debilitated in **Scorpio** and **Sagittarius** Enemies: **Aries, Cancer, Leo, Pisces**	**Strengths** Strong in **Pisces** Exalted in **Scorpio** and **Sagittarius** Friend's house - **Aries** Strong in **3rd** and **11th** houses, but best for moksha in the **12th** **Weaknesses** Debilitated in **Taurus** and **Gemini** Enemies: **Cancer, Leo, Virgo, Libra**

Rahu and Ketu - The Karmic Axis

Rahu and Ketu are the names given to the North and South nodes of the Moon. The nodes are 180° apart at the two points on the ecliptic, where the path of the Moon around the Earth crosses the apparent path of the Sun around the Earth. Their axis moves through the signs of the zodiac in retrograde motion, taking about 18 years to complete their cycle.

Solar eclipses (on a new Moon) take place at 0 - 18° from the nodal axis; lunar eclipses (at full Moon) take place within a band of 0 -11° from it. For this reason the Moon's nodes have an important place in Vedic astrology, on a par with the planets. Symbolically, they are a point of harmony, the coming-together of the three most important influences in our life - the Sun, the Earth and the Moon.

Together Rahu (the north node), and Ketu (the south node) are called the **Chayya Grahas** (shadow planets). They have no physical substance, yet their influence is full of potency and spiritual significance. They work in unison - two opposite points in the zodiac with a mission to churn up our lives in order to externalise hidden potential and wisdom. In keeping with their shadowy nature, they work on a psychological level so it is always difficult to gauge their effect; their main concern is with our emotional make-up and we might be unaware of what exactly is happening to us at the time. During eclipses Rahu and Ketu symbolically 'swallow' the two luminaries, and it is this capacity to darken the Sun and the Moon that makes them the most powerful influence in the zodiac. The Sun, around which the other planets and the solar system revolve, and the Moon which controls life on earth, are obscured by Rahu and Ketu during eclipses. They represent Cosmic Law which everyone and everything, including the Sun and Moon, has to obey.

An eclipse can blot out the Sun (consciousness) or the Moon (mind); it darkens our perspective in order to bring in new light. The energies created are powerfully psychic, pregnant with new information and the influence of that which is hidden and the period after the eclipse is considered a rebirth of the Sun and the Moon. The function of Rahu and Ketu in this powerful alignment of the Sun, Moon and Earth gives them the role of the ultimate controllers of destiny. If the soul's lives on earth are the pearls on a necklace, the thread which holds the pearls together is Rahu and Ketu. The purpose of the soul in this life is to act out its given karma, destroy the illusions of the materialistic life and progress towards self-realisation; to move over to the astral planes where pleasure and pain do not have the capacity to hurt, the mind is still and at peace. Its journey in a particular lifetime and its connection with eternal life is indicated by the position of Rahu and Ketu in the natal chart. Ketu is said to be the keeper of the knowledge of past lives. Rahu externalises karmic flaws, emphasising desires so that we can learn to overcome them.

The symbol for Rahu and Ketu is **Naga**, the snake, and it is a powerful mystic symbol in Vedic culture, representing both wisdom and poison. We all know that knowledge can be used for good or ill. Likewise poison can cure (modern medicine uses poisons as antidotes) and kill. Snakes remind us of our mortality, but the process by which snakes shed their skins has come to symbolise transformation, death followed by rebirth.

The myth behind Rahu and Ketu

Naga Vasuki was the serpent who ruled the **Patala Loka**, the underworld. There was a great war between the gods and the demons for control of the universe; at first Vasuki helped the gods. They tied him around the spiritual mountain, **Mandara,** and used him like a rope wound around a rod to churn the ocean while they looked for **Amrita**, the nectar of immortality. When they found it the gods wanted to keep it for themselves as they rightly felt the demons would use it for personal glorification and materialistic happiness rather than universal good. They plied the other demons with wine, women and song to distract their attention; Vasuki, though a demon too, was wiser than the others and he wasn't fooled - he saw through the gods' ploy and drank the nectar of immortality secretly. The Sun and the Moon complained to **Lord Vishnu**, creator of the Universe, who grew very angry at this deception. He threw a wheel called the **Sudharshan Chakra** at Vasuki cutting him in two; but of course Vasuki was immortal now as a result of drinking the Amrita and could not die. He thus remained in the skies as Rahu (the head) and Ketu (the tail), a permanent reminder to the other planets (gods) of the darker side of life which we have to defeat in the pursuit of immortality.

The myth of Naga Vasuki is an allegory of life. Without the help of Vasuki the gods could not find the secret of immortality; in the same way we, as humans, cannot find our higher selves without understanding the lessons of Rahu and Ketu. Our inner emotions are like the ocean being churned; within this ocean are treasures but also poisons and dangers and we have to learn to distinguish the precious from the dross and finally find Amrita - the secret of immortality or true happiness. The conflict is between our attachment to materialistic achievements (the domain of Rahu) and the liberation of the soul through eternal bliss and tranquillity (Ketu is the Moksha karaka significator for spiritual realisation).

Vasuki wasn't taken in by the illusion that deceived the other demons. He wanted to achieve the very highest pinnacle of perfection, so he didn't do what was expected of him. Likewise, Rahu is very ambitious; it has the kind of ambition that is never satisfied and the necessary drive to achieve whatever it desires. However, Ketu is there reminding us that we each have past life issues that have to be addressed, and without attending to them we will not make any real, spiritual progress. Ketu represents the cycles of change in life - we can't always demand that life goes according to our own plans.

The Sun and the Moon are considered the enemies of Rahu Ketu because they told Lord Vishnu what Vasuki had done; any conjunctions of Rahu and Ketu are full of esoteric and karmic significance.

To interpret the influence of Rahu and Ketu in our charts we must understand their shadowy nature. As they are only symbolic points in the zodiac they are unable to act on their own; they take on the characteristics of the planet that rules the sign they are in. Conversely the dispositor itself is influenced by Rahu Ketu.

The Karmic Axis

So what are the major karmic issues we bring with us? Which areas will be churned up while we try to navigate through the stormy waters of life? Each incarnation focuses on certain areas which have arisen from the deep consciousness of an individual and have to be faced. Those areas represent a karmic axis which is indicated by the position of Rahu and Ketu in the chart; other planets or other areas of our life are also controlled by this axis and we use them to try to understand and work with the dominant theme.

If we aware of the subtler levels of energies at work, it can become easier to overcome the difficulties represented by the karmic axis.

The axis pinpoints the areas where we struggle within ourselves, it highlights past life issues and focuses on present day experiences. Our previous actions, karma we have made in past lives, fashions how we will act today. The karmic axis is not an easy area of the chart; it throws up situations that require knowledge and wisdom to work through and at times it can be very uncomfortable. However, these issues don't go away if you ignore them! They will come back at different times and in many forms until they are resolved.

Rahu Ketu together indicate the kundalini, the latent power within us. The symbol for this is also a snake; Rahu as the mouth of the snake has to taste and experience life, while Ketu as the tail learns from Rahu's experience and turns it into intellect, knowledge and perception. How your karmic axis works depends upon the way the Rahu Ketu energy is harnessed. The nodes represent a psychic power which needs knowledge, wisdom and perception to truly understand; the process can take years.

The axis works on two different levels. During youth we reject any idea of karma and issues of destiny; we fight against the mental blocks created by the nodes, and experience life to the limit. We over-reach, overdo life in the areas represented by the position of the nodes. Then as we live through these experiences and grow older we learn to control the axis and move towards its subtler energies. If the early experiences are too extreme, we may never allow ourselves to truly understand the axis which represents both the restrictions and the enhancement of our life. With these thoughts in mind we'll look at the effect of Rahu Ketu through the houses.

Rahu in first/Ketu in seventh house

Your karmic axis is about yourself and relationships. This is the issue which dominates your life. You will always feel dissatisfied with your relationships for some unknown reason - you may be involved in a relationship which is envied by the world but it will never be good enough for you. In the same way your own success will not satisfy you. It is important to understand that the success you seek in the outer world may not give you satisfaction and in fact you need to work within yourself; are you are overdoing things? It can indicate ambitions which can get you into trouble - like the seriously rich industrialist who risks his last penny for an even bigger slice of the cake. Being over-ambitious can lead to loss.

With Rahu placed in the first house, you want to experience every shade of life, which can make you selfish and self-centred if you don't recognise it. Rahu in this house can make you an intensely materialistic and ambitious person as the desire to achieve wealth and power is very strong. Rahu drives you to impose your personal mark on society. You are likely to experience frustration, with feelings of non-achievement and disenchantment, despite being successful. However, if you immerse yourself in humanitarian work you can find deep satisfaction.

Ketu in the seventh house destroys the chance of finding true happiness in relationships if you don't understand the subtle lessons your relationship is bringing to you. Ketu is the planet of moksha, spiritual enlightenment, in the house of sensual relationships. The two energies do not combine. You can meet people who are carrying the guilt of other relationships with them. As you feel internally dissatisfied with your relationship you may well create situations which hurt your partner, so it is important to remember that your partners may decide to leave you and break away from your selfishness. Ketu in the seventh can teach you a painful lesson in relationships. If you are able to work with the deeper levels of this axis, the challenge is to retain a sense of individuality within the relationship. There could be the feeling of having given it all up for a relationship in a past life, so now it's your turn - but the ideal is to find a balance. Two contented individuals in a relationship can achieve much - like the theory of synergy: the whole being greater than the sum of (in this case) the two parts.

Rahu in second/Ketu in eighth house
The second house is to do with speech, wealth, early childhood, potential and insight, while the eighth house is associated with longevity, death, transformation and the secret knowledge of past. This karmic axis is considered one of the most difficult as many of the associations are things we cannot change - we are born into them. The connection with material wealth, talents and speech can be both negative and positive.

People born with this axis can feel that the world owes them a living. They have a tendency towards financial dependence on others and towards self-destructive habits This attitude arises from Rahu's link in the second house with past life potential; Rahu feels it should get merit for all the past actions and is anxious to externalise everything for its own profit. The link with speech can give a very harsh way of speaking which needs to be controlled as it can alienate others. Rahu in the second gives tremendous insight into life. There is usually a side that wants family inheritance and wealth, involving fights through litigation and wills. There is a need to escape from past life karma and learn that the world does not owe anyone a living. You have to be responsible for your own karma. Of course these extremely negative issues can be modified greatly if one learns to be self-reliant.

As the second house deals with eating and what we take into our bodies, Rahu can lead towards eating and drinking the wrong kind of food and drink. Ketu, on the other hand, is the more spiritual energy in the hidden eighth house and can be a good placement if one is looking for spiritual attainments; materialistically though it causes problems. It can lead you into the world of hidden powers and deep knowledge of the past. Energy for acquiring occult and psychic powers is evident. The eighth house energy is unfathomable as it works at such a deep level. Ketu allows you to look into this as deeply as you desire. Be aware though that looking into hidden areas may throw up issues you are not prepared to deal with as yet; a mature soul is required to deal with the influence exerted by Rahu Ketu in this axis.

Rahu in third/Ketu in ninth house

This axis is concerned with the relationship between the lower mind and higher mind: your practical instincts, idealistic desires, your personal efforts and paternal influences. This axis can work when you are self-confident and don't allow others - especially the father - to control your actions; seeking and following your own counsel rather than following existing religions or philosophies is preferable. You will want to be both different and extremely successful.

Rahu placed in the third house is a very good position, giving ambition, courage and a sense of adventure. You want to do your own thing and find it difficult to take other people into account; forming relationships will be a problem. You really need to be involved in intellectually interesting and stimulating work, otherwise a short attention span will make you restless.

Ketu in the ninth house shows a strong need to follow the path to enlightenment, perhaps through philosophies and teachings not of one's culture. Relationship with the father would be very difficult - either through separation or alternatively an extremely close relationship which you may physically want to sever but the emotional, psychological ties keep you close. Later on in life, you may surprise everyone by cutting these ties. Ketu here will also give you a guru who has a great insight into spiritual matters. Make sure this is a person who is trustworthy and ethical. The main problem of this axis is the unwillingness to listen to advice; some need to make and learn from their own mistakes.

Rahu in fourth/Ketu in tenth house

The fourth house symbolises karma from past lives while the tenth indicates future karma. This is a powerful karmic position - but Rahu deals with the future and Ketu with the past: placed in the chart in this way, the energies of past and future are mixed up. If you have Rahu and Ketu here it is important to pay attention to what you are doing. The confusion between past and future indicates that work started in the past is not complete and there are still problems to be sorted out. The karma of work would have been very important in a past life and one can show insensitivity on the surface, ruthlessly pursuing career goals without bothering about others. You must try to understand the need for a simpler life and not let work rule your life. You can do this by becoming more involved in your home environment. The fourth house is concerned with inner feelings and Rahu's placement there can cause conflict between inner and outer desires. Some can express desires too forcefully or be scared of accepting them. The inner world may seem to be full of darkness. Try to understand that if you look into that darkness your eyes will get used to it and the fear that you hold within will slowly disappear. Rahu in the fourth house often indicates a difficult relationship with the mother.

Ketu in the tenth house is afraid to express its full potential. You might pursue an 'alternative' type of career, or one in history, antiques or astrology. You are likely to be afraid of what the future has in store, and may be stuck in the past - the immediate past or a past life where you didn't sort out some personal issues. This makes it difficult for you to express your self in the outer world. Your life is always connected to maternal issues. You will need to sort them out in your mind to be happy with yourself.

Rahu in fifth/Ketu in eleventh house

This karmic axis is about creativity and the fruits of life. This creativity can be expressed through children, ideas, higher and abstract thinking. The fruits of one's efforts can be material or spiritual. Children become very important for you and it could also be that your children are creative. The fifth/eleventh axis sometimes brings problems with having children or experiences with them where you may not have control over what happens. On a creative level, you can be very fertile. Rahu makes one ambitious to achieve the highest form of creativity - but Ketu is not necessarily interested in getting the material results from it. This axis will forever draw you to the intangible areas of your life but you must pay attention to the practicalities as well - otherwise you will be a genius with no idea how to handle money or finances.

With Rahu in the fifth house finding your true identity is the most important lesson. It can often focus on children - the lesson you must learn comes through them. Many writers and artists also have Rahu in the fifth house, though there can be overindulgence in creativity which can isolate you from others if you're not careful.

The eleventh house is the house of gains. Ketu is not interested in work on a materialistic level, so placed there it can give you so many financial problems that it focuses your mind on higher principles. But if you are looking for gains on a spiritual level, it can bring forth those in immense quantities. Ketu has a mystical side to it which can suddenly give untold financial gains and the ability to make lots of money. However, what usually happens is that you may want to give this money up through philanthropic activity or maybe you find little pleasure in financial success; generally speaking it has no attraction for you, but that does not necessarily stop it coming to find you!

Rahu in sixth/Ketu in twelfth house

This axis links the sixth house (service, obstacles, enemies and disease) to the twelfth house (loss, imprisonment, sexual pleasures, clairvoyance and moksha) and is a strong position for Rahu Ketu. Rahu has the ability to fight against every obstacle put in front of it and Ketu naturally wants to move towards enlightenment. This axis may create obstacles to be overcome in the early years; one might be overly attached to sexual pleasures and sexual needs - there will definitely be issues connected with it - either one is are afraid to enjoy sex or some may have overindulged. There may be obstacles regarding work, disease or enemies, but only at a level that can be dealt with. The earlier years of life will be devoted to dealing with mundane problems, then comes a move towards controlling personal desires through meditation and yoga. Once that stage is achieved, the natural progression will be towards moksha or spiritual realisation.

Rahu in the sixth house will remove obstacles lying in your path. It can help to slay the inner demons. Enemies will be strong, but you will be able to handle and destroy them. However, you will need to learn how to assess people close to you: are they friends or foes? You can also suffer from mysterious illnesses which are hard to diagnose and which can disappear as suddenly as they appeared.

Ketu as the moksha karaka is in its own house - a powerful instrument for those seeking spiritual fulfilment and higher understanding. You are introspective and will need to be alone a great deal. Ketu in the twelfth house represents knowledge gained as part of karma, from the continuing chain of lives and deaths, which is going to be useful in finding final salvation.

Rahu in seventh/Ketu in first House

This axis again is about self and relationships, but is subtly different from Rahu in the first and Ketu in the seventh house. Here Rahu's position indicates that relationships will dominate your life - there is a need to experience them in every hue. This can make for a promiscuous personality and also a dissatisfied one regardless of how many relationships are experienced. It is important here to recognise an inner antipathy which will not be fulfilled by another relationship, but by trying to work out the present one.

With Rahu in the seventh you will need relationships a great deal. However, as a loner and being rather self-centred, selfishness will tend to alienate others. You have to learn how to relate to others and acknowledge that there are always two sides to any story.

Ketu in the first house indicates a karmic connection with a past life; a clinging to issues on a psychological level. You may be blocking yourself through guilt and there will be a tendency to blame oneself for the actions of others too. Take care not to view yourself from a completely negative standpoint. Some will have contacted at an early stage of life people who were not very nice, and their behaviour can have an lasting impact. Ketu in the first house gives an ability to hold onto memories; you still remember and feel past events which you should have dismissed. There is a real need to have an emotional clear-out every so often otherwise you may find yourself suffering physically or psychologically. Learn to let go.

Rahu in eighth/Ketu in second house

This axis is a difficult one. Both the second and the eighth houses have a powerful connection with hidden potential - negative or positive. The eighth is a multi-layer house dealing with the hidden areas of life, and it is difficult to gauge how the subtle energies will be experienced. Rahu has the thirst to experience everything and may not be able to distinguish between the good and the bad. This is the position or axis where the underworld is activated and our latent power is located. The kundalini rests dormant here. Rahu here will have the urge to activate the kundalini, but are you ready for it? A good teacher is vital here to help bring forth these powerful energies? This axis creates a direct link between creative potential and the underworld. There has to be transformation and change, but knowledge and wisdom are needed to deal with these energies successfully.

With this placement the urge to explore the dark reaches of society, to dive into the still dark waters of human knowledge, is very strong. Unless it is properly harnessed, this need for the knowledge that others fear can lead to dark alleyways of human weakness, even to involvement in crime and drugs. Understanding this potential and using it to gain higher wisdom can bring immense power. People with this placement of Rahu Ketu can become scientists, researchers, astrologers, archaeologists. Rahu in the eighth can express itself in drug addiction, manipulation of the mind and psychological control issues.

Ketu in the second house can symbolise a difficult childhood. Because this area is linked to speech Ketu will create problems with the way we talk - for example people with speech defects. You may communicate in very straightforward way without the usual social niceties which can alienate others; yet the heart is pure and clean; alternatively you may be very sweet in your speech but hold onto resentment and anger within.

Rahu in ninth/Ketu in third house

Here the positions are reversed from the third/ninth axis but the issues are still connected with the higher and lower mind. Rahu is now in the ninth house where it has the need to experience issues like higher knowledge, teaching, gurus, the dharmic path of life, and Ketu is linked to the practical issues of life - the personal efforts, ambitions and desires. Ketu usually wants to give up material issues and is connected to the abstract mind. Here it will work in an abstract, unusual eccentric way; it will not be bound by material ties. Rahu will want to impress others with its knowledge and power. This is usually a position seen in politicians who try to influence the minds of others through their thinking. On a negative side this axis could bring manipulation with the ideas and philosophies of present life or a new and innovative way of presenting these ideas.

The paternal relationship can be difficult. There is a separation from him or a father who believes in control and dominance. It is not usually an easy relationship as paternal issues will be dominant.

With Rahu in the ninth you will need to control people through knowledge. You have the potential to become a great teacher, but poorly placed it can lead to extreme self-righteousness and teaching the wrong kind of doctrine with no regard for the good of others. Cult gurus and politicians often have this placement!

Ketu in the third suggests living life in an unusual way. There is a strong past life contact with your siblings.

Rahu in tenth/Ketu in fourth house

Rahu as the node concerning the future, is well-placed in the tenth house; this is where future karma is laid down and it indicates living one's life on a larger canvas. If you are not expressing yourself properly you could feel frustrated. There is a link between past life karma and present life actions - some can find it hard to cope with the emotional issues in life. This usually suggests a difficult relationship with the mother which forces the offspring to live life in the outer world - and some sort of pressure is exerted (maybe through guilt) that keeps the maternal ties strong. You could feel lonely and disenchanted within but others will only see the successful side of your nature. Fulfilling one's potential in the outer world can ward off depression.

With Rahu in the tenth you have the capacity to sway the consciousness of many people and a strong sense of destiny, a belief that you must make a name for yourself. Women especially also have a strong attachment to their home, but also a longing to give up that comfort and lead life in the public arena. Many world leaders and personalities are born with this configuration.

Ketu, the node of the past, is very strong in the fourth house, the area connected with past life. The more challenging side is the emotional problems and a difficult relationship with the mother.

Rahu in eleventh/Ketu in fifth House

This is one of the best positions for Rahu and it can bring much material success. Rahu in the eleventh will bring money, financial rewards and respect from others, but a certain dissatisfaction with personal achievement. Ketu links you with abstract knowledge and a real, deep, understanding of life. Here the intellect will be very powerful and give the ability to express ideas in a new and innovative form. Past life knowledge can be expressed very positively; the fifth house shows how to translate them into creative activity in this lifetime; Ketu represents the past life that you brought into this one and which does not allow you to let go. You will have to find a way to make all the achievements of your past lives work for you this time.

However, Ketu in the house of children can cause problems with them or with other creative enterprises. It will always be difficult to find true creativity until you start using it for the good of others. Ketu in the fifth will also give the ability to be a very unusual writer - you will be able to present old themes in a new and exciting way.

Rahu in the eleventh is very strong, giving great earning ability and the capacity to make real profit. However, there is a need to do this in your own, individual way - learn to be a true 'new ager', more of a free spirit. Leaving behind the old philosophy of I/Me will make it easier to interact with others.

Rahu in twelfth/Ketu in sixth House

This axis indicates that one is meant to understand the lessons of the twelfth house in this life. It represents loss, endings, expenses, sexual pleasures and enlightenment. On one level the twelfth house reflects hidden indulgences through extravagance or sexual activities, but on the other hand it represents the highest achievement that the soul can experience: enlightenment and the breaking away from the cycles of life and death. Rahu will have to experience this house in all its shades. This is a powerfully sexual situation. It could be that you have a great need to enjoy pleasure but can take it to a negative extreme. Again this indulgence will not find happiness.

It is important to understand that in the same way as spending a lot of money can give a momentary thrill, sexual orgasm also only leads to momentary relief. There is inherent dissatisfaction connected with this axis unless there is a desire to understand and control the positive energies of Rahu in the twelfth house, and accept the cycles of life and death. Those not on an enlightened path will find this placement very difficult, because Ketu in the sixth house creates powerful enemies (real or imagined), and a certain disenchantment with work. Sudden illnesses can block the path of material success. Ketu can also cause great unhappiness in the pursuit of daily life.

For those already seeking higher consciousness, Rahu creates a desire for the highest level of karmic salvation and transformation leads you to the right spiritual path - the urge to explore unknown lands and achieve true nirvana is very strong. On a very non-spiritual level, Rahu can lead to you over-spending and wasting energy on a strong sexual appetite.

Past Life Connections

Planets in the same houses as the nodes indicate the past life connections we bring into this life, some issues which still have to be worked out and others which by focusing on them intensely we will take to new heights. Planets develop unusual traits when they are with Rahu or Ketu. They lose their natural abilities. Rahu usually enhances the basic quality of the planet and the issues the planet represents become issues we need to experience to their fullest extent. Ketu overshadows the planets - it pinpoints karma which we are still attached to from previous lives and need to give up, but the subconscious sometimes finds it difficult to let go.

In Vedic astrology planets which conjunct Rahu or Ketu are described as 'eclipsed'. This is not a physical phenomenon but a description of what Rahu and Ketu do to the planet involved, releasing psychic energy and causing inner turmoil so that the planet behaves contrary to what would generally be expected. Because Rahu and Ketu are the opposite ends of an axis, conjunctions with Rahu also means oppositions to Ketu, and vice versa.

Note: Planets will be conjunct Rahu or Ketu if they are in

the same sign in the same house; orbs of influence regarding the aspects are not used as they are in western astrology.

The Sun and Moon
The Sun and the Moon suffer the most from conjunctions to Rahu or Ketu. In the myth of Naga Vasuki, the Sun and Moon were his enemies. Their ability to eclipse the light of the Sun and Moon makes a conjunction with either of the nodes very difficult.

Past life connections with Ketu
Ketu represents past lives, particularly misdeeds or insufficient effort, which now form a negative part of karma in this life. Ketu is the sting in the Rahu Ketu tail - it takes away what it has given during its dasha cycles of seven years and is generally thought of as coming of age when you are 48; up until that time you are likely to experience its negative side and tendency to take. As you grow older Ketu takes less and starts to give.

Your birth chart will indicate areas or people in your past lives where you have unfinished business. It can come forth as guilt that you have carried over from a past life. Ketu has a tendency to remember all the experiences - so it absorbs everything and finds it difficult to let go. When planets are conjunct the Ketu part of the axis, it shows issues that have to be worked out on an inner level. These experiences or issues cannot be resolved by new experiences but by understanding old ones and letting them go.

The aim of Ketu is renunciation. Conjunct any planet, it will encourage you to give up something to do with that planet's energies; as the planets signify various relationships (Sun - father, Jupiter - husband etc.) Ketu conjunctions show unresolved issues carried over into this life.

Ketu and the Sun
Ketu conjunct the Sun indicates a powerful past life karma which obstructs growth in this life, blocking the light from the future unless adverse issues are dealt with. The blocks usually work on the mental plane and at times it is difficult to recognise them without deep reflection. You need to let go of past problems and create new karma in their place.

Ketu conjunct the Sun can also appear in a materialistic form; a loss of reputation is possible. However, Ketu with the Sun shows itself most often in difficult relationships with the father - there will be a mental distance between you.

I have noticed that several of my clients with this conjunction feel rejected by their fathers in some way.

Ketu and the Moon

The Moon represents the mind and Ketu is the keeper of knowledge of past lives as well as being moksha karaka, the significator for spiritual salvation. Their conjunction is not an easy combination. Ketu conjunct the Moon gives great psychic powers and the ability to look into the past. Many events in this life will have their roots in powerful past life connections, particularly problems with mothers, which must be addressed in this life. It is possible to become confused by past-life knowledge - Ketu causes injury and the psychic powers of Ketu and the Moon can come out as irrational fears, self-abuse (both physical and emotional) and tendencies towards suicide. There is a struggle between the Moon's enjoyment of physical pleasure and Ketu's ideal of renunciation. Self-knowledge, better control of psychic abilities, and more understanding of the higher principles of life will help you to live with Ketu and the Moon. You have to let go of the unhappiness due to maternal relationships as well as emotional needs left over from a past life which are not relevant to you now. Be strong, release the past and move on.

Ketu and Mars

A Ketu and Mars conjunction indicates you are retaining past life issues about anger, violence, courage and experience of new be-ginnings. Ketu acts like Mars and they are similar energies, both prone to anger, violence and a tendency to cause accident and injury on a negative level; on a positive level they aim for the highest, purest objectives and have the courage and ability to reach for them despite the obstacles faced. This combination indicates that you have a special connection with your brother or brothers in this life. If you do not have a brother, then you will find that you feel the lack of this relationship strongly and may have platonic male friends who act as substitutes.

You may fear violence or have some past life experience which was connected to war, blood and violence which you are carrying in your subconscious. With Ketu and Mars you will need to calm down and control your tendencies to anger and impulsive, often violent behaviour. However, they are the qualities which are needed to make a good leader in the police or armed forces.

Ketu and Mercury

Ketu keeps the 'book of life' and also represents the knowledge of astrology, the Vedas, Tantra etc. Mercury is the intellectual mind. Although Ketu and Mercury may block your ability to use your mind well, this is a very good situation for abstract thinkers. Here the intellect has the knowledge contained within Ketu to use - you can be intuitive, psychic and clairvoyant. You may not have used your intellectual energies properly in previous lives, but here you need to use it for the benefit of others through teaching or writing. Ketu will also give you the ability to forget what is too painful to remember, but at the same time unless the mind is used actively you may feel unfulfilled and unhappy.

Mercury is the significator of childhood and in this position indicates childhood issues brought from past life which have to be experienced in this life.

Mercury has the ability to be two-faced and the combination with Ketu can lead to deviousness and underhandedness. This highlights the poisonous aspect of Ketu and the past life. It is a matter of choice how you are going to use your abilities - for the good of others or for negative purposes. Here one needs to be aware of how karma created now can affect one at a later stage.

Ketu and Jupiter

Jupiter conjunct the karmic axis of life shows that relationships, children and knowledge are the big issues in life. This conjunction in a woman's chart, where Jupiter represents her partner, may show itself in the choice of someone who is not socially acceptable, who doesn't do the correct thing and is not bothered about appropriate rituals. Even showing itself more positively, a woman with Ketu and Jupiter is not likely to marry someone run-of-the-mill! You may have brought into this life some unfinished business with partners and consequently there is a need to understand relationships on a much deeper level than the purely physical. Ketu and Jupiter can also indicate a karmic relationship with sons, especially the eldest. You may experience separation, extreme attachment or guilt connected with them.

You might feel a strong attachment to certain types of philosophy with a strong past life connection and may experiment with different faiths or religions till you find the right one; maybe a doctrine you were unable to follow in a past life.

Ketu and Venus

This shows a definite karma with relationships. The relationships you experience will be so unusual that others may not understand what you are getting out of them. You are still trying to work out a past life karma here, and unless you understand the subtle realities of your relationship patterns, the experiences could be painful or unhappy. You attract partners who carry lots of emotional or spiritual baggage - this would be true for either sex. It could also lead to experimentation with sexuality through gay or lesbian relationships. The Ketu Venus combination brings an unresolved past life relationship into the context of the current life.

As with Ketu and Jupiter in a woman's chart, a man with Ketu and Venus may choose a partner who is not acceptable to his caste or class, or to his family.

More generally, Ketu and Venus indicate a marriage relationship that is very unusual, or unorthodox in some way; or that you will relate to people only on a spiritual level.

Ketu and Saturn

Ketu and Saturn show specific past life issues which crystallise now. The houses where the karmic axis falls will show the areas you are likely to have tough experiences - but of course they do not have to be difficult. Faced with problems, you develop an ability to deal with them and this actually gives you immense strength. As Ketu acts like Mars, Ketu and Saturn are seen as the greatest enemies in the zodiac. Although they do share the same purpose, of guiding you towards your true, spiritual path, they act in very different ways. Saturn separates, Ketu renounces. Saturn operates in the here and now of the real world; Ketu operates on the inner person.

Saturn keeps you firmly anchored in the material world and insists that you face issues that must be confronted in this lifetime. Ketu wants you to renounce the material world and move on; it will not necessarily want you to face up to the issues Saturn is pressing on you. It will try to block your mind.

Past Life Connections with Rahu

Rahu and the Sun

Any connection between Rahu and the Sun is considered an eclipse. This is usually a difficult combination. Firstly Rahu creates problems with the personal connection to the eternal soul. A person with Rahu conjunct the Sun will make an immense mark on the world. Rahu enhances the qualities of the Sun. Your life has a clear direction and success is indicated: a high social position, political career, fame and achievement are all likely. However, as Rahu behaves like Saturn and Saturn and the Sun are not friendly, the negative side of the Sun is also enhanced: over-ambition, selfishness and a rigidity of ideas. There may be strong foreign connections in your life; foreigners can sometimes harm your reputation and you could be involved in a scandal in some way. You might be also afraid to let your own light shine.

Rahu and the Sun may also indicate problems with, even a separation from, your father. You will be always connected to paternal issues in life. Your father could have a dominant influence which you may secretly want to break away from. You will not gain any personal satisfaction from this relationship, but all the same may well feel the need to follow in his footsteps.

Rahu and the Moon

The Moon is afraid of Rahu, which represents darkness. If the Moon is placed with Rahu all those things which the Moon represents - the mind, mother, the emotions - will suffer. Rahu causes fear, anxiety and distrust. Issues from the past will obstruct your growth in this life, usually in the form of fear or phobia that you cannot rationalise and for which there is no explanation. You may lean towards taking drugs or drinking too much. The relationship with your mother is eclipsed in some way (perhaps you were separated from her while very young) and there are hidden factors in your relationships with women in general.

Just as in the myth of Naga Vasuki the ocean was churned up, so with Rahu and the Moon your emotions are always in turmoil. However, in the myth, the nectar of immortality was discovered, so the consequences of having Rahu conjunct the Moon need not be all negative. People with this combination should meditate and practice yoga and mantras. This will help overcome the influence of Rahu and the fear of moving towards the future. The house placement is very important with this conjunction; obviously it will be much harder to deal with in the eighth house than in the ninth.

Rahu and Mars

Rahu acts like Saturn, which is no friend of Mars, so this is a tense, difficult conjunction. You are always testing your power and courage. It could show outward courage and inner fear. Mars does not like limitation. Mars placed within the karmic axis will be concerned in externalising all its previous powers and may not be able to control its potential. Rahu highlights athletic prowess but makes the Martian energy over sexual. Passion, courage and an adventurous spirit are emphasised and this is a good combination for an achievement-orientated career in which these qualities are required. But they can bring unexpected consequences. Rahu and Mars together can make one accident prone and also give you an impetuous temper, even an inclination towards violence.

However, this combination can be a great boost if you choose to follow a spiritual path. Mars and Rahu placed in the tenth or sixth house become very powerful.

Rahu and Mercury

This is a good combination, for Rahu and Mercury are friends. Mercury represents pure intellect and Rahu highlights this to its greatest extent. Past life intellect now has a channel for the strongest possible expression. Together they can give a powerful intelligence, a sharp mind, good powers of communication and knowledge of the hidden side of life. However, Vasuki was a demon, using his powers for his own gain and both he and Mercury are ambivalent energies. You may be intelligent, flexible and charming but perhaps not especially honest! You might use your powers of mind to promote yourself rather than for the greater good. Of course, in today's world that is quite acceptable but it may not help you on the path to true enlightenment.

Rahu and Jupiter

Jupiter's connection with the karmic axis suggests that you are experiencing expansiveness and beneficence. This conjunction enhances good luck. The presence of Jupiter creates a balance between Rahu and Ketu, teaching them wisdom and knowledge of rituals and higher philosophies. As Rahu represents where we are heading in life, Rahu/Jupiter encourages you to seek the very highest knowledge and learning. Rahu represents foreigners - so you could be drawn to foreign philosophies and religions. This is fine in most societies but may prove frustrating within a more traditional environment where such exploration is not acceptable.

On the material level, there can be an abundance of financial gains and you need to be careful that you do not overdo things. However, Rahu and Jupiter do not necessarily give happiness, just wealth.

Jupiter enhances the karmic axis of life making the karmic issues easier to understand. But the connection of Rahu to Jupiter spoils the energy of Jupiter in its pure form.

In a woman's chart, Jupiter represents her partner; Rahu is the significator of foreigners. A woman with Rahu/Jupiter may be attracted to foreign men. She might also be attracted to men who have hidden qualities which can be used in devious ways; she might never know what her husband is up to! Here Jupiter will not give her a traditional marriage partner which nowadays is not so much of a problem.

Jupiter also represents the eldest son. It might mean that your eldest son is somehow foreign to you - the conjunction is often associated with adoption.

Rahu and Venus

Venus and Rahu are friends, so this combination can give financial and material wealth. Rahu emphasises the charm and beauty of Venus, but it can take away its purity. Rahu does not recognise caste or class, so if you have Rahu with Venus you will be able to move freely in any society.

Venus represents marriage generally, and in a man's chart specifically, the kind of woman he will marry. Here, Rahu/Venus can be a difficult combination. A man may be attracted to foreign women or women who are not of his caste or class. He might be attracted to a woman who has had sexual experience without being married: in the past in India such a woman would have been a social outcast. Or he might be attracted to a woman who has seen it all - sex, drugs etc. - and lived through the fear.

Rahu and Saturn

Rahu acts like Saturn and in conjunction they can be doubly malefic. Rahu is an achiever, Saturn an ascetic; with this combination there is a double dose of wisdom through limitation and separation, with the purpose of encouraging detachment from this world. The difficulty is the level at which they operate: Saturn acts physically, Rahu operates through psychological struggles. If you are patient and able to acknowledge the positive energy of Saturn as the teacher of ultimate truths and the guide to your spiritual direction, Rahu and Saturn will give you immense patience to understand the karma of life represented by the nodes. You will learn to recognise your limitations, the cosmic law and your part in Rahu Ketu's learning process. It is a difficult position and understanding it requires great maturity of the soul.

Saturn placed with the karmic axis indicates that the issues of life will be experienced not only on a psychological level but also on a physical level. You have no option but to face them.

73

Rashis - The Signs of the Zodiac

In Vedic astrology the zodiac is referred to as **kalpurusha**, the eternal time which has no beginning and no end - in the Vedas the ecliptic is described as the **Sudarshan chakra** - the wheel in the hand of Lord Vishnu, creator of the universe. The whole chakra is 360°, divided into twelve parts or **rashis** of 30° each, representing twelve constellations, the signs of the zodiac. Together they tell a story of the cosmic evolution of the soul. Each constellation creates a special area of influence which forms the characteristics of that zodiac sign and shows how the sign directs its energy. Unlike Western astrology, each rashi rules one house of your natal chart and so helps describe the part of your life represented by that house. You will need to reflect on how the signs manifest themselves in your own chart. Everyone's experience of them will be slightly different.

Characteristics (swabhava) of the Rashis

Chara (cardinal) signs

Aries, Cancer, Libra and Capricorn are the cardinal signs. Cardinal signs are positive and action-orientated with an outgoing nature. They emphasise leadership, impulsiveness, ambition, wilfulness, and self-confidence. On the negative side, strongly cardinal individuals can be too forceful, arrogant, overambitious and overly active.

Sthira (fixed) signs
Taurus, Leo, Scorpio and Aquarius are the fixed signs. They are reflective, thoughtful, fixed in their ideas, rigid, placid and determined. They are neutral and stable. They like continuity in life and are unwilling to make changes or modify their ideas. They can also be lazy, stagnant and stubborn.

Dwi-swabhava (mutable) signs
Gemini, Virgo, Sagittarius and Pisces are the mutable signs. They are dual-natured and negative, changeable, quick-witted, irate, subtle, adaptable and introverted. They are thinkers and communicators. On the negative side, they can be unstable, erratic, unreliable and great worriers.

Male signs
The male signs are the odd-numbered signs - Aries, Gemini, Leo, Libra, Sagittarius and Aquarius. They have a predominantly masculine nature which in Vedic literature is often described as 'cruel'. Planets in male signs are more dynamic; they take action and tend to accomplish more. Their energy is more outgoing, ambitious and expressive.

Female signs
The female signs are the even-numbered signs - Taurus, Cancer, Virgo, Scorpio, Capricorn and Pisces. Their nature is soft and benefic. Grahas in female signs are more passive, introverted, supportive and reflective. They can take action but to do this they need an outside impetus.

Each sign has the characteristics of one of the elements: fire, earth, air and water.

The fire signs - Aries, Leo and Sagittarius
They are dynamic, strong-willed, determined, independent, forceful and dramatic. They can be argumentative, wilful, vain, egoistic, domineering and self-promoting. They make good leaders, entertainers, sportsmen, actors and other public personalities.

The earth signs - Taurus, Virgo and Capricorn

They are practical, enduring, reliable, committed, materialistic, sensuous and physical. They can also be coarse, overly attached to material goods, unimaginative and resistant to any form of change. They will do well as bankers, gardeners, doctors and farmers and in other types of work emphasising the practical side of life.

The air signs - Gemini, Libra and Aquarius

They are communicative, changeable, full of ideas, inspirational, creative, social, independent, very mentally and intellectually orientated. They can also be impractical, confused, unwilling to face facts, deceptive, unrealistic and nervous. The air signs make good journalists, writers, media people, philosophers, lecturers and intellectuals.

The water signs - Cancer, Scorpio and Pisces

They are intuitive, reflective, emotional, caring, compassionate, intense, secretive and family-orientated. They can be overly emotional, destructive and muddled with a tendency to stagnate. The water signs make good healers, teachers, nurses, chefs, cooks, psychics and creative writers.

As in ayurvedic medicine, each sign and planet (graha) is classified as a specific body type or **dosha**. There are three types: **vata, pitta** and **kapha**. When the three are in balance in the body, we are healthy. When one dosha predominates, it creates illness.

Vata	Vata means wind, or breath
Vata rashis	Taurus, Virgo and Capricorn
Vata grahas	Saturn and Rahu
Attributes	Perception, enthusiasm, inspiration, ability to communicate, exercise, action, dryness.
Pitta	Pitta means bile
Pitta rashis	Aries, Leo and Sagittarius
Pitta grahas	Sun, Mars and Ketu
Attributes	Hunger, thirst, suppleness of body, cheerfulness, intelligence, vision.

In India it is thought that fire is required to digest food. Pitta produces heat and controls the digestive system.

Kapha	Kapha means phlegm, the cold moisture of the body
Kapha rashis	Cancer, Scorpio and Pisces
Kapha grahas	Moon, Venus and Jupiter.
Attributes	Kapha produces stability of the body, potency, strength, supple joints, forbearance.

Tridhatu	A combination of all three humours
Tridhatu rashis	Gemini, Libra and Aquarius
Tridhatu graha	Mercury

The air signs and Mercury share the ability to show the characteristics of any of the basic doshas. The placement of the ruler of the sign in question and Mercury's position will indicate which dosha will predominate. The dosha that is dominant in any chart is indicated by the dosha of the rising sign and its ruler. Looking at the rashi that rules the chart's sixth house, and that rashi's ruler will show which dosha, if any, is likely to become out of balance during your life.

The Rashi Chakra

Each birth chart contains the twelve signs of the zodiac so in some way we are affected by all of them.

Aries - Mesha		0 - 30° of the circle
Number: 1	Guna:	Rajasic
Ruler: Mars	Dosha:	Pitta
Element: Fire	Quality	Cardinal
Male	Symbol:	The Goat

The first sign of the zodiac - a birth or rebirth from a primordial source into matter. The start of a new cycle of life with its pleasures and pain. Its glyph is like a sprouting seed. Wherever Aries is in the birth chart there is newness and a sense of adventure, of moving into unexplored territories.

That the process of creation carries with it immense knowledge and spiritual energy is often missed in the interpretation of the Aries impulse. The important thing to understand here is that Aries represents a new cycle; the many things the Aries individual has learned in past lives may not be of any use to them now. They will need to relearn the lessons of life. They are impulsive and lacking in fear as they have not experienced it before. They may live their life at a low spiritual level, in selfish pursuit of lower desires such as sexual conquest. However, a more mature soul experiencing the Aries new beginning can bring with it healing powers and knowledge.

Mars rules Aries

Giving birth requires physical strength and courage; as a new beginning and a new way of life, Aries needs the rulership of the warrior Mars with his conquering powers and ability to lead. Aries is a pioneer. It requires courage to venture into the unknown, to experience what no other person has experienced. Mars is passionate. In Aries it is always searching for an ideal - searching but never finding.

The Sun is exalted in Aries

In Aries, the Sun (the soul) is still so new it can be totally pure. It has not yet become contaminated by the process of earthly living.

Saturn is debilitated in Aries

Saturn is the planet of death - death of life, death of illusions. It does not want Aries' new life and brightness. The two have opposite characteristics - Aries is impulsive, Saturn is rigid. Aries rushes forward, Saturn tries to delay. Saturn tends to show its worst side in Aries, but even Saturn begins a new cycle when entering that sign. Grahas in Aries act very youthfully!

Taurus - Vrishibha		30-60° of the circle
Number: 2	**Guna:**	**Rajasic**
Ruler: Venus	**Dosha:**	**Vata**
Element: Earth	**Quality:**	**Fixed**
Female	**Symbol:**	**The Bull (Nandi)**

Taurus represents creative potential - sex, procreation and nurture. The need to procreate is part of the soul's mission, the second stage of cosmic evolution. Its symbol is the Nandi bull, Lord Shiva's steed. Nandi is considered very lucky in India. Women pray to it to give them children: Taurean energy is feminine and needs the bull's male impetus to make it fruitful. In Taurus desire predominates, and physical and material needs are paramount. The soul recognises its limitations and its need for nurture, working solely on a material level. Despite an innate laziness Taurus is action-orientated, though it tends to resist change.

The Taurean's sphere of influence is always on a practical level. As well as being a symbol of male potency, the bull is important economically, for tilling the land and as transport. Taureans are suited to careers in business, trade and commerce.

Venus rules Taurus

Venus is very sensuous and loves the finer things in life: money, good food, art, music and beauty. Its desires are essentially materialistic. It likes an atmosphere of permanence.

The Moon is exalted in Taurus

The Moon likes comfort and good things and loves the sensuous promise of Taurus. In any chart, the Moon represents life on Earth and in Taurus the Moon enjoys all life's pleasures. It is happy contained in the earthiness of Taurus.

However, Rahu is exalted here and Ketu debilitated and, like the planets, they have an important psychological effect. Rahu's domain is the Earth, and the Taurean impulse for creation, wealth and stability sees Rahu acting at its best. Ketu, the moksha karaka, feels extremely uncomfortable in Taurus. Its spiritual potential is restricted by Taurean materialism. Grahas in Taurus will be happy to work hard, but they are never in a hurry! Taurus nurtures the qualities of grahas placed in it.

Gemini - Mithun		60-90° of the circle
Number: 3	Guna:	Triguni (sattvic, rajasic and
Ruler: Mercury		tamasic)
Element: Air	Dosha:	Tridhatu
Quality: Mutable	Symbol:	The Twins
Androgynous		

At Gemini, the third stage in the cosmic cycle of the signs, the intellect is born. Gemini's symbol, the twins, symbolises the meeting of universal consciousness and material reality; it also represents the birth of the intellect, the mental (not sexual) joining of the opposing male and female impulses to make **ahamkara**, the ego. Once we have an ego the gunas are formed, because it is only then that we begin to ask questions and to recognise ourselves as something special. The guna senses (rajas, tamas and sattva), live within each of us and they are all contained in Gemini.

There is a duality and an ambivalence within Gemini: male/female, objective/subjective, harmony/chaos, spiritual/material. Gemini energy is about mental agility, understanding the other side, the other point of view. Geminis are intellectuals, changeable and quick-thinking. They lack stability and peace of mind, and can seem very fickle. Looking for ever-higher mental satisfaction, they exist in a state of discontent. They need to be in less of a hurry to change.

Being so capable of deceiving themselves and others, they are difficult to get to know.

Gemini people are good at making money; a practical goal rather than a spiritual one. Being dual-natured, Geminis can intellectualise and be businesslike at the same time! Their purpose is to understand all the workings of earthly life.

Mercury rules Gemini

Mercury represents the rashi of pure mind. It is quick-thinking and quick-moving - there is no stillness here. The need for mental activity and for independence is very strong. Geminis need to be careful that in their search for higher intellectual satisfaction, they do not lose sight of their present goals.

No grahas are debilitated in Gemini; although Mars is uncomfortable with its duality, its intellectual searching and restlessness.

Cancer - Karkata		90-120° of the circle
Number: 4	Guna:	Sattvic
Ruler: The Moon	Dosha:	Kapha
Element: Water	Quality:	Cardinal
Female	Symbol:	The Crab

The symbol of Cancer is the crab which lives in water but moves onto the land. At this stage of cosmic evolution, the soul is still immersed in universal consciousness (water) but is learning to live the practical reality (Earth). The ten feet of the crab are the ten sense organs of man, five working inwardly and five outwardly. In Indian numerology the number ten represents perfection. Cancer people are seeking perfection in this life. The crab has a hard crust and the shedding of the shell represents the continuity of the soul through various physical reincarnations.

The sattvic quality of Cancer is very pure and high-minded and these people often feel that their journey through life will involve making sacrifices.

Cancer's skills are best used in the material realm. Cancer is very aware of money and deals with finances well.

The Moon rules Cancer
The Moon waxes and wanes and there is some change to be seen in it every day. It is outgoing but introspective, mysterious and secretive. Cancer has the ability to reflect all those characteristics. The Moon is the fastest moving planet in the zodiac and Cancer people are never still. They need to recognise that their personality waxes and wanes with changes of mood like the Moon's phases. Being a water sign, Cancer people are emotional, possessive and very adaptable.

Jupiter is exalted in Cancer
Cancer nurtures Jupiter's wisdom and Jupiter understands and guides Cancer's energy.

Mars is debilitated in Cancer
As a planet of action without reflection, Mars finds the moody emotionalism of Cancer (Cancer is kapha) difficult. Cancer disperses Mars' energy/focus.

Grahas in Cancer look at life through subjective eyes: they feel rather than think.

Leo - Simha   120-150° of the circle
Number: 5   **Guna:** Sattvic
Ruler: The Sun   **Dosha:** Pitta
Element: Fire   **Quality:** Fixed
Male   **Symbol:** The Lion

Leo allows the inner being to express itself. Leo is about individuality. Its element is fire, so it is virile and independent, active and larger-than-life. It is sattvic and retains its idealism at the same time as recognising the need to live life on the practical level; it is essential for the soul's progress towards maturity. You must experience life on Earth to be able to move beyond it.

The Lion represents power and male potency. In the Vedas goddesses like **Durga, Uma, Kali** and **Vaishno devi** all rode on lions, uniting that male potency with the power of the female. Leo's self-expression blends male and female powers on a universal level.

Their leadership qualities draw people to them. They are very steady people, but with a tendency to resist change.

The Sun rules Leo

In Indian philosophy the Sun is the ruler of the universe and the planets revolve around it. However, there is an element of loneliness about the Sun in Leo - no one can get close to so much fire. Kings rule alone.

Mars is very happy with Leo's fiery energy, its idealism and power. No graha is debilitated in Leo - they become more fiery, powerful and creative in Leo.

Virgo - Kanya		**150-180° of the circle**
Number: 6	**Guna:**	**Tamasic**
Ruler: **Mercury**	**Dosha:**	**Vata**
Element: Earth	**Quality:**	**Mutable**
Female	**Symbol:**	**The Virgin**

At this stage in the cosmic cycle the karma of past lives dictates that the soul in this life must be completely involved in the material world; careers in business and commerce suit them well. However, involvement solely in these concerns doesn't nurture the inner self. The soul knows it must fulfil its material role in the divine plan, but without spiritual consciousness to sustain it, material satisfaction brings emptiness and despair. The material world has become an obstacle in the way of true happiness. Virgo is a stage of divine discontent.

Virgo is the only sign with a human symbol so it has the strongest human influence. The Virgin symbolises the perfection of the pure feminine and this purity is what the Virgo's inner self craves. Virgos need to find a balance between their inner and outer selves and to recognise the inner self lost under sheaths of materialism. Mercury rules Virgo and so there is a duality and a changeability present. Through yoga and meditation, Virgos have the ability to transcend the limitations imposed by their karma.

Mercury rules Virgo and is exalted there

As ruler of Virgo, Mercury represents the power of the intellect to overcome practical limitations. Virgos tend to be very thought- and plan-orientated. The exaltation of Mercury in Virgo symbolises the intense mental activity undertaken by Virgos in trying to overcome the limitations imposed on them by karma from previous lives.

Venus is debilitated in Virgo

The obstacles faced by Virgo and its striving for perfection makes sensuous Venus question itself. It ceases to enjoy life as it comes and starts questioning everything that comes its way.

Grahas in Virgo become heavily involved in the material world. They also have a great need to focus their attention on objective (rather than subjective) analysis.

Libra - Tula		180-210° of the circle
Number: 7	Guna:	Rajasic
Ruler: Venus	Dosha:	Tridhatu
Element: Air	Quality:	Cardinal
Male	Symbol:	The Scales

Libra is the halfway point of the zodiac and as such represents the end of our material dreams and the beginning of our spiritual ones. (In Indian philosophy relationships are part of the material world). We realise how we have lost our inherent spirituality through too great an involvement in the darkness of the material world. The start of the journey towards higher wisdom and consciousness is represented by Libra; it guides us towards achieving a fine balance, in which we experience material life to the full but are no longer trapped in it. It is here we finally begin our spiritual quest.

Decision-making in any form is difficult for Librans, and action as opposed to non-action is usually at the root of the dilemma. To marry or not to marry? Dependence or independence? Conflict or compromise? Company or solitude? Squash or meditation? It is a constant battle to find a balance between the extremes that present themselves on a daily basis. If there is a persistent lack of balance the Libran becomes uncomfortable; however, achieving it is very difficult. Symbolically it is represented by the point in Shiva's Dance where he balances on one foot. Libra is an air sign and the only sign of the zodiac solely represented by an inanimate object. Librans will search for balance throughout their lives, which can make them seem very detached and impersonal to others. Libra is male energy and rajasic. Librans are action-orientated and make good leaders.

Venus rules Libra

Venus desires the good things of life, but in Libra it has a more important role. Venus was known as **Bhrighu** in the Vedas and was the advisor to the demons - the highly evolved souls who have lost their purity in the pursuit of self. Venus's rulership of the crucial sign of Libra indicates the need for guidance on the route towards higher consciousness. However, Venus doesn't initiate. If you are ready to begin your spiritual quest, it will help you. If you are not, it is happy to wait and enjoy the ride.

Saturn is exalted in Libra

Saturn's mission is to move individual consciousness on the final journey to spiritual liberation, so it is exalted in the sign where this journey begins. Saturn knows that a materialistic outlook isn't everything and that sooner or later every individual will have to look for something more. Then Saturn will direct the mind towards its true purpose. Libra is the sign for relationships - Saturn breaks away from the relationships of illusion on earth to the more permanent relationship of the soul with the divine.

The Sun is debilitated in Libra

In Libra, the purity of the Soul (the Sun) is sullied by such emphasis on the physical world.

Grahas in Libra are usually pulled in two different directions, and are always seeking a sense of equilibrium.

Scorpio - Vrishchika		210-240° of the circle
Number: 8	Guna:	Tamasic
Ruler: Mars	Dosha:	Kapha
Element: Water	Quality:	Fixed
Female	Symbol:	The Scorpion

Scorpio is the sign in which our material ties loosen and where the kundalini, the latent power within us, resides. Both negative and positive in quality, the hidden knowledge is very potent - proper understanding of these forces can give great power but activated in an immature soul it is extremely dangerous.

The symbol of Scorpio is the Scorpion, which lives in a hole in the ground and is associated with occult power. (Vasuki, the ruler of Patal Loka who helped the gods and became Rahu and Ketu, lived in a hole too.)

Scorpio is the stage at which Vasuki's churning begins in an individual's life. All the emotions are in turmoil (the Moon is debilitated here) because the search is for the Amrita, the nectar of immortality. Scorpio is the abode of Rahu and Scorpios face a great deal of negative issues from past karma. Material life is no longer enough, its bonds have to be destroyed and the kundalini aroused. It is a very painful process. The kundalini can be only activated by the complete annihilation of the individual personality; the activation of the chakras and the search for the higher self is very dangerous and even individuals who are spiritually ready will need great self-discipline. The churning is like a death, a stripping-away of the outer layers to reveal an inner purity; the higher an individual's incarnation this time around, the more painful the churning.

Vedic astrology considers Scorpio to be one of the most difficult signs in the zodiac. It is intense, complex and difficult to comprehend. As a water sign it is psychic and very deeply emotional. However, it is a fixed sign and water needs to flow. Scorpios need to ensure their emotions do not stagnate. Scorpio is kapha, and its strength of feeling can often result in health problems. Its guna is tamasic. It has to deal with material issues but wants to move towards spirituality and purity and the struggle between these two creates great dilemmas.

Scorpio has great powers and spiritual energy but these gifts come with a great deal of psychological distress. Scorpio is the point of the death of illusions and of past ways of life, where we realise that our lives will never be the same again.

Jyotish does not make the Western connection between Scorpio and sex - it is simply part of everyday life. There is an underlying sexual energy in Scorpios which is not satisfied through just the physical expression and indicates an inner quest. When the female scorpion has mated, she kills the male: the route of the spiritual life is one we must follow alone.

Mars rules Scorpio

The courage, leadership and strength of Mars is essential for those who are on a spiritual quest. Aries is where we are born into a new cycle of life. In Scorpio an old self is destroyed so that a new one can be born. Spiritual courage is needed here to consciously choose a material death. Mars is active and has a need to conquer. In Scorpio the enemy is your own desires. Aries is bright. Scorpio is full of darkness but a journey through the darkness will lead to the final light.

Ketu is exalted and Rahu debilitated here.

The Moon is debilitated in Scorpio

The Moon represents the mind. The Moon is content with material happiness. It doesn't want emotional trauma or to recognise its own mortality.

Grahas in Scorpio become very intense and do not expect or receive simple answers.

The glyph for Scorpio is often described as the sting in the tail. But is also an arrow in a powerful spiritual direction - an arrow leading into the next sign.

Sagittarius - Dhanus		240-270° of the circle
Number: 9	Guna:	Sattvic
Ruler: Jupiter	Dosha:	Pitta
Element: Fire	Quality:	Mutable
Male		

Symbol: The Centaur, and the Bow and Arrow

The Centaur is half-man, half-beast. Sagittarius is the stage in the cosmic cycle where the animal turns into a human, striving to control its lower impulses so that the soul can move ahead on its final journey. Sagittarius is a warrior. The sign's name, Dhanus, links it with Arjun, the warrior to whom Krishna gave his divine message in the Bhagvad Gita. Arjun aspires to divine consciousness but finds that in order to achieve it, he has to conquer those he holds dear. The backdrop of the Bhagvad Gita is the battlefield where Arjun is fighting his own family. In the midst of the battle Arjun decides to stop fighting rather than injure or kill those he loves. Lord Krishna appears to Arjun and helps him decide what he should do next by guiding him towards the duty (dharma) which is his destiny. The recognition of our duty to life, our true destiny, takes place in Sagittarius. On a spiritual level, the war between Arjun and his relatives is the war we fight everyday in trying to conquer our human desires. To reach the final path of our spiritual mission, the temptations of the material life have to be resisted. Lord Krishna gives Arjun a clue about how to overcome them. That is Jupiter's message - how to move beyond being merely animal, a slave to our own human desires.

As we move along the path of self-discovery, our choices become increasingly difficult; the churning of our emotions begun in Scorpio continues. There is conflict between our sexual impulses and our spiritual ones. Material achievements no longer satisfy us, but our spiritual growth is still in its infancy. Discipline and austerity, aspiration and discipleship will help us enter into the secrets of hidden knowledge.

Jupiter rules Sagittarius

Jupiter is the teacher, guide and spiritual initiator. It is also the planet of plenty, and of good fortune, especially in the non-material areas of life. No grahas are either exalted or debilitated in Sagittarius.

Capricorn - Makara **270-300° of the circle**
Number: 10 **Guna:** **Tamasic**
Ruler: **Saturn** **Dosha:** **Vata**
Element: Earth **Quality:** **Cardinal**
Female **Symbol: The Crocodile**

The sign of Capricorn provides the bridge between Man and the Supreme and now the individual is consciously co-operating with the divine plan. It is an initiation into a different stage of life. The newly-emerging Man realises that on the spiritual path, as in the material world, there are goals to be reached (Capricorn is the cardinal earth sign and Mars is exalted there).

Initiations are painful. This stage in the cosmic cycle is one of taking on problems, of deliberately making it difficult for yourself in order to evoke any negative karma and deal with it now. When it has been dealt with you can move beyond your own problems to a state of more universal awareness. Paying the price for past actions (karma) is not an easy choice. Qualities of renunciation and self-sacrifice are being developed in order to activate the deeper levels of the soul. Capricorn is the sign of duty and hard work and Capricorn's temperament fits them for working. Capricorns are very steady people, serious and with a heavy sense of responsibility. They have a tendency to suffer from depression.

Makara is the crocodile and fittingly Capricorn is the sign opposite Cancer. Whereas the crab lives in water and moves towards earth, the crocodile lives on the riverbank but is also at home in the water (the universal soul). The life of the crocodile symbolises the Capricorn stage, where you are still living in the material world but moving along the final path towards the submergence of your individuality in the universal sea.

Saturn rules Capricorn
Saturn will act like its true self in its own sign but Capricorn brings out its heaviest qualities. Saturn is the graha of karma and in Capricorn the individual is faced with the results of actions in past lives. It also represents austerity and denial, acting through restriction and limitations to force people to change.

Mars is exalted in Capricorn

In the sign of Mars' greatest enemy! But he relishes being amongst his foes - and you will need his courage to face the challenge of Capricorn.

Jupiter is debilitated in Capricorn

The heavy demands of Capricorn require the right kind of action. It is not a time for expansion, optimism or looking forward. Jupiter's rituals and philosophical debates cannot flourish and are not appropriate. Grahas in Capricorn act more slowly and feel heavyweight.

Aquarius - Kumbha		300-330° of the circle
Number: 11	Guna:	Tamasic
Ruler: Saturn	Dosha:	Tridhatu
Element: Air	Quality:	Fixed
Male	Symbol:	A pitcher holding water

Aquarius is an air sign and the word Kumbha is associated with **kumbhaka**, a yogic practice of breath control. Breath is prana, the life within us. If we are able to retain and control our breath, we are able to control life. Symbolically then, we are able to understand the secret of life and death.

The symbol of Aquarius is the pitcher, representing the human ego. Water gives life and can turn base metal into gold. It is used in purification rituals. The Aquarian water-bearer symbolises the merging of the individual with the universal life force. It is at this stage in the cosmic cycle that the crown chakra is activated, giving knowledge of the cosmic plan. The individual finally understands the true meaning and purpose of this life; there are no more goals to be fulfilled. However, Aquarius is ruled by Saturn and is not an easy sign. There is still work to be done. As the individual starts to break free from his individual ego and work in accordance with cosmic law, traditional ideas and worldly attachments are inevitable destroyed. Saturn is ruthless in forcing you to recognise the final goals. The Aquarian impulse is on a thinking level not an emotional one. The pitcher can only pour forth its water of universal life if it is broken - symbolising the need for the final breaking down of the individual personality. In Aquarius you are forced to work for the good of all rather than for personal ambitions.

Saturn rules Aquarius

Again, Saturn acts like its true self in its own sign. Again, responsibility and duty are highlighted but this time it is the responsibility of the individual to work for the good of all. You have all the world's problems on your shoulders. However, there are rather fewer lessons to be learned in Aquarius than in Capricorn.

There are no grahas in exaltation or in debilitation in Aquarius. It has moved beyond the personal to the universal and grahas placed here will tend to act for higher causes, not for personal gain.

Pisces - Mina		**330 - 360° of the circle**	
Number: 12		**Guna:**	Sattvic
Ruler: Jupiter		**Dosha:**	Kapha
Element: Water		**Quality:**	Mutable
Female			

Symbol: Two fish facing in opposite directions

The last stage of the cosmic cycle is where individual consciousness merges completely with the universal. The Pisces fish are not like the Cancer crab or the Capricorn crocodile - they cannot live out of water. Pisces people have to merge their individuality with cosmic forces. The great ocean is infinite and silent. The process of merging does not necessarily bring peace, but it does bring calm. Understanding the universal truth frees us from bondage to the cycle of life and death. Pisces people know we all have to bow to cosmic law and they have the strength to face the ups and downs of life; they accept the restrictions of the material world and allow their minds to become submerged in the eternal.

Pisces is a mutable sign. Theirs is a dual, changeable nature, very difficult to assess. Free from the bonds of personality, knowing the secret of life, these people can merge themselves with anything and anyone - but risk becoming victimised or an extension of their partner. They make good writers and actors.

Jupiter rules Pisces

Jupiter is true wisdom and the great teacher.

Venus is exalted in Pisces

Venus signifies semen and therefore birth and procreation; the conception of a new life, which links the ending of one cycle with the beginning of the next.

Mercury is debilitated in Pisces

There is no need for an intellect identified with the individual in Pisces. The knowledge of Pisces is on another plane.

Planets in Pisces are passive and more concerned with universal than with personal energies.

Bhavas - The Houses

In Vedic astrology the natal chart is known as the **Bhava Chakra** or the **Rasi Chakra**. In Sanskrit **bhava** means a division and **chakra** means a wheel - so the bhava chakra is the full 360° circle of life, divided into parts. It also represents our own personal way of enacting the energies in that wheel. The bhava chakra shows what we bring into our life, how we are going to express it, what obstructions we are going to face and what good fortune will be there to make things easier for us.

The bhavas are imaginary divisions, designed to show the whole wheel of the zodiac as it relates to earth but reduced to the size of a horoscope chart. Several different systems are used by Vedic astrologers to try to overcome this problem of down-sizing; the two main ones are:

Bhava Chakra (similar to the Porphyry system in the west)
This house system takes the degree of the sign rising at the eastern horizon (the ascendant) and the degree of the sign overhead (the Midheaven) and divides the number of degrees between them into three. This is repeated with the degree of the ascendant and the Nadir (the point opposite the Midheaven; and the Nadir and the degree of the sign descending at the western horizon (the descendant). These calculations identify the boundaries of each house; the cusp

is the point in the middle of the two boundary lines. The houses will not necessarily contain the same number of degrees.

Rashi Kundali (known as the Whole Sign system)
With this system each house is 30° across, like the zodiac signs; it's more straightforward to use as, regardless of the actual degree of your ascendant, if your rising sign is say, Libra, then Libra will be your first house, Scorpio your second - and so on, around the signs with each sign covering one house. The rashi kundali is the most commonly used system in India, and it is the one I use in this book.

General Rules Governing the Houses

The Kendras - the cardinal houses
These are the first, fourth, seventh and tenth houses.
Planets that are placed in the kendras are strong. Benefics (Jupiter, Venus, the Moon and Mercury) become malefics if they rule a cardinal house in your chart. Conversely, the malefics (Saturn, the Sun and Mars) become benefic when they rule a cardinal house. Planets placed in cardinal houses have a great deal of energy.

The Trikonas - the trine houses
A trine is a beneficial aspect linking signs in the same element. The trikona houses are the first, fifth and ninth. The fifth and ninth houses both trine the first house which represents you personally; the first house is also a kendra.
    The rulers of the trikona houses are always auspicious and bring wonderful results, although the ruler of the fifth house is not as powerful as the ruler of the ninth. The rulers of the fifth and ninth houses will bring good luck even if they also rule negative houses. Planets placed in the fifth and ninth houses will flourish, as will the houses they in turn rule, whilst planets placed in the first house highlight personal issues.

The Upachayas - the developing houses
These are the third, sixth, tenth and eleventh houses.
Planets ruling upachaya houses act negatively and have the capacity

to cause harm. Malefic planets flourish in them and benefic planets do not give such good results - their energy tends to be restricted. In addition, the tenth house is a cardinal house (see previous page). The third house is the weakest upachaya house and the eleventh the strongest. Planets located in upachaya houses gain in strength as you mature; you tend to feel their more negative side when you are younger.

The Sama - the neutral houses

These are the second, eighth and twelfth houses.
They usually act in the same way as the other house ruled by their planetary ruler. In practice, however, the rulers of the eighth and the twelfth houses are always malefic (see below).

The Dusthana - the evil houses

These are the sixth, eighth and twelfth houses.
The normal behaviour of planets placed in these houses is spoilt as is their strength over the houses they rule. Planets placed here usually indicate problems on a material level which are telling you to redirect your energy to a higher sphere. The ruler of the sixth house can cause injury and disease. The ruler of the eighth house destroys the significations of the house where it is placed. The ruler of the twelfth house causes loss of some kind.

The Karakas - significators

Each house has one planet which is more significant to it than any other. It is important to consider the karaka planet when looking at the quality of any house. The karaka and its placement in the chart can alter the interpretation of a particular house by altering its benefic or malefic influence. (See the notes on the individual houses for details of their karakas.)

Maraka or death-giving planets

Maraka planets have death-giving powers. They create situations during your life when something dies - a relationship, a career, a cherished idea - resulting in periods of mourning and personal transformation. When the time is right, the transformation will be physical death itself. In each natal chart there are two maraka planets, the rulers of the second and the seventh houses. However, the death-giving powers they have can be mitigated in certain situations (see the individual rising signs). The death-giving situations are created by your own maraka planet or planets during their dasha periods (these are discussed in the Dasha chapter of this book) when the events which are promised in the birth chart will occur.

At one time one of the most important things a jyotishi in India would include in the reading of the natal chart was the time of physical death - but this practice is no longer as common as it used to be, and it is non-existent in the West. However, the rulers of first and the eighth houses indicate how long you are likely to live and I do refer to this in the section on the eighth house.

Lagna - The Ascendant and First House

The **lagna**, or ascendant, is the first moment of contact between the soul and its new life on earth. There is a clear distinction between this and the tanu bhava; the lagna is the exact degree of the sign that is rising on the Eastern horizon at the moment of birth and determines the ruler of the ascendant, while the tanu bhava is the **whole** of the first house. In practice however, the term lagna is often used as a way of expressing them simultaneously. As each sign also has its nakshatra divisions, two and a quarter in each sign, the degree of your rising sign will give you the rising nakshatra as well. It connects on subtler levels to your previous births and contains all the mysteries of your past lives; in Indian philosophy all new beginnings have a past. Your destiny is the sum of the karma of your previous lives, and these are represented by your first house - a new cycle in the journey of the soul.

On the physical level the lagna represents the body characteristics, physique, skeleton, complexion, texture and colour of the hair and overall appearance. It rules the head, brains and skull, and also indicates how well you withstand illness or disease. The lagna indicates your personality and nature - how you approach life and overcome obstacles, being the 'first impression' we all pick up on meeting somebody new. The karaka planet for the ascendant is the Sun - self, atma, soul.

The line from the degree of the lagna to the point 180° opposite joins the east and west horizons and divides the houses into two groups: 2 - 6 are below and 8 - 12 are above the horizon, with the first and seventh houses actually being cut in two by the line. Planets below the line and therefore below the horizon indicate past karma you will face in this life over which you have no control - but it is neither good nor bad: your ability in this life to play music or learn foreign languages easily comes from your past karma. Planets above the horizon are more active. They offer opportunities to create fresh karma during this lifetime. Only if there is an even balance of planetary influences above and below the horizon will the energies be balanced. Looking at the grouping of the planets relative to the line of the horizon is a good way to begin to interpret an individual chart. You will be able to make a quick assessment of the person's overall personality and how, in general, the planetary energies are likely to work in them.

The lagna ruler - Lord of the ascendant

The planet ruling the sign of the lagna becomes the most important planet in the birth chart and is known as the Lord of the ascendant. You will take on some of the characteristics of the planet which is Lord of your lagna. The house it occupies, the planets that are placed with it, which sign it is in, and whether the sign is friendly to the rising sign or an enemy, what aspects it is making: all these are important components to evaluate. (See the Graha chapter.) If the lagna ruler is in exaltation, in its mooltrikona, or its own house it can give the individual the ability to face adversity with strength. If it is debilitated or in a house ruled by an enemy planet, it will create problems which can be overcome with a struggle.

In chart interpretation I always study the ascending sign and its ruler before anything else as they will tell you a great deal about the overall focus of the individual's life and what they might expect from it, on the physical as well as the spiritual level. Each lagna has planets which act negative or positively for it.

When we say a person is an Aries or a Scorpio in Vedic astrology, we mean their ascendant is Aries or Scorpio.

The Ascending Signs

A malefic planet can change its function relative to the lagna, in the same way that benefics can change their characteristics. Saturn is considered the greatest malefic but becomes the best planet for those with a Taurus or Libra lagna. In the same way Jupiter, which is considered the best benefic, functions as a malefic for Taurus and Libra rising. Mars, another malefic, is good for Cancer and Leo lagna. I'll go into this in more depth within each lagna section.

Aries - ruled by Mars

Action is the key word here. If your lagna is in Aries you will need to contribute to the world in a positive way. Mars will give you courage, strength and determination. An Aries individual is usually average in height and well-built. Eager to take the initiative, new challenges are a must, and routine work will always bore you. Aries people are freedom-loving and the restrictions of Saturn are the greatest test. If your lagna is Aries, Mars will also rule the eighth house of longevity. If it is well-placed in the chart Mars will indicate a long life, though the responsibility would be your own. However a debilitated Mars could indicate muscle problems and blood disorders. Saturn, Mercury and Venus act negatively with this lagna. The Sun and Jupiter are very positive although Jupiter can sometimes cause problems because it rules the twelfth house of loss as well as the auspicious ninth house. Venus is the maraka planet for Aries rising.

Taurus - ruled by Venus

Venus rules the good things in life and Taurus being an earth sign, the good things have to be practical and earthy: food and sex! These people admire beauty and enjoy luxury. People with Taurus rising are usually physically attractive, with a thick neck and broad shoulders, although they have a tendency to put on weight. Venus also rules the sixth (difficult) house - guard against putting obstacles in your own way. Venus can also show itself here as relationships with partners from foreign countries. The Moon, Mars and Jupiter also act negatively for people with Taurus rising. The good news however, is that the normally difficult Saturn functions at its best here and the Sun and Mercury are also good. Mars is the maraka planet for Taurus.

Mercury can be too as the ruler of the second house, but as it also rules the benefic fifth house its maraka qualities are not emphasised.

Gemini - ruled by Mercury

People with Gemini rising are usually tall, slim and attractive, with large hands and feet; they have lovely eyes and sharp features. This sign is all about mental activity. Lagnas in Gemini have a dual personality and the ability to see the other point of view. However, they can sometimes be deceitful, even to the point of self-deception. Mercury also rules your fourth house, and when a benefic planet rules a cardinal house it becomes malefic, so Mercury can create problems in the first house (your self) as well as the fourth (mother, your intimate feelings). Similarly so with Jupiter, which rules the cardinal seventh and tenth houses. Mars' rulership of your sixth and eleventh houses gives it the capacity to create problems, as its purely physical energy doesn't work well with intellectual Mercury; and the Sun, ruling the negative third house, has an inherently adverse relationship with Mercury. Even Mercury's natural friends can create problems for the Gemini lagna. Saturn rules the auspicious ninth house and the inauspicious eighth house while Venus rules the positive fifth house but also the negative twelfth house.

In common with Virgo, Gemini does not have a planet that acts in a wholly positive way. This lagna suggests that major issues will have to be reconciled in the current life. The Moon and Jupiter are the maraka planets for Gemini rising.

Cancer - ruled by the Moon

People with lagna in Cancer are of medium height with a moon-shaped face. Like Taureans they have a tendency to put on weight. If you have Cancer rising you will need to be especially aware of the waxing and waning phases of the Moon as these will greatly affect you. Lagnas in Cancer are very moon-like - mysterious, changeable and secretive. Cancer is a water sign so you are likely to be very emotional. Water has the ability to boil as well as freeze. The Moon is the significator of the mother and you will always feel a great need to nurture others. You are able to adapt easily and will feel at home in any situation.

Venus is a benefic planet, but ruling the cardinal fourth house and the eleventh house, it is not positive. Mercury is also negative as it rules the third and the twelfth houses. The Moon is afraid of Saturn, the death-inflicting planet for Cancer, and those with lagna in Cancer have Saturn ruling their seventh and eighth houses. The Sun is not always positive. Mars is the Moon's great friend as it rules the auspicious fifth and the powerful tenth houses, and is raja yogakaraka - a planet that can make kings. Even if Mars is debilitated in the chart it still gives very good results. Jupiter is a benefic planet, only creating problems as ruler of the negative sixth house. The Sun and Saturn are the maraka planets for Cancer rising.

Leo - ruled by the Sun

Leo is a royal sign and its symbol, the lion, is called the king of the jungle. People with Leo rising have a regal appearance with a broad face with strong bones. However, Leo men can have a receding hairline with a tendency towards baldness. If you have lagna in Leo you will be basically materialistic but like to be spiritually aware. You will be both an idealist and ambitious. You have the ability to take sudden action, and can become extremely involved in a project or romance, only to give it up with no warning. Lagnas in Leo tend to expect others to fit in with what **they** want. As Saturn, the Sun's enemy, rules the seventh house, relationships can be a difficult area, with struggles for power and clashes of ambition. Leo, Saturn, Mercury and Venus are negative planets for you: Saturn rules the sixth house as well as the seventh, Mercury rules the second and eleventh houses, and Venus the third and tenth. Jupiter can be a good planet but it can cause problems through its rulership of the negative eighth house. The Moon is generally considered neutral for Leo rising, but depending on its overall strength in the chart, can sometimes bring emotional stress and mental suffering connected with loss. Mars is the best planet for this lagna as it rules the fourth and ninth houses and is a raja yogakaraka - a king-making planet. It can give great success and happiness.

Mercury has a special quality for Leo rising: it rules the two houses of wealth - the second and eleventh. If Mercury is well placed it will yield good results financially, but it can create problems elsewhere. Mercury and Saturn are the maraka planets for Leo rising.

Virgo - ruled by Mercury
Virgo is a practical and materialistic sign. Virgos often have an air of innocence about them. They are usually of medium build and fair, with a broad face and shy eyes. With a lagna in Virgo you will be a good, successful worker in an office or business environment, as a lawyer or diplomat, or in administrative work. However, you may find it difficult to live up to your own high standards - Virgo seeks perfection. Jupiter, Mars and the Moon are the negative planets for you: Mars rules the third and eighth houses, both malefic; the Moon rules the eleventh house and the eleventh house ruler is always negative. In addition, Jupiter is a benefic planet made malefic by ruling the cardinal seventh house (it also rules the fourth). The Sun rules the negative twelfth house.

Venus rules the auspicious ninth house, making it the best planet for lagnas in Virgo. Saturn is Mercury's friend but in a chart with Virgo rising it rules the difficult sixth house as well as the benefic fifth and so is unable to give completely positive results. So like Gemini, the other Mercury-ruled sign, Virgo does not really have a planet which acts completely positively. This situation indicates that on a spiritual level, lagnas in Virgo have some major issues to work out during this life.

Venus rules the second house for Virgo rising, however its maraka qualities are lessened as it also rules the benefic ninth house. Jupiter too is a maraka planet for lagnas in Virgo.

Libra - ruled by Venus
People with lagna in Libra are of average height, slim and attractive with long faces and soft eyes. As Libra is an air sign, communication is important. They are sociable and need to be appreciated.
Libra's symbol is the scales and lagnas in Libra need to balance their life on all levels - trying to achieve this can result in overdoing things. There is a tendency to be judgmental; as the scales are the only non-human symbol of the zodiac somebody with Libra rising can detached and impersonal.

With Venus as the ruling planet they will have a great liking for the fine things in life. However, Venus also rules the secretive eighth house and lagnas in Libra are often responsible for causing their own problems here. Jupiter, Mars and the Sun are negative influences: Mars rules the second and seventh houses and is the maraka planet, Jupiter rules the difficult third and sixth houses, creating obstacles and sudden transformations, and the Sun rules the eleventh house. Saturn is good for lagnas in Libra as it rules the cardinal fourth and auspicious fifth houses. For them it is a raja yogakaraka planet. It ensures success. A conjunction of the Moon and Mercury is good for Libra rising.

Scorpio - ruled by Mars

People with Scorpio rising are beautiful with a well-shaped body, which can very sexy too. There is great emotional sensitivity, but there is always have a sting in the tail so you will be capable of great vindictiveness and nurture a tendency to be secretive too. The conflict between this base self and a strong spiritual side will dominate in life. Mars rules the sixth house as well as the first, so there will be times when you are your own worst enemy. You won't need other people to cause you harm; you'll do that very well for yourself! With Scorpio rising, Saturn, Mercury and Venus will be negative influences. Mercury rules the eighth and eleventh houses and Venus the seventh and twelfth. Saturn is your ruling planet's greatest enemy. Ruling the third and fourth houses it will put obstructions in your path which the Martian energy will find difficult to accept.

The Moon (ruling the ninth house) and Jupiter (ruling the fifth) are very positive influences and you will also have the Sun ruling the powerful and karmic tenth house. Jupiter rules the second house if you have Scorpio rising, but it also rules the fifth, so its maraka qualities are lessened. Venus is your maraka planet, through its rulership of your seventh house.

Sagittarius - ruled by Jupiter

People with lagnas in Sagittarius are tall with a broad face, long neck, sharp nose and large ears. If you have lagna in Sagittarius, Jupiter's influence will make you philanthropic, religious and wise, with a great need for freedom. It also gives you a tendency to give others advice which may be unwanted! You will make a good teacher. You like the outdoor life and may be good at sport.

Jupiter also rules your fourth house; unfortunately, when a benefic planet rules a cardinal house it becomes malefic, so in this case you can have problems dealing with its expansive energy. Unless it is strongly placed, Mercury will also turn from benefic to malefic, ruling the seventh and tenth houses. For Sagittarius rising, Venus is the most negative planet as it rules both the sixth house and the eleventh, both of which can signify injury and disease in your life.

For lagnas in Sagittarius, Mars and the Sun are positive planets - the Sun particularly so, as it rules the very auspicious ninth house. Any conjunction of the Sun and Mars is very good for Sagittarius rising. The Moon can give you problems, ruling the dark eighth house. Saturn, ruler of the second and third houses, is a maraka planet for lagnas in Sagittarius, and so also Mercury, as ruler of the seventh.

Capricorn - ruled by Saturn

Lagnas in Capricorn are usually tall with a well-built upper body. They usually live a long time, especially if Saturn is strong in the chart. If you have lagna in Capricorn you will have an essentially pragmatic approach to life and be patient, hard-working and persevering but perhaps rather distant on a personal level. With Saturn as your ruler, you will have a tendency towards depression and negativity, but Saturn will also give you the ability to face trials in the process of achieving your goals. Beneath the materialism you will have a strong spiritual side and the ability to endure a great deal of hardship if you choose to follow a spiritual path. Jupiter, Mars and the Moon will be negative influences for you: Jupiter rules the third and twelfth houses and Mars the fourth and eleventh. Relationships will be challenging as Saturn's enemy the Moon rules the seventh house. Eighth house issues will also be difficult, as that house is ruled by the Sun, enemy to Saturn. However, Venus and Mercury are more positive influences. Venus rules the fifth and the tenth house and so becomes a raja yogakaraka planet, powerfully enhancing the chart. Mercury rules the sixth and the ninth houses and is generally a good planet for you although it can create some problems - you will be tempted to flit from one subject to another, rather than settle down to study something in depth. Saturn itself rules the second house, and the Moon the seventh, so they are the maraka planets for Capricorns.

Aquarius - ruled by Saturn

In Vedic astrology, Aquarius is considered the most difficult rising sign as Saturn rules the first house as well as the twelfth house of loss. We consider that lagnas in Aquarius indicate very evolved souls who will have to bear a great deal of suffering, karmic in nature; working for something more than just the obvious rewards will give you more fulfilment. Aquarians are not necessarily physically beautiful but they do have strong personalities. Jupiter rules the second and eleventh houses and, like Mercury in Leo, can help financially but may bring problems in other areas. Venus is a yogakaraka planet, giving success, and it works well with Saturn. Mercury is usually neutral with this lagna as it rules the fifth and eighth houses.

Mars, the Moon and the Sun will act negatively - Mars rules your third and tenth houses and the Moon rules your sixth. The Sun is always the enemy of Saturn and ruling your seventh house it indicates that there will be testing times with marriage and other partnerships. Jupiter and the Sun are your maraka planets.

Pisces - ruled by Jupiter

Pisces lagnas are usually large people with deep mysterious eyes. As Pisces is a water sign, it is likely that you will be intuitive and very emotional, possibly psychic and clairvoyant. Working for the good of all will bring you greater happiness and more success than a career based on personal fulfilment. You will probably have a great interest in astrology and other esoteric areas that encourage your awareness to expand. Life will improve as you grow older and you will gain great success in the form of respect for your empathy and good advice.

With Pisces rising Jupiter becomes malefic because it rules a cardinal house, your tenth house. This change from benefic to malefic applies also to Mercury, which rules your fourth and seventh houses. Saturn, the Sun and Venus are negative planets for you - Saturn rules the eleventh and twelfth houses, the Sun the sixth and Venus the third and eighth.

For Pisces rising Mars is a yogakaraka and thus a positive influence. The Moon's influence is also good (it rules the fifth house). Mars rules the death-giving second house for those with lagnas in Pisces; however it is not the maraka planet because it rules the auspicious ninth house and is very friendly to the lagna ruler, Jupiter. Saturn and Mercury are the maraka planets.

The Lagna Ruler Through the Houses

I find that you can discover a lot about somebody's motivation and focus just by looking at the lagna ruler and its relationship with the planets in the chart. For example, if the Lord of the ascendant is above the horizon, active and laying down karma for future lives, it can cause conflict in a chart dominated by planets below the horizon and vice versa. The lagna ruler is always considered auspicious and it enhances the house where it is placed.

First house

This placement produces good health, long life, self-belief, ambition and the ability to lead. However, exactly where the lagna ruler is relative to the horizon will make a difference to the purpose of what you do - if the lagna ruler is below the horizon, you will react strongly to the karma of previous lives, whereas if it is above the horizon, the need to create new karma will be the focus of your life this time.

Second house

This placement will show itself as an interest in music, education and family wealth. The accent will be on youthfulness. Past karma will have an important effect on you, perhaps as attachment to your place of birth or your ethnic roots. If the influences on the lagna ruler are mostly negative, this placement of it can indicate a possible separation from your family, unhappiness during childhood or that issues first apparent in childhood will dominate the rest of your life.

Third house

The lagna ruler's placement here indicates a need for self-expression, probably through writing (journalism or other forms of communication) and a life continually on the move (the third house rules short journeys), perhaps in a job that requires frequent travel. It shows a person who is self-motivated and ambitious. Changes in your life may take place at regular intervals. If the Moon is your lagna ruler these intervals may be monthly; yearly if the ruler is the Sun, Venus or Mercury; every two years if Mars is the ruler; twelve years for Jupiter; twenty nine and a half years for Saturn.

Fourth house
If your lagna ruler is here, it indicates a great attachment to your mother, home and inner emotions. It will link you with wealth and property in some way. If the ruler is conjunct Rahu or has another aspect to it, this can create feelings of fear with no obvious outer cause. This placement will often bring an interest in politics.

Fifth house
Your main focus will be on creativity whether it is by producing children or other means (writing, painting or acting, for example). You will enjoy taking risks. The fifth house is considered to be auspicious: it is where new karma is created with the help of good karma from the past, and the lagna ruler's placement here can lead to the kind of success which gains you the respect and admiration of others. However, if malefic planets aspect the lagna ruler, your creative endeavours (children or otherwise) can bring you great unhappiness.

Sixth house
Your lagna ruler being placed here will focus your attention on health and healing. You will need to be of service to others. This placement will put obstacles in your way but it also gives you the conditions and the ability to conquer those obstacles. Connections with people from other countries may be important in your life and at times you will feel more appreciated by them than by people from your own country. Your enemies or detractors will respect you.

Seventh house
Your life will be focused on personal relationships. The link with your partner will be especially strong, perhaps emotionally or perhaps because you feel that they reflect your personality. The lagna ruler placed here may also make you restless, with a need to travel and change your environment constantly. If you do not achieve the balance between your outer physical needs and your inner spiritual self it can make you very dissatisfied with your life. Take careful

note of the exact degree at which your ruling planet is located: is it above or below the horizon line? If it is below the horizon, your past karma will control your current destiny; if it is above the horizon, you will actively seek to move from satisfying only your physical needs towards greater emphasis on your spiritual ones.

Eighth house

This is a difficult house, concerned with death, transformation and secrets. You may be a very secretive person yourself. If your lagna ruler is here, you will have a great need to release the kundalini energy within you in order to strive towards higher consciousness. This process may involve powers which you will find difficult to control. You will seek out people who seem to have access to the knowledge you desire, which could lead to involvement with drugs. Less harmfully, your quest for hidden knowledge might involve work in hospitals or in the forensic sciences, or an interest in history, archaeology, antiques or pathology.

Ninth house

If your lagna ruler is here you are especially blessed. This is the strongest house of the zodiac, where past karma works favourably for you, giving you luck and allowing you to develop your higher mind without much struggle. You will travel to foreign lands and be able to meet wise teachers. In time, you will become respected for your own wisdom. This position can also indicate a particularly beneficial relationship with your father.

Tenth house

This is a cardinal house and any planet situated here will become highly charged with energy, so this is a very strong position for the lagna ruler. The tenth house indicates your karma in this life. Your career will be of great importance to you and you might pursue it in agriculture, government or public service or in the financial world. This placement gives strong leadership qualities. You will be ambitious, with a great need to express yourself on a wide canvas. You will strive for success and achieve it.

Eleventh house

When the lagna ruler is placed in the eleventh house you will reap the reward of work done in the tenth. The eleventh house is concerned with material profit: moreover on the spiritual level, the eleventh house may activate the sahsara (crown) chakra, enabling you to understand the true meaning of life. This is a good position for the lagna ruler as it indicates achievement and rewards for ambition.

Twelfth house

The lagna ruler is in its most difficult position here because the twelfth house is concerned with loss, both emotionally and financially. You may give yourself to others but your selflessness will not be appreciated. The twelfth house is also known as the house of imprisonment. You may well work in a prison or similar institution or in some way always be a loner, frequently retiring within yourself. You might make strong foreign connections and go to live abroad. It is also the house of efforts which are not rewarded, and of energy spent on wasteful pursuits. However, the twelfth house is also the house of moksha and you will have a very strong urge towards spiritual realisation.

Dhana Bhava - The Second House

The second house is difficult to understand; astrologers connect it with the material aspects of life, but in fact it has very deep associations with past lives and the potential we bring forward from them into this one. In the myth of Samudra Manthan the gods and demons fought for control over the ocean, which carried in its depths the nectar of immortality, as well as gems, jewels and poisons. This potential for positive and negative is related to the second house. The five main things connected to the second house are: wealth, family relationship, speech, eyesight and death. These are aspects of ourselves over which we have no control. The karaka planets are: Jupiter, gives wealth, but not always in the strict financial sense; Mercury - speech and childhood; Venus - family; the Sun and Moon - the eyes and insight.

The second house ruler through the houses:

In the **first** house it links the house of wealth to yourself - so you could make your wealth work for you. There is a strong family influence in your life.

In the **second** house it indicates wealth, either through inheritance or astute saving. The second house governs the voice and speech - so this will be affected by the ruler of the house.

In the **third** house you may create problems with impulsiveness; you can make the best of yourself by planning what you are going to do and sticking to it. Things will improve in time.

In the **fourth** house - your mother is a strong influence in childhood; inheritance in some form is likely from her.

In the **fifth** house, children play an important part in your life. This is also a great position for a writer as the second house potential is expressed very positively through the fifth house energy.

In the **sixth** house, it indicates strained family relationships. Separation from your partner, money problems; these situations can be reversed if one puts in a lot of personal effort. There could be problems with your eyes. This is a good position for working for the benefit of others.

In the **seventh** house it indicates more than one marriage or relationships with people more successful than yourself. Relationships are important for your own growth.

In the **eighth** house, the second house ruler gives problems on a physical level. You may have problems with your eyes or teeth as well as low energy levels. There could also be financial difficulties or loss of inheritance. If you can cope with this it can lead to opening of a deep inner potential, which will far outweigh the problems you struggle with. This indicates legacies and wealth but an inability to keep them.

In the **ninth** house this indicates riches, wealth from your father, inheritance and gains without making effort. This is the best position for the second house ruler.

In the **tenth** house your potential is expressed through achieve ment in your career.

The **eleventh** house is the house of gains and the second house is associated with wealth, so the connection between the two gives a great ability to make money. This also shows ability to earn from your other potentials - like singers who make a living with their voice.

In the **twelfth** house, there can be a loss of inheritance due to carelessness, or not really bothering to do what you are good at. On a positive level, this indicates using your energies for the good of others.

Signs in the Second House

Aries - ruled by Mars, which also rules the ninth
You evaluate your potential with a fresh point of view. You have high ideals and a willingness to discharge your own obligations and use your abilities to their best advantage. The position of Mars is vital. A strong Mars as the ruler of the ninth house as well gives great wealth and the ability to make the best of yourself. A weak or debilitated Mars can create obstacles or distance from family and you may not have their unqualified support in life. There is a need to go it alone.

Taurus - ruled by Venus, which also rules the seventh
Attachment to family and their material wealth. A desire to acquire jewellery, gems, minerals, precious metals like gold. You need to have material security. A strong Venus can give the ability to sing.

A weak Venus not only creates problems with your partner but also with your family.

Gemini - ruled by Mercury, which also rules the fifth

Gemini ruling the second house gives the ability to be a clever speaker; this is an important area as Mercury, the significator of speech rules the sign. Mercury also rules the fifth house of creativity; so the duality of Gemini can give you mastery over two talents. On the negative side, Gemini here can lead to somebody being sneaky or deceptive in their communications with others. A negatively placed Mercury could give speech disorders.

Cancer - ruled by the Moon

The Moon waxes and wanes and is emotional and changeable. In this house is shows the changeable quality of your family relationships. Your style of speech can be very touching which gives you the ability to influence others through their emotions too. The ability to spend money on a mere whim can be strong. A difficult Moon could also indicate eye problems.

Leo - ruled by the Sun

Leo in the second house represents the ability to command others through speech, but beware - it can also make for an autocratic personality. Leo is the sign where we move towards the materialisation process, so some measure of wealth is important. If the Sun is strongly placed the chances of unearned wealth are strong. The second house deals with eyesight and vision - so the Sun becomes a double significator as does the Moon. The Sun in a difficult position gives problems with eyesight but can also give the inability to see beyond the obvious.

Virgo - ruled by Mercury, which also rules the eleventh

This is a very good position for financial stability, if Mercury is strong, as it rules the second house of wealth and eleventh of earnings. Virgo has a good business head. The combination of all three can be the makings of a good business person. You are able to earn and save at the same time. Beware of the Virgo tendency to be verbally critical and dissatisfied with your own achievements; this could alienate you from your family.

Libra - ruled by Venus, which also rules the ninth

With Libra ruling the second house there's every chance you could benefit from others financially; it also rules the lucky ninth house, and can create very good financial conditions for you. You will have a pleasant voice and other enjoy listening to you. There is an attraction to both material goods as well as wanting to gain spiritually through your talent.

Scorpio - ruled by Mars, which also rules the seventh

Partnerships dominate your life. Scorpio ruling the second house indicates a potential which can be either elevated or poisonous. If unaware of the power you have, you can be vindictive and hurtful. The mystical potential of Scorpio can go either way and in this house it indicates a need for balance. But you are always wrestling with the inner demons. (See the chapter on Rahu and Ketu for more information on Vasuki and the kundalini.)

Sagittarius - ruled by Jupiter, which also rules the fifth

This links you to dharma and the need to do the right thing. The result of this is that you feel uncomfortable using your money for unethical causes and will be inspired to speak up for good causes around the world. It is important to remember here that the ascendant will be Scorpio and the ability to use your rhetoric, wealth and family relationships properly depends on the Scorpionic struggle between the higher and lower aspects of your consciousness.

Capricorn - ruled by Saturn, which also rules the third

Capricorn in the second house indicates that you will face financial restrictions. It usually brings up issues to do with family, childhood and wealth as Saturn, the ruler of Capricorn, requires you to face these in your search for the higher self. Family can appear as a great responsibility. Your speech may be harsh and you don't believe in 'small talk', which could alienate you from others. Your childhood may be overshadowed by a sense of duty, but here Saturn also rules the third house of self-motivation and courage, so there's every chance these restrictions can be overcome through self-reliance and action.

Aquarius - ruled by Saturn, which also rules the first
Aquarius ruling the second house indicates that the potential for altruistic efforts. Saturn's placement is of prime importance as it rules the self as well as the inner potential. It can constrain or release through its restrictions. It's likely you will be careful with your acquired wealth. Family relationships and the experience of childhood will not necessarily be easy as you feel drawn to communication on a wider, less personal scale.

Pisces - ruled by Jupiter, which also rules the eleventh
Jupiter here rules both the houses of wealth, the second and the eleventh, so if well-placed will give good financial security. Pisces in the second usually shows that there a lot of collective karma which has to be dealt with; you have enormous potential in this area which can be used for the good of others or for yourself.

Sahaja Bhava - The Third House
This is the house of those actions for which we ourselves take responsibility. It signifies your mind (memory, mental strength and agility) and how you will communicate; also your immediate environment including colleagues and friends; and again siblings (except for the eldest one, which is the eleventh house). It is a very materially-orientated energy. It rules short journeys by air and road, and changes of location (whether and how you will make them). If its ruler is badly placed in the chart, the third house can indicate an unsettled existence and a desire to be on the move all the time, even a lack of confidence and cowardliness.

The third house indicates when your parents are going to die. A note of explanation here: in Vedic astrology we count on around the chart to get information about the house in question from other houses which have some kind of relationship to it. The third house indicates parental death because, starting at the fourth house (mother), and counting onwards around the chart, we arrive at the third house when we have counted to twelve - thus the third house has in this case taken on the indications of the twelfth house (loss etc.). The maraka house for the father (represented by the ninth house) is the seventh house from it, so counting the ninth house as one, we end up back at the third house by the time we get to seven. This is a technique used frequently and well worth the struggle to understand! The third house is also considered to be the secondary house of longevity as it is the eighth house from the eighth. Karaka planet: Mars - brothers, valour, the courage to take action.

The third house ruler through the houses

In the **first** house it indicates that you will express yourself well, but there may be a tendency to act out your impulses before thinking them through properly. Siblings will also be a strong influence.

In the **second** house it connects the house of action with the house of inner potential, also the third house of reception to the second house of transmission. It focuses our activity in relationship to what we brought into this world - family, speech, and unearned wealth.

The **third** house ruler works very well here, in its own house. It can make you brave, physically strong, motivated and self-confident; financial success is indicated.

In the **fourth** house the third house ruler gives you the ability to earn through property and fixed assets. Your home is an important expression of your self worth.

In the **fifth** house is the placement for writers and actors and generally brings great fame. The third house represents motivation, confidence and the ability to make things happen, while the fifth acts as the conduit for expressing it. A good placement for astrologers, singers and actors.

In the **sixth** house, it indicates that relationships with brothers can be difficult. This is a good position for those who are in the military forces or the police. It also indicates that you will need to work for a living to get the best out of your life, although the circumstances may be difficult.

In the **seventh** house it indicates a lack of independence. Partners bring out the best in you either in your private life or at work.

Placed in the **eighth** house, the third house ruler indicates a difficulty in expressing yourself openly. Your actions can be secretive, private; issues of power or control can become important. This shows are great interest in the hidden side of life.

In the **ninth** house this indicates that you will follow in your father's footsteps; it is important for you to follow the correct path of life. There is a conflict between your earthly needs and those of your spiritual self. This placement gives you great confidence in dealing with people who communicate and express themselves well.

The third house ruler works well in the **tenth** house. It shows a need to be successful and have the ability to achieve. High status and a successful career are possible.

The **eleventh** house is the house of gains and the third house is all about effort; you could make money through writing, communications or travel.

In the **twelfth** house, there can be a loss of siblings or friends through death or separation. You are not very interested in worldly issues. Your main motivation is to move towards finding your spiritual roots.

Signs in the third house

Aries - ruled by Mars, which also rules the tenth
Aries in the third house shows a person who enjoys challenges and adventure. There can be many new beginnings in life. Mars is the natural significator of brothers and courage, so any aspects to it would also have an effect these two issues. A strong Mars as the ruler of the tenth house as well, gives good motivation with the ability to focus your energies in the direction of career. A weak or debilitated Mars would create lack of confidence and varying success with your career due to your own actions - or lack of them.

Taurus - ruled by Venus, which also rules the eighth
Taurus in the third indicates attachment to the everyday material pleasures of life, and the risk of being too easy going. It also suggests that you can be very creative and generous. Venus here rules both the houses of longevity (third and eighth), so its condition in the chart is also a double significator of life.

Gemini - ruled by Mercury, which also rules the sixth
With Gemini ruling the third house you have a natural ability to communicate. Mercury also rules the sixth house of service, obstacles, health and healing, so your focus is very much towards working for the good of others. Gemini is about mental agility and your work should be connected with your abilities. As Gemini is a mutable sign it can cause you to think constantly about changing direction of life and thus feel unable to settle for one goal.

Cancer - ruled by the Moon
In this house the Moon brings a changeable, emotional quality to any decisions. The Moon also understands the deep spiritual aspects of the hidden areas of life as it is the lord of the night and sleep. You can seek the physical pleasures of life at the same time as understanding its esoteric mysteries.

Leo - ruled by the Sun
Leo in the third house represents the ability to command others. This is a warrior who is a royal leader as well, which in turn indicates

isolation of some sort as the Sun, or Leo's mission, has to be one of loneliness. Through your actions you can motivate others and give them courage and confidence - but they will always know that there is a difference between you. Leo here indicates knowledge of a special mission in life.

Virgo - ruled by Mercury, which also rules the twelfth
Virgo in this house indicates actions and involvement in the material aspect of life. The goals to achieve are all material but at the same time there is a dissatisfaction about them as you know instinctively that the soul is enmeshed in the material sheath. Mercury rules the twelfth house as well, so there is need to act selflessly if you want to achieve happiness.

Libra - ruled by Venus, which also rules the tenth
Libra ruling the third house indicates that there is a need to keep a balance between a totally materialistic approach to life and a spiritual one. This indicates a soul hidden within layers of material impulses. Venus ruling the third and tenth houses shows you can succeed in a creative field. You can also create problems for yourself through impulsive actions.

Scorpio - ruled by Mars, which also rules the eighth
There is never any balance as far is Scorpio is concerned - it is either positive or negative and there is tension between the opposing polarities. The third house is concerned with action and the position of the ascendant ruler indicates exactly how the Scorpio energy will manifest. Mars has the potential here to create problems as it rules both the third and the eighth houses. (The Rahu Ketu chapter goes into this in more depth.)

Sagittarius - ruled by Jupiter, which also rules the sixth
Jupiter is known as the most benefic planet in the zodiac but placed here means it rules the two negative houses for a Libra ascendant (3 and 6) and it will create problems. Jupiter's natural inclination is to teach and spread knowledge with no obvious need for reward, and Libra represents the material world; you can see there will be conflict. Your siblings may be more spiritually inclined and you may

find it hard to understand their motivation.

Capricorn - ruled by Saturn, which also rules the fourth

Capricorn in the third house indicates responsibility and duty - your main concerns as far as your motivation is concerned. You need to have a strong practical basis to your life; in fact you would be very happy creating a real estate empire. Property and financial security are important to you but only so that you can look after others. The relationship with the siblings or your friends can be distant. You feel somewhat resentful of Saturn's restrictions in this house.

Aquarius - ruled by Saturn, which also rules the second

Aquarius in the third house indicates that Saturn rules the second house as well. The fashioning of your early years through Saturn's restrictions were not necessarily good for you. It shows that your childhood (second) and teenage years (third) were both under the shadow of Saturn, which is of course the planet of old age. Responsibilities were thrust upon you at an early age when you may not have had any say in the matter. There is much deliberation before you take any action. Aquarius in this house shows a person who is not much interested in the material realities of life.

Pisces - ruled by Jupiter, which also rules the twelfth

Pisces in the third wants to merge with the eternal, which of course is in direct conflict with the Capricorn ascendant and its ruler (Saturn). Capricorn's brief is to experience karma, while Pisces, as ruler of the third house (of action) and twelfth (of enlightenment) is concerned with letting go rather than experiencing life. Jupiter rules the negative third and twelfth houses and will create problems wherever it is placed.

Sukha Bhava - The Fourth House

This is a very subtle and complex house, the seat of emotions and thus of that secret self not revealed to others. The fourth house rules inner feelings and private life, the home and all related feelings. Sanchita karma (the good and bad karma you bring into this life) is reflected here so there is a need to study the fourth house when looking into past lives. Your own sanchita karma can show very clearly in your mother, the kind of person she is and your relationship with her. Those of us who have had difficult relationships with our mothers find the inner scars very difficult to deal with.

Because of the fourth house association with home and feelings, problems with the fourth house can lead to difficulties with partners. Indian astrologers consider that a happy home life is vital for marriage and always study the fourth house when asked to assess potential marriage partners. Karaka planet: the Moon - the emotional mind, mother, life on Earth.

The fourth house ruler through the houses

In the **first** house, you focus very much on your own needs and putting yourself first. This indicates that a comfortable home is high on your list of priorities.

In the **second** house it indicates a strong family connection. There is some gain or inheritance from mother - here the inheritance need not be in money terms only - it could be talent or wisdom.

In the **third** house it suggests that your hopes and dreams can be achieved through your own actions. This would create difficulty in the relationship with your mother as the fourth house ruler (mother) is placed in the twelfth house (the house of loss) from itself. (This is again using the system of counting on round the houses as described in the Third House)

In the **fourth** house it forms one of the Panchmahapurusha yogas. Malavya yoga here is specially powerful as it is also the best location for Venus to be situated. (See Yoga chapter.)

119

In the **fifth** house, creativity is highlighted and children will bring happiness. It indicates a good relationship with the father as well as ability to gain from his good deeds.

In the **sixth** house, it suggests a difficult relationship with your mother, or that she has health problems. An unsettled home life is also indicated.

In the **seventh** house, an early marriage is likely. Relationships are important for your inner happiness.

In the **eighth** house it indicates a separation from home, perhaps by living abroad. Definitely a difficult relationship with the mother.

In the **ninth** house this indicates luck from your mother. You may follow in you father's footsteps. You need to work at reconciling the physical needs of everyday life with your spiritual journey. This placement gives great confidence in dealing with learned and wise people.

In the **tenth** house it shows the ability to achieve inner aspirations. This indicates a person who will be prominent in their field.

The **eleventh** house is the house of gains. The focus of the ambitions is not necessarily on career but on what you can earn from it. A difficult relationship with your mother is suggested as the eleventh house is the eighth house from the fourth.

In the **twelfth** house, there can be a loss of the mother through death or separation. This is another indication of living abroad. It can also show lack of peace of mind - perhaps even mental illness.

Signs in the Fourth House

Aries - ruled by Mars, which also rules the eleventh

Aries in the fourth house shows a person who would like to reveal their talents to a wider audience, but in the process of doing so and looking for more excitement may find it difficult to settle at home. This usually indicates more than one marriage. A strong Mars can bring gains in the form of property. Aries in this house can also indicate someone prone to anger and aggression in the home.

Taurus - ruled by Venus, which also rules the ninth house

Taurus ruling the fourth house shows that home and assets (in general) must be of the best quality available. With Taurus here you are likely to be sensuous and pleasure loving; good luck shines on you now, as good deeds from past life give comfort and satisfaction. Venus here rules the fourth and the ninth houses and so becomes a raja yogakaraka or a king making planet. It has the ability to bestow power, success and happiness.

Gemini - ruled by Mercury, which also rules the seventh

Mercury rules both the home and relationships. Any negative aspect to Mercury will create problems in both areas. Gemini in the third house shows a mind which is very agile. There is a connection with the past life as Mercury is the planet that connects the eternal to the physical. It can at times make a person who is dependent on others for their happiness. Partnerships are important.

Cancer - ruled by the Moon

The Moon has a deep connection to the eternal forces of nature and Cancer ruling this house shows a deep and intuitive understanding of the subtle realities of life. Cancer here will draw you to develop and express this wisdom through study and meditation.

Cancer in the fourth is naturally loving and happy. If the moon is waxing you will be an extrovert but if it is waning you are more likely to treasure your privacy.

Leo - ruled by the Sun

Leo in the fourth house can make you detached from other people.

They may feel uncomfortable in your company as you radiate a special energy which sets you apart. Leo is ruled by the Sun, the eternal soul and ruler of the universe, so you are likely to behave in a regal manner, but your emotions are very intense. You are aware of a higher purpose but find it difficult to express this in the company of friends, with the result that they may see you as rather a cold person. Your warmth is genuine but not everyone can relate to it.

Virgo - ruled by Mercury, which also rules the first

Virgo in the fourth house shows you use intellect and logic when expressing your inner feelings. You may well feel you would like to achieve material goals but the only way you can find happiness is by working selflessly and for others. Virgo in this house shows a soul which feels bound by its material restrictions and dissatisfied with mundane achievements.

Mercury rules the first and the fourth houses so it is responsible for your life-focus and the inner emotions. The relationship with your mother will influence your actions.

Libra - ruled by Venus, which also rules the eleventh

Tolerance, calmness and happiness are connected with Libra in the fourth. In common with your mother you will seek a balanced, slightly detached quality in your life. The past life connection brings you to the threshold of your spiritual life but the direction from that point will be decided by the position of Venus in the chart. Venus also ruling the eleventh house of material gain does indicate that the life will have a very practical aspect to it.

Libra in the fourth house also shows a person who is charming and flirtatious.

Scorpio - ruled by Mars, which also rules the ninth

Scorpio in this house indicates strong karmic influences from previous lives. As with most situations involving Scorpio you are being pulled between your higher and lower selves. Mars also rules the ninth house of duty in this life, so your Scorpionic impulses will have the chance to aim higher if Mars is strongly placed. The right attitude to life is important here for your potential to unfold.

The urge to live out past life experiences will be strong. There is a desire to express yourself on the mundane level but that in itself will never be enough.

Scorpio in the fourth indicates the relationship with your mother can be intense and difficult.

Sagittarius - ruled by Jupiter, which also rules the seventh
Sagittarius in the fourth house shows the aspirations of the individual are of the highest level. You bring forth knowledge and wisdom. Learning is important an expression of this life. You will wish to achieve the impossible but can feel restricted with the practicalities of life. (Virgo the ascendant has to operate on a material realm.) Jupiter rules the seventh house as well and therefore it suffers from the dosha of a benefic ruling a cardinal house. Unless Jupiter is strongly positioned, it can create problems with fulfilling your aspirations.

Capricorn - ruled by Saturn, which also rules the fifth
Here Saturn rules both the fourth and fifth houses so becomes a raja yogakaraka for Libra ascendants. Saturn has an extra-special part to perform here. It can give a very good life and ensure that you achieve all you desire. Capricorn in the fourth shows a mother who was detached from you. It could mean a strict upbringing so you later on have difficulty in expressing your emotions. It also indicates that you are ready from your experiences in a past life to lead this life on a mundane level and face your karmic responsibilities head on.

Aquarius - ruled by Saturn, which also rules the third
Saturn ruling your third house of self-motivation and fourth house of aspirations links the two together. It becomes very important here for you to take responsibility for your own happiness as well as achieving your ambitions. You are capable of undoing your earlier good work by your own actions. Here it is important to remember the Scorpio ascendant which can also create its own problems and Saturn which forces you to face your karmic issues in this life.

Pisces - ruled by Jupiter, which also rules the first

Pisces here shows the capacity to look deep into spiritual issues. The ability to feel what is happening on a psychic level and work with intuition is strong. The emotional relationship with your mother and the nurturing received from her will have a profound effect. Here again Jupiter as a benefic ruling a cardinal sign can have a negative influence, suggesting that you can sometimes put obstacles in your own way.

Putra Bhava - The Fifth House

This is considered one of the luckiest houses in the natal chart because here we can react to our past lives and create kriyamana karma, the karma for this lifetime. Wherever it is located, the ruler of the fifth house is always auspicious. The fifth house represents our impulse to be creative. It rules children, especially the eldest, and the business of having them, including conception pregnancy: also the inability to conceive, miscarriage and abortion. It rules all self-expression, also tantra, **sadhana**, religious practices and deep knowledge of the spiritual side of life. Karaka planet: Jupiter - wisdom, sons; Mercury - intellect.

Personal deities and the fifth house

In India there are many different gods and goddesses, and we each direct our devotions to a particular one. To find out which is your special deity, refer to the list and see which planet either rules the fifth house or is located there.

Sun	Vishnu, the preserver
Moon	Saraswati, the goddess of knowledge
Mars	Hanuman, the god of strength
Mercury	Vishnu, the preserver
Jupiter	Brahma, the creator
Venus	Durga, the eternal mother
Saturn	Shiva, the destroyer of ignorance

Brahma, Vishnu and Shiva represent the Holy Trinity of the cosmos.

The fifth house ruler through the houses

In the **first** house, you can work creatively on your own, without needing ideas or motivation from anyone else.

In the **second** house it links your creativity (fifth house) and ability to create wealth (second house). This is also an indication of writing abilities. It shows knowledge and that you are very articulate in expressing your wisdom. It can also show inheritance.

In the **third** house it indicates living life on an everyday level, where you are very good at using your talents.

In the **fourth** house, your creative energies are best used around your home, where you feel comfortable and happy due to the link with past karma. Your mother is an especially important influence in your life in the realm of help and advice.

In the **fifth** house, you are very creative. The birth of children as well as happiness from them is indicated.

In the **sixth** house, you can have difficult relationship with your children. Unless you understand the difficulties presented by the sixth house, its energies can be very frustrating and effectively block your self-expression of creativity. The ruler placed here can also indicate adoption.

In the **seventh** house it indicates marrying the love of your life. Romance is important in relationships. It can sometimes leads to affairs outside of relationships.

In the **eighth** house, there can be a loss of children or separation. You are able to focus your intellect in the hidden areas of life. Issues of power can dominate.

In the **ninth** house this is a distinctly advantageous position. It indicates fame, success, happiness from children and wealth.

In the **tenth** house, your creativity is connected to your career. This is a very good position. It shows an ability to express your actions on the highest level.

The **eleventh** house is the house of gains, so this shows you are able to make money through your natural abilities.

In the **twelfth** house, loss through gambling, or separation from children. This can also indicate children living abroad.

The Signs in the Fifth House

Aries - ruled by Mars, which also rules the twelfth house
Aries in the fifth house indicates somebody with an interest in sports. There is also an intellectual restlessness that needs new horizons to keep it satisfied; this can lead to you taking risks just for new experiences. Aries, being a male sign ruling the house of children, indicates the ability to have sons. It is also an active way of expressing your creativity.

If Mars is in the seventh house this can make a person very sensuous and romantic: the fifth house is romance, the seventh relationships and twelfth house is pleasures of the bed.

Taurus - ruled by Venus, which also rules the tenth house
Taurus ruling the fifth house makes Venus a very powerful planet as it rules the tenth as well. Venus becomes a Raja yogakaraka for Capricorn ascendants and therefore has the ability to grant success, money and power. Any negative aspects to Venus can, however, create problems. Advisory powers and the ability to use them for your career are indicated.

Taurus being a feminine sign in the house of children and procreation, will indicate daughters.

Gemini - ruled by Mercury, which also rules the eighth
Mercury rules both the auspicious fifth and the negative eighth houses, so is not necessarily always good. As Mercury is an asexual planet there can be difficulty producing children. The fifth house deals with

intellect and as Gemini is the sign where the intellect is born, it can show a person who is both intellectual and well-informed.

Cancer - ruled by the Moon
Cancer ruling the fifth house shows a person who has a retentive memory and the ability to absorb details. The desire for children and on a non-physical level, the need to leave an imprint of your thoughts and ideas behind for others will be a priority. A strong waxing Moon is desirable and the further it is away from the Sun the better. The Moon is a reflection of the eternal soul, the Sun; in this house it is ideal for expressing the way to use positive karma.

Leo - ruled by the Sun
Leo in the fifth house connects one to the eternal aspect of life. There can be health problems, the heart especially being affected if the Sun is aspected by Rahu, or if the Sun or the fifth house are under malefic aspects. If Sun itself is placed in the fifth house you can be sure that any creativity will be expressed in a very individual way. Leo in this house also indicates successful sportsmen and actors.

Virgo - ruled by Mercury, which also rules the second
Virgo ruling the fifth indicates the birth of daughters. It also suggests someone who is very intellectual but doesn't make a fuss about their abilities. Mercury rules the second house of potential and the fifth house of creativity - which can produce a good writer, orator, singer or actor. On the negative side, malefic aspects to Mercury would create problems with children as well as difficulty with speech and self-expression.

Libra - ruled by Venus, which also rules the twelfth
Venus can give very similar energy to Aries in terms of sexual energy. It rules both the fifth and twelfth houses, and if it is placed in the seventh house, personal relationships and romance will be of great importance; this is considered a good placement for family life and producing children. Libra is about communication and sound judgement, which results in a very creative nature when it is placed in the fifth house - others will come to you for wisdom and advice.

Venus rules refinement: music, acting and drama so a strong Venus would highlight these abilities.

Scorpio - ruled by Mars, which also rules the tenth
A raja yogakaraka is created here for the Cancer ascendant as Mars rules both the fifth and the tenth houses. Mars alone can bring success, wealth and happiness. Here even a debilitated Mars will give good results as it will be placed in a trikona ninth house. An exalted or over-strong Mars would create a dominating personality. Generally Scorpio in the fifth is connected with good karma; you are benefiting from the trials of a previous life where you made wise decisions.

Sagittarius - ruled by Jupiter, which also rules the eighth
Sagittarius here shows a person who is very interested in sports and has the ability to be a good athlete. In this house Sagittarius signifies sons, but if there are malefic aspects to Jupiter there can be problems with children. Your karma will be best expressed if you fulfil the goals you have set yourself; this is likely to be in using your ability to give others the benefit of your knowledge and intellect. Higher education and teaching is indicated here.

Capricorn - ruled by Saturn, which also rules the sixth
Saturn here rules the lucky fifth house as well as the difficult sixth, so it could create obstacles in your path and problems with children. There will be a Virgo ascendant if Capricorn rules the fifth house, which shows that self-expression has to be connected with being of service to others. Recognising the karmic difficulties as well as the opportunities will help you to fulfil this dual role.

Aquarius - ruled by Saturn, which also rules the fourth
Here Saturn rules both the fourth and fifth houses so becomes a raja yogakaraka for Libra ascendants. Saturn has an extra-special part to perform here. It can give a good life where all desires will be granted. Aquarius here shows a responsibility to others. You will not be looking for shallow ways of expressing your creativity or your karma. It usually causes some restriction with children; they are not necessarily your best audience.

Pisces - ruled by Jupiter, which also rules the second

Pisces ruling the fifth house shows an intellect which is deep and profound. Here the Scorpio ascendant needs to be noted as there is sometimes the temptation to misuse intellect but there is never any doubt that you are indeed knowledgeable. You carry within yourself the experience of past lives which can be fluently expressed. You subtly recognise your restrictions and can enhance your creativity within these limits. Jupiter here also rules the second house of wealth and if strong it can give a lot of wealth specially if it is in contact with the fourth-house ruler, Saturn.

Ari Bhava - The Sixth House

Here is where difficult karma is be found, so it is considered to be an inauspicious house. Negative karma appears here as obstacles to your progress: illness and injury, hardships (such as the loss of a partner), enemies, struggle, litigation or the grind of daily work. It is also the house of foreigners and foreign-ness and learning lessons from other cultures.

The sixth house is the house of service, and of healing. As long as you do not create new negative karma which will return through the sixth house of a future life, undergoing the sixth house emphasis in this lifetime should lighten the karmic load, helping the soul to develop and grow in wisdom. Accepting sixth house karma can bring the peace of mind which is achieved by learning to overcome difficulty. Karaka planets: Mars - accidents, but also the courage to face obstacles; Saturn - disease, delay, limitation.

The sixth house ruler through the houses

The important thing to note here is that the ruler is a malefic and wherever it is placed it will create problems.

In the **first** house it will show inner conflict. Health issues can dominate your life and it may feel as if there is always an obstacle in the way. If you have this placement it is very important to look after your health as a general lack of vitality is indicated.

In the **second** house it will show problems with childhood. It can also indicate that there may be problems associated with family wealth or savings. Healthwise, there can be problems connected with face, eyes (especially right eye), teeth and speech.

In the **third** house it shows the ability to face up to problems on a practical level. You will deal with issues though courage and self-motivation. There can also be problems with your siblings, either through separation or argument. The right ear, throat, neck and windpipe can be weak or subject to injury.

In the **fourth** house - this shows problems in relationship with the mother. It could indicate you are either separated from her or that she has weak health. The chest, lungs and breasts could be the weak areas.

In the **fifth** house, there can be testing times with children. Either they have health problems or you feel they are stopping you doing the things you want to do; the sixth house ruler here can also show you are separated from them in some way. Health wise, for women it can indicate difficulties with conception, even miscarriage or abortion. General health issues are the heart, the upper abdomen, stomach and liver.

It is well placed in the **sixth** house. It gives the ability to fight off disease and fend off enemies. It also indicates Harsha yoga, which will bring success.

In the **seventh** house it indicates there could be tension in relationships, or that your partner is in poor health. In terms of your own health there could be weaknesses in the pelvis, lower urethra, bladder, prostate or uterus.

In the **eighth** house - this can sometimes show long-term health issues. Whereas this position is good for dealing with obstacles, it is not so good for health, where weaknesses in the sexual organs and rectum are indicated; there may be a weakened constitution.

In the **ninth** house, shows loss or separation from father, or a generally difficult relationship with him. It won't be easy for you to find the teachers you seek, or the relationship with them may not be constructive. Your weak areas are the hips and thighs.

In the **tenth** house - this is a good position for the sixth house ruler as hard work and dealing with obstacles will enhance the quality of the house. An Upachaya planet in another upachaya house gives growth over a period of time. Healthwise, the weak area will be knees, but you can improve their flexibility with time.

The **eleventh** house is the house of gains. The sixth house ruler placed here indicates profits from facing obstacles, through hard work and personal effort. Health wise there can be problems with legs and the left ear.

In the **twelfth** house, you may suffer from insomnia or deliberately avoid having a comfortable bed and nice surroundings in your bedroom. This can also show secret vices or desires. You can try to deal with problems of life through meditation or living in retreats for a while. Health-wise, you may have problems with your feet.

Signs in the sixth house

Ari in Sanskrit means 'the enemy of mankind' and usually refers to the six instincts that keep us attached to the materialistic side of life: Kaam (desire, passions), Krodh (anger), Madh (intoxicants like drugs and alcohol), Moh (attachment) Lobh(greed), Ahankara (ego, arrogance) and Matsaya (jealousy). The sign that rules the sixth house indicates the struggles that will be faced on a soul level.

Aries - ruled by Mars, which also rules the first

Aries ruling the sixth house shows you are fearless in dealing with obstacles. Here Mars becomes the planet of the self and of your personal difficulties - this is why Scorpio is called the sign of self-undoing. Ego can be a problem; it will distance you from friends. Your life direction is indicated by Mars in the natal chart, as well as issues which you need to work with - personally and health-wise. A weak Mars suggests the head is a vulnerable area. Mars here will create a Harsha yoga which brings success through taking correct decisions.

Taurus - ruled by Venus, which also rules the eleventh
Taurus ruling the sixth house shows attachment to physical desires, which could create a state of total tamas inside. (See Guna Chapter). Here Venus rules both the houses which can create difficulty, so its placement becomes critical. Venus placed in any of its own houses (Taurus or Libra), is fine as it will not create problems in other areas, but Venus placed in the eleventh will aspect the fifth house and can indicate heartache over children. There can be health issues with the face, teeth and mouth. Venus placed here creates a Harsha yoga which brings success through helping others.

Gemini - ruled by Mercury, which also rules the ninth
Gemini in this house shows you create anxiety for yourself through struggle on an intellectual level. There is always a polarity of thought - two different ways of working out the same problem. This makes for inner doubts but can also indicate a person who is rather fickle; however, you can overcome this by recognising that a problem exists. Mercury here rules the difficult sixth and the auspicious ninth so its placement can create difficulties as well as enhance your life. The weak area is the arms. Mercury placed here creates a Harsha yoga which will bring you happiness and success through intellectual understanding

Cancer - ruled by the Moon
Recognising emotional needs will be the greatest struggle. You should try to develop a quiet mind through yoga and meditation. Other may think you are too detached, cold even, but this is probably a mask presented to the world as you struggle with changing emotional issues. Recognising your sensitivity will make life easier. Your weaknesses are the chest and heart. The Moon placed here creates Harsha yoga, resulting in success through caring for others.

Leo - ruled by the Sun

Arrogance, ego, power and superiority will be life or death struggles. Although you could feel invincible and somewhat egotistical, there is also the need to let this go so that you can move further along your spiritual path. The drive to do this can be intense, but others see only your powerful side and don't realise how you feel inside. This is your soul lesson and confronting it will bring peace. The Sun placed here will create a Harsha Yoga giving success through using your power properly.

Virgo - ruled by Mercury, which also rules the third

Virgo in the sixth house shows struggle with intellectual restrictions. In many ways there is recognition of a different, more spiritual path to be experienced, but life is controlled by practical day to day issues. This can bring intellectual unhappiness which can result in stress-related stomach problems. Mercury rules both negative houses here, so it can create problems wherever it is placed. Placed in Virgo it will give Harsha yoga which indicates success through academic prowess.

Libra - ruled by Venus, which also rules the first

Libra in this house shows that the soul is involved in satisfying the more materialistic desires and wants the best in life - money, beauty and relationships. This idealistic standard is difficult to achieve in real life, so there will be a constant struggle until you learn that happiness will not be found this way. Venus also rules the first house which puts the responsibility of your health or life struggles in your own hands. Your weakness is the kidneys.
Venus placed here becomes a Harsha yoga which indicates success through judgement and balance.

Scorpio - ruled by Mars, which also rules the eleventh

Sexual desires and passions cause problems here. There can be an unnatural attachment to secrets or a secret way of life which isn't shared with others. This can be unpleasant when the truth comes out, so your lesson is to be more open about sexual needs. Hiding away will be counterproductive. The Mars energy here is the most difficult one for you to deal with as its association with passion and action are directly opposite the intellectual side of your nature - the ascendant here will be Gemini. You may have to confess to having diseases connected to sexual organs and the rectum. Mars placed here becomes a Harsha yoga which shows success through externalising the inner power.

Sagittarius - ruled by Jupiter, which also rules the ninth
The struggle here is with the philosophies and religious rights of others. Some are driven to change spiritual direction. The soul struggles with its physical needs but at the same time has a great capacity to overcome physical limitation through study, knowledge, meditation and rituals. Fighting one's desires is very prominent here, but Jupiter's wisdom helps in this process. Jupiter rules the auspicious ninth house as well and the dual rulership enables achievement of the highest ambitions. Jupiter will create both benedictions and obstacles wherever it is placed. Your weak areas physically are the hips and thighs. If Jupiter is placed in the sixth house, it will give rise to a Harsha yoga which will bring success through knowledge.

Capricorn - ruled by Saturn, which also rules the seventh
Capricorn ruling the sixth house shows the soul struggling to merge its consciousness with the eternal. The life is essentially concerned with the detail of everyday existence but the soul is pulling it in a spiritual direction; this can lead to tension in relationships. Recognising the practical realities of life and accepting them will go a long way to resolving this inner conflict. As Saturn here rules the sixth and the seventh houses it shows that karmic experiences will be connected with relationships. Knees can be a weakness physically. Saturn here will give a Harsha yoga which brings success through hard work.

Aquarius - ruled by Saturn, which also rules the fifth
Aquarius here struggles with others' needs and genuinely wants to give himself in the service of others. The letting go of ego and breaking the ties which bind are of paramount importance. This can be misunderstood by other people but it is the main lesson for you; it is hard for you to understand why they don't see the pure shining soul within. By being aware of this problem with image, you will

be able to overcome your dilemma. Legs are your weak point. Saturn in its own sign here will give a Harsha yoga which brings success through working for others.

Pisces - ruled by Jupiter, which also rules the third

Here you allow yourself to merge with the eternal and that in itself can be your problem. What you would really like to do is give your life to service: healing, caring and not thinking about yourself, but you have to learn to deal with the physical world first and fully before you can relinquish it; philanthropy while living an essentially practical existence is a must. Feet can be your weakness. Jupiter placed here will give a Harsha yoga which results in success through profound thinking.

The Yuvati Bhava - The Seventh House

This is the house which is opposite the ascendant, where the actions of this lifetime will be played out. It shows how to use the energy given to you at birth; it is where the soul rests from its spiritual journey and becomes involved with the world of matter. The seventh house rules the earthly ties of relationships, both personal and business, including your sex life and the way you deal with people who oppose you - it is the house of opposites and reflections. Experiencing the realities of life is part of the soul's purpose in being born; however in Hindu philosophy too much involvement in the material life is viewed as a hindrance to those on a spiritual path; we also see sexual activity as energy that is wasted by being used for personal gratification rather than spiritual ends. All partnerships are attachments; they highlight our lower instincts and prevent the development of higher consciousness. The planet which rules the seventh house is the second maraka (death-giving) planet which will create deathlike situations during your life. Karaka planet: Venus - marriage and wife; Jupiter - husband.

The seventh house ruler through the houses

In the **first** house, relationships are very important - your partner will be a great influence in your life and the decisions you face.

In the **second** house it indicates that a partner has great influence over you and also that they have some kind of family wealth. If the second house is mutable it can indicate more than one marriage.

The seventh house ruler in the **third** house indicates that your partner works with you to achieve your ambitions on the material level.

In the **fourth** house, this is an indication for happily married life and good relationship between partners. Home is an important part of your relationship.

In the **fifth** house, it indicates a love marriage. Romance is very important to you. It can also mean more than one marriage.

In the **sixth** house, you may have an inimical relationship with your partner. There can be fights and aggression between you and obstacles in marriage. This can also mean a partner who has health problems.

The **seventh** house ruler is well placed in its own house. Although planets are not considered to be good in the seventh house, the effect is nullified to some extent when it is the house ruler.

In the **eighth** house, you may lose your marriage partner through death or divorce. Issues of power can dominate your marital life. Partners may be secretive.

In the **ninth** house, this is very beneficial. It indicates fame, success and happiness from children, and wealth. Your partner will probably be interested in philosophy and religion.

In the **tenth** house, your partner will be interested and support you in your career. Partnership will enhance your career. There will be an increase in prosperity after marriage.

The **eleventh** house is the house of gains. Here you have the chance to make money through the association with your partner. This is a good position for the seventh house ruler.

In the **twelfth** house there could be marriage to a foreign partner. Strong sexual energy.

Signs in the Seventh House

Aries - ruled by Mars, which also rules the second
Aries in the seventh shows youthful partners, who can also be selfish and controlling; they are very active and need their freedom. They need passionate partners and you need to find new ways to keep yourself youthful and exciting. Aries is very forceful in this house so you will have to work with this energy to avoid making your marriage a war zone - compromise will be necessary.

Mars is a double maraka planet here as it rules both the second and seventh houses. Its strength is important in giving long life. Mars in Aries makes a Ruchaka yoga, which is good for general success, but not for relationships; as a planet of action and impulse it does not create harmonious partnerships.

Taurus - ruled by Venus, which also rules the twelfth house
Venus becomes a very sensuous planet here through its connection with Taurus and the twelfth house. Any conjunction with Mars will make for a relationship dominated by passion. Your partners will be hard-working with a sense of responsibility. Taurus is a sign of creativity and children will be important in this relationship. Taureans can be selfish so this part of your relationship will need to be worked on. Taurus ruling the seventh house shows that the soul is concerned with the material aspects of life. Venus placed here would create a Malavya yoga, indicating marriage to a special person, success and material wealth.

Gemini - ruled by Mercury, which also rules the tenth house

Mercury rules both the seventh and tenth houses and is therefore subject to the dosha of benefics ruling kendra houses, which is not always good. Also as Gemini is a mutable sign there is the possibility of more than one marriage. Partners can be two-faced and if Mercury is afflicted, deceptive as well. It does however show partners who are intellectually gifted. Mercury placed here would create Bhadra Yoga, which indicates success and a strong relationship.

Cancer - ruled by the Moon

If Cancer rules your seventh house you may have difficult relationships. Saturn, as ruler of the ascendant, is an enemy of the Moon and this is reflected in its position here. Those of you with this combination might find it hard to adapt to the changing nature of Cancer and the Moon. It is important to recognise and respect the individuals in the relationship, which can work if you realise that you operate according to different planetary principles. In many ways Saturn is the most difficult lesson for the Moon to learn. Here is a naturally difficult combination; how it works out depends on where the rulers of the signs are placed. The Moon in its own sign can be very sensitive and emotional. It is a magical, mysterious sign that Capricorn finds difficult to comprehend.

Leo - ruled by the Sun

Leo's ruler has a difficult relationship with Saturn, the ruler of the Aquarius ascendant. Both are strong individuals and will fight; for this relationship to survive there has to be room for independence and self-expression. These two signs usually find any partnership very testing because they are so different: Aquarius is concerned about the world and Leo thinks about its own needs. You need to look at the position of the Sun and Saturn to find out how this one will work out. The Sun in Leo will illuminate the seventh house, but your partner's radiance may overshadow your own. They may become involved with other partners.

Virgo - ruled by Mercury, which also rules the fourth

Mercury rules both the fourth and seventh houses and is therefore subjected to the dosha of a benefic that is ruling kendra houses;

this is not always good. As Virgo is a mutable sign, more than one marriage is indicated. Virgo partners will often try to dominate the relationship, having very high ideals that you find difficult to live up to. They seek perfection and feel restricted on a spiritual level.

Mercury placed in its own house here would create a Bhadra Yoga, indicating success and a strong relationship. It is also exalted in Virgo.

Libra - ruled by Venus, which also rules the second house

This indicates attractive partners. As Libra is an air sign it needs independence and Aries as the ascendant can be very possessive. You need to allow each other space here. Venus is a double maraka as it rules both the second and seventh houses. Any afflictions to it could cause problems in the longevity of relationships and life itself. A combination of Mars and Venus would suggest a passionate relationship.

Venus placed here would give a Malavya yoga, indicating marriage to a special person, success and material wealth.

Scorpio - ruled by Mars, which also rules the twelfth house

Scorpio in the seventh house indicates strong sexual energy in relationships. In this case there will be a Taurean ascendant which further emphasises the sexual aspect. Scorpio is an intense energy and it relates to moving your soul from materialism to a higher energy. Scorpios usually struggle against this higher energy. Any combination of Mars and Venus in this chart would suggest an overemphasis on relationships and therefore a struggle for individuality. The area in which this happens will be shown by the house where the combination takes place.

Mars here indicates Ruchaka yoga which shows strong partners. It can also mean a relationship centred on power and dominance.

Sagittarius - ruled by Jupiter which also rules the tenth

Here Jupiter represents both the seventh house ruler and is the significator of the husband. If Jupiter is strong so will the relationship be strong, but a weak or afflicted Jupiter will bring problems to the partnership.

Sagittarius is a mutable sign, so here again, there can be more than one marriage. The Sagittarius partner will need freedom and independence in the relationship as they pursue the search for the higher self. There can be harmony if the two of you understand that you are individuals.

Jupiter in Sagittarius would create a Hamsa yoga, which indicates a wise an intellectual partner but also overall success in relationships.

Capricorn - ruled by Saturn, which also rules the eighth

Capricorn ruling the eighth house usually indicates difficult relationships. The ascendant ruler, the Moon, is an enemy of Saturn. Those who have this combination will find it hard to adjust to the rigid energies of the sign and its ruler, Saturn. You both need to recognise and respect that you are individuals and work in different ways. In many ways Saturn is a difficult lesson for the Moon, but one it must learn. How this works depends on the signs occupied by the rulers. Saturn placed in its own sign will create a powerful Sasha yoga. Your partner could be more concerned with their work than with paying attention to you.

Aquarius - ruled by Saturn, which also rules the sixth

Aquarius in the seventh and its ruler, Saturn, both have a difficult relationship with the Sun, the ruler of the ascendant. Both are individuals, and for the relationship to survive there has to be some freedom of expression. There is an inherent conflict between the two planets, which is why they find it hard to relate in partnerships. Saturn placed in its own sign will create a Sasha yoga; this means they may be more interested in looking after the less fortunate that being with you.

Pisces - ruled by Jupiter, which also rules the fourth

Pisces in the seventh would indicate a partner who is very amiable and willing to move with your ideas and thoughts. Sometimes Pisces partners can be difficult to understand. As the twelfth sign of the zodiac there are mysterious depths associated with the Pisces person and it may be hard for you to relate to their higher dimensions. They can be indecisive and impractical which can be trying for someone who is practical. Here Jupiter represents both the seventh house ruler and the significator of the husband, so there will be a strong relationship if the planet is well aspected. If Jupiter is afflicted it could create multiple problems in relationships.

Jupiter in Pisces would create a Hamsa yoga, which indicates happiness, success and strong partnerships.

Randhara Bhava - The Eighth House

This is the house that indicates longevity. It is also the hiding place of the kundalini energy, the latent power activated when we reach a certain stage of maturity. Without kundalini energy the chakras remain dormant. Once awoken, kundalini energy can lead to death, knowledge or spiritual realisation, so the eighth house is one of very turbulent emotions. It is the point at which one forsakes the material world to begin the spiritual quest: a journey not to be undertaken lightly.

The areas signified by the eighth house are seen as difficult and stressful: length of life, physical death, serious and/or long-term illness. Planets located in your eighth house will always be challenging energies for you; however, they can help to develop psychic awareness when treated with respect. Karaka planet: Saturn - rules the length of your life.

Assessing the Length of a Life

A word of warning here: it needs a very experienced astrologer to weigh up the various factors which will influence the length of a person's life. The information below is given so that you can understand the principles behind the assessment. As you move towards greater understanding of the complexities of Jyotish, you will be able to make the assessment yourself but I suggest that you analyse the charts of people already dead to see how the principles work in practice. The eighth house indicates a person's life-span, and the mode of their death. To determine the mode of someone's death we need to look at the first and eighth houses and their rulers.

There are four main factors:

The strength of the ascendant and its ruler

The strength of the eighth house and its ruler

The strength of Saturn, as significator of longevity

The strength of the ruler of the third house, another significator of longevity

If two of the four factors are weak, the life-span is considered to be short - up to 32 years. If three out of the four are strong, the life-span is considered to be of medium length - up to 64 years. If all four factors are strong, the life-span will be over 64 years.

The eighth house ruler through the houses

The eighth house ruler is considered a malefic planet. Its position will indicate problem areas and difficulties which need to be overcome, and it is also important here to looks at the ruler's aspects with the rest of the chart.

In the **first** house, can show some kind of health problems. It indicates a weakness of constitution. Also you can be a private person. It also shows somebody with an interest in politics.

In the **second** house it can cause problems with family life. It can create friction in childhood. From the second house, the eighth house ruler will aspect its own house, thereby strengthening longevity.

In the **third** house it shows you probably don't have siblings. It can also indicate problems with self-confidence.

In the **fourth** house, loss or separation from the mother is possible. You may live in a foreign country. The fourth and eighth houses are concerned with moksha, so you may be aware of past life connections which draw you towards a deeper understanding of your present life.

In the **fifth** house, this indicates a loss of children or separation from them. The eighth house ruler here can either give a deep spiritual connection or it can make you very manipulative.

In the **sixth** house, it can enable to combat disease, obstacles and difficulties.

In the **seventh** house it will indicate problems within marriage. There can be issues of power with your partner; there is an indication of divorce or separation and sudden endings.

In the **eighth** house this creates a Sarala yoga which gives power and riches. It also shows a long life.

In the **ninth** house it will create problems with your father. There can be sudden separation or a loss, and in the process of coming to terms with it you may be drawn to someone whose intentions are less than honourable.

In the **tenth** house, there is a possibility of working abroad. Also you could be involved in office politics. There are possibilities of having an unusual career: astrology, yoga, or as a spiritual teacher. The power of the eighth house is immense and if people are on the correct path, the inherent knowledge gained can be used in a very positive way.

In the **eleventh** house you could face a sudden loss of money, leading to a change in long-term earnings.

The eighth house ruler placed in the **twelfth** house can make for a highly sexual personality as it links the eighth house of sex to the twelfth house of the pleasures of the bed. Here is a person who wants to use their hidden power to probe the ultimate truths or moksha. There is positive need to activate the kundalini. Both the eighth and twelfth are moksha houses and any connection with the fourth, another moksha house, allows you to merge with the unconscious or the greater reality. On the negative side it can make one secretive, controlling and manipulative.

Signs in the eighth house

Aries - ruled by Mars, which also rules the third
Here Mars rules the sign of action as well as the house of longevity. It suggests wanting to express the hidden knowledge represented by the eighth house quite fearlessly in your quest to experience the mysteries of life. No doubt this will lead you into realms that are very dangerous, either mentally, physically or emotionally. Mars placed here would create a Sarala yoga, which indicates success, prosperity and long life.

Taurus - ruled by Venus, which also rules the first
Taurus ruling this house can give a powerful sex drive, with indulgence in sensual pleasures. Here Venus rules both the house of the self, and the house of longevity: in effect this is giving you responsibility for your own life. If Venus is well placed in the chart there will be long life, but a weak Venus may cause it to be shortened. With the eighth house influence there is a tendency towards many affairs or secret romances. Venus placed here would create a Sarala yoga, indicating success, long life and a sensual personality.

Gemini - ruled by Mercury, which also rules the eleventh
Here Mercury is ruling two malefic houses, so its particular placement in the chart can cause problems. Gemini ruling the eighth house usually shows somebody who is torn by conflicting desires for sensuous fulfilment and highly spiritual aspirations. The subconscious plays a large part here and one should try to listen to it. Mercury placed here will create a Sarala yoga, which will give powerfully intellectual personalities who have the ability to work with their subtle and astral energies.

Cancer - ruled by the Moon
Cancer in the eighth house suggests you can live both in the spiritual as well as in the material world. You do have sensuous desires but at the same time want to explore the deeper spiritual self. A well-placed Moon would indicate a long life and give good results in its dasha and antardasha if it is waxing and in good houses. In practice I have not found this to be true; the eighth house ruler will always create dramatic a situation that leads to transformation. The Moon here will give a Sarala yoga, a combination for success and power.

Leo - ruled by the Sun
Leo in the eighth house indicates a desire to uncover the power of the kundalini. Dissatisfaction with the material world leads into all kinds of activities that allow for experimentation in this area. As Leo is concerned with power this hidden knowledge proves very attractive. Again the Sun's rulership of this house (like the Moon) is not said to give problems during its dasha, but I feel you can never discount its rulership of the eighth. The Sun in its own house will give the opportunity to meet many exalted souls and becomes a Sarala yoga, a combination for success and spiritual power.

Virgo - ruled by Mercury, which also rules the fifth
Mercury rules both the auspicious fifth and difficult eighth houses, and here the eighth house is very strong because it is the sign of Mercury's mooltrikona. Virgo seeks perfection in its pursuit of spiritual awareness; Mercury acts as the mental link between the physical and eternal. This can cause frustration and unhappiness with the material side of life until you recognise your limitations; then you will find peace and your true life direction. Mercury placed here will create a Sarala yoga as well as suggesting foreign travel and fame abroad.

Libra - ruled by Venus, which also rules the third
With Libra ruling the eighth house you have a tricky balance between your sensuous desires and your spiritual ones. You want to explore the darker side of life, but at the same time you are restricted by the material needs of a day to day existence. However deep your interest in the occult, you will always try to fulfil your other

commitments as well, which could mislead others as to your true intentions. Venus placed here will give a Sarala yoga, bringing success and true balance in life.

Scorpio - ruled by Mars, which also rules the first

Here Mars rules both the houses of longevity. The first indicates the fundamental vitality and the eighth how long you will live, so the quality of Mars is very important. This is the natural house of Scorpio so there will be a strong connection with the occult. There is an intensely sensual but unsatisfied side to Scorpio; clandestine relationships, experimentation with sex and drugs are all very likely, but the conflict will not be resolved until the energies are redirected to higher levels. Mars in its own sign will create a Sarala yoga, giving success and power through action.

Sagittarius - ruled by Jupiter, which also rules the eleventh

Jupiter is not a good planet for Taurus ascendants as it rules the negative eighth and eleventh houses; wherever it is placed it can stir up deep-rooted problems. On the positive side Jupiter can bring financial gains from contacts with foreign countries. There is a need to delve into esoteric knowledge, but not necessarily the wit to use it in everyday life; it can be stored for another time. Your outer persona will be essentially materialistic and possibly sensuous, but not attached to anything or anyone in particular. Jupiter in its own house creates Sarala yoga, which indicates success and power through knowledge.

Capricorn - ruled by Saturn, which also rules the ninth

Saturn here rules the dusthana eighth and the auspicious ninth houses. As Saturn's mooltrikona is in Aquarius it will give a ninth house effect during its dasha/bhukti period. A strong Saturn denotes long life as it signifies both longevity and also rules the house of longevity. In this house Capricorn wants to investigate further the deep mysteries of life and it is not afraid of issues arising from it. Saturn in its own house will give rise to Sarala yoga, which also gives long life.

Aquarius - ruled by Saturn, which also rules the seventh
Aquarius here focuses on the eighth house as it is the mooltrikona sign. There is an idealistic quest for knowledge which will be used for the benefit of all rather than just for oneself. This can also indicate living in a foreign country or away from your birthplace. Saturn in its own house will give rise to a Sarala yoga, which gives longevity; it also rewards keeping the interests of others close to your heart.

Pisces - rules by Jupiter, which also rules the fifth
When Pisces rules the eighth house it indicates a soul who has interest in the deepest, most inaccessible mysteries of life. Here is someone who is performing as expected on the material level, but whose thoughts are really directed inwards towards a spiritual connection. Other people probably aren't even aware of it as outwardly what shows is power and an enjoyment of the sensual side of life. A well-placed Jupiter will give long life. Placed here it creates a Sarala yoga which shows deep wisdom and knowledge.

Dharma Bhava - The Ninth House
The ninth house is the most auspicious house of the natal chart, the seat of your positive sanchita karma and your positive prarabhda karma, which will bring you unexpected help and good fortune in this life. It rules luck and fortune (**baghya**) and the wealth of your parents, but does not necessarily mean that you are going to be rich. Knowledge and inner spirituality are also part of the good fortune we have earned in a previous life and will come to our aid now, in terms of making life easier for us.

Dharma means religion, custom, ethics, morality and justice and as the house of dharma, the ninth house reflects all these factors. Dharma is our duty is to others as well as to ourselves. It is a very profound house deserving much study. Understanding our dharma in the larger context of the word makes it easier to deal with the contentious issues in our lives.

The destiny of the individual is also connected with the ninth house. Here the consciousness unfolds and brings us to a higher realisation; we are given the knowledge to learn about the higher things in life and we begin our spiritual journey towards the higher levels of attainment. Being the twelfth house from the tenth house of career and material achievements, the ninth house reflects our need for inner development rather than a search for the outer, material self.

The ascendant ruler placed in the ninth house is considered a very powerful destiny for the individual. It is also very good if the ninth house ruler aspects the ascendant as it indicates you have a protective energy around you.

Vedic astrologers are divided about which house in a natal chart signifies the father. Many look at the tenth house, but I have always used the ninth house to signify the father and your relationship with him. The karaka planets are: Jupiter - the guru (teacher), spiritual quests and higher learning; the Sun - the father, the soul.

The ninth house ruler through the houses

In the **first** house, you are an influential person. People find you attractive. Ethics, religion and your dharma are important to you.

In the **second** house, which is connected to wealth, it indicates the inheritance of property from your father and birth into a wealthy household.

The **third** house is the house of self-motivation, courage, writing, short journeys and brothers. The ninth house ruler placed here will aspect its own house, therefore increasing all its significations. There will be some kind of guru to guide you in your earthly duties - your daily life will have a spiritual emphasis.

In the **fourth** house is an indication for a happy married life. You may well own a lot of property. There is strong attachment to the mother. Both parents will have a strong influence on your thinking.

In the **fifth** house, this is very good positionThere will be fortune and good luck. Knowledge and insight are highlighted.

In the **sixth** house it indicates a difficult relationship with your father. You face opposition in the course of trying to find your destiny. It represents struggles and hard work to get what is rightfully yours.

In the **seventh** house it is in a good position, indicating good luck in your marriage partners. Although planets are not considered to be good in the seventh house, the ninth house ruler here reduces the negative effect to a large extent.

In the **eighth** house there can be separation from the father through loss. This does indicate inheritance of property and unexpected gains in life. You may follow a religion which is unacceptable to your family.

In the **ninth** house this is a great position. It indicates fame, success, happiness from children, wealth. Extreme good fortune. You will be protected throughout life.

In the **tenth** house indicates a raja yoga. Much success with your career. Past karmas act positively to help achieve your ambitions.

The **eleventh** house is the house of gains. This is a good position. You have the ability to make good money without too much hard work. This is a money yoga and usually indicates financial success.

In the **twelfth** house the loss of your father is indicated. This also indicates foreign settlement or making money from other countries. You are not concerned about worldly goods but are moving towards spiritual enlightenment.

Signs in the Ninth House

Aries - ruled by Mars, which also rules the fourth
Aries in the ninth house indicates individuals who will express their dharma in an individual way. They will be looking for ways to move onto a new level and won't lack courage in doing so. This can bring about good fortune and success through initiative. Usually a malefic planet, Mars works well here, producing good results from its position and aspects.

Taurus - ruled by Venus, which also rules the second
This indicates someone who is aspiring towards higher knowledge, but still wants to fulfil a materialistic karma - financial success is important to you. Venus is the best planet for you, and wherever it is placed will enhance the qualities of that house. Venus rules the second house of wealth and the ninth house of good luck, so in a strong position it can make for wealth. Inheritance from the paternal side is also indicated.

Gemini - ruled by Mercury, which also rules the twelfth
Mercury here rules the ninth house of luck and the twelfth house of loss. The mooltrikona of Mercury is Virgo, so it will express twelfth house issues. Having Gemini in this house allows you to work on two levels at once, both materially and spiritually, however this can make others doubt your commitment on either level.

Cancer - ruled by the Moon
Cancer in the ninth house shows religious inclinations, depending on where the Moon is placed, the benefic and malefic aspects and whether it is waxing or waning. It suggests you play out your dharma on the world stage and have successful connections with authority figures. Cancer in this house indicates that the Scorpio ascendant will be headed towards its higher aspirations. Jupiter placed here would give extremely good results.

Leo - ruled by the Sun
With Leo in the ninth house, its ruler, the Sun, becomes the best planet for you. It is an indicator of the soul, the father and works

to its best advantage in this house. You will feel naturally linked to higher energies with a pressing need to express yourself on this level. The position of the Sun in your chart guides you both on the soul level and the physical one.

Virgo - ruled by Mercury, which also rules the fourth

Mercury is the best planet for you. It rules both the difficult sixth and the auspicious ninth houses, but as its mooltrikona sign is Virgo it will give a ninth house effect; it gives very good results here. There has to be a practical expression of dharma here, especially as the Capricorn ascendant has to deal with its duty on earth to progress towards enlightenment. Virgo further highlights those issues.

Libra - ruled by Venus, which also rules the fourth

The Aquarian ascendant combined with Venus ruling the fourth and ninth houses creates a raja yogakaraka and the ability to do great good. Its dashas and sub-dashas will be especially strong for you. Libra as the ninth house sign shows you are evenhanded and use good judgement in your life. You could be a good teacher as you are impartial. You will desire both material success and spiritual fulfilment which could cause conflict.

Scorpio - ruled by Mars, which also rules the second

Here Mars rules the second house of wealth and the ninth house of good fortune, so it gives very good results. As ruler of the second house it becomes the maraka planet for a Pisces ascendant, but here it is said to lose that power because it rules the ninth house and is also the best friend of the ascendant ruler, Jupiter.

Sagittarius - ruled by Jupiter, which also rules the twelfth

Jupiter is the best planet for you. Its mooltrikona is Sagittarius, so wherever it is placed it will be beneficial. It is also the natural ruler of the ninth house, so the desire to teach and study further will be strong. Even if Jupiter is in Capricorn, its sign of debilitation, it would be in the strong tenth house and therefore subject to Neechbhanga rajayoga - the cancellation of debilitation.

Capricorn - ruled by Saturn, which also rules the tenth

As ruler of the ninth house, the normally difficult energies of Saturn become helpful. In this case it will also rule the tenth and becomes raja yogakaraka - the best planet for you. A strong Saturn will give you rewards from hard work done in previous lives. This does show that you are very motivated by material ambitions and have the ability to achieve them. Saturn's mooltrikona is Aquarius so here the ninth house ruler will help with career and success.

Aquarius - ruled by Saturn, which also rules the eighth

Saturn will act positively for you here as its mooltrikona sign is Aquarius and also as ruler of the ninth house. There will be interest in the occult, which will be used positively for the benefit of others and foreign connections that bring you success.

Pisces - ruled by Jupiter, which also rules the sixth

Jupiter becomes the best planet for you. If it is placed in exaltation in the ascendant it will bring you extraordinary luck. Jupiter can sometimes act negatively as it also rules the difficult sixth house, which is also its mooltrikona sign. Pisces in the ninth shows great concern for the preservation of life; your dharma is connected to spiritual realisation, which is something you will work towards throughout life.

The Karma Bhava - The Tenth House

The tenth house is the strongest of the kendra houses. Planets in kendras or cardinal houses are powerful in building the foundations of this life and in the tenth house they are specially energised. This house is intimately connected with the fourth house of inner hopes, dreams and the connection to past lives. The way we fulfil our hopes and dreams from here are shown in the tenth house. These are our karmas; the things we do now, through personal effort, will bring out our soul's best potential and as they are connected to the kriyamana karma which is our free will, our actions also create karma for future lives.

There is an intrinsic link between the luminaries and the fourth and tenth houses, which goes beyond the everyday associations of the parents and career. The Moon nurtures us and acts as a connection to past lives, while the Sun draws us towards our highest spiritual potential. These days our careers are deemed to be all-important and high on the list of personal achievement, but our potential can be expressed on any level.

Less personally, the tenth house rules government and administration, monarchy, glory, business and commerce. It also rules adopted sons and, for some Vedic astrologers, the father (see ninth house). Karaka planets: Mercury - the material world, the business of life; Jupiter - fortune; the Sun - power, authority; Saturn - hard work.

The tenth house ruler through the houses

In the **first**, you fulfil your ambitions without help from anyone else. Career is a priority. At times there is confusion between personal needs and worldly outer goals.

In the **second** house it is the ability to become wealthy through famil connection and inheritance.

In the **third** house it indicates that you will achieve your ambitions through your own efforts, a career in communications is a possibility. As the third house is the sixth from the career house (tenth), it shows that to a certain extent you might create your own obstacles on the way to achieving your goals.

In the **fourth** house it suggests that your outer ambitions and your inner aspirations are in harmony. This would indicate a natural inclination to work from home. Can indicate a strong maternal influence in your life.

In the **fifth** house, enhances the creative connections of your career and can give you tremendous insight. Your creative instincts might get in the way of finding your true vocation.

In the **sixth** house it indicates success through hard work. Both the sixth and the tenth are upachaya houses, so they improve with time.

In the **seventh** house - your career is connected with partnership issues. It could be you need others to work with or you can make a good career where relationships are involved- a relationship therapist, marriage counsellor etc.

In the **eighth** house, it suggests a career in research, astrology, history or issues around reincarnation. The tenth house ruler in the eighth can also lead to scandals connected with career.

In the **ninth** house this indicates luck. It creates a combination for success through knowledge, teaching and higher learning.

In the **tenth** house this makes you a prominent personality. Career, ambitions and your sense of independence are strong.

The **eleventh** house is the house of gains. This shows the ability to realise your ambitions and make money.

In the **twelfth** house it shows success away from home. There is also connection with institutions, hospitals and those who work for the benefit of others.

Signs in the tenth house

Aries - ruled by Mars, which also rules the fifth
Aries in the tenth house shows an ambitious person reaching for the highest pinnacle in life. Working on your own and success in business is indicated. Mars is a raja yogakaraka planet here as it rules the fifth house as well, and brings gains from property. Mars placed in the tenth house will give create the powerful Ruchaka yoga, resulting in success and power. Here your career has to be one of authority and independence: as an entrepreneur, industrialist, engineer, or maybe in the armed forces.

Taurus - ruled by Venus, which also rules the third

Taurus ruling the tenth house shows the ability to work hard for personal success. There is an enduring quality to your career, and a determination to succeed in life; you are happy to wait for the results of all the hard work. Taurus here would indicate a career in accountancy, finance, banking, art, farming, food retailing, cooking, fine arts or other aesthetic professions. Venus here will create Malavya yoga which will bring success from careers in fine art, finance etc.

Gemini - ruled by Mercury, which also rules the first

Mercury rules both the self and career; you need a career to allow Mercury full range. You will judge your personal success on how well you do in the outer world. The Gemini career would involve intellectual pursuits, writing, travel, publications, authors, actors. Mostly when Gemini rules the tenth house there is the likelihood of more than one career, but constantly changing direction will lead to dissatisfaction and disappointment. Mercury here will create Bhadra yoga which will bring success through intellectual excellence.

Cancer - ruled by the Moon

Cancer shows a deep and intuitive understanding of the subtle realities of life and you can use this to further your ambitions. As the natural cycle of the Moon is to wax and wane, this can indicate the fluctuating state of your career. You may want different things from it at different times of life. Careers likely for Cancer in the tenth are medicine, water related activities, caring for others, catering and anything connected with food. As Cancer is a cardinal sign, it also has the ability to be a leader or an entrepreneur.

Leo - ruled by the Sun

Leo in the tenth house shows leadership potential. You have powerful ambitions and need to be right up at the front in your career. If the Sun is placed here there is a strong soul connection. It is also a great position for success. Suitable careers for Leo in the tenth would be high level positions in industry, government, acting, politics, the military organisations and sports. Leo here indicates that you need to be able to work on your own and with accepted authority.

Virgo - ruled by Mercury, which also rules the seventh

Virgo ruling the tenth house shows intellect is important in the pursuit of your career. Virgo aspires to the highest ideals but can show great practical capabilities which bodes well for your career. If Mercury is placed in the tenth house it will indicate a powerful Bhadra yoga, enhancing career prospects.

Mercury rules the tenth and the seventh houses, which shows that strong relationships will lead to promotion. You need intellectual stimulation in your work, so mathematics, technical work, support roles, librarian, accountancy and management level jobs would all suit you.

Libra - ruled by Venus, which also rules the fifth

Here Venus become a yogakaraka planet and its strength can greatly enhance the quality of your life and enhance ambitions. If Venus is placed here, it would indicate great success in the field of arts, music, luxury goods, finance and diplomacy. Venus would also create a powerful Malavya yoga. Libra careers are usually linked to the fine things in life. Other careers involve: the legal profession, acting, directors, jewellery designing and retailing, high finance and advertising.

Scorpio - ruled by Mars, which also rules the fifth

Mars will be very powerful planet for you. As a raja yogakaraka its strength will bring ambition and success. If Mars is placed in the tenth house, it will make a Ruchaka yoga which will ensure success and achievement. Likely careers for you are: astrology, science, study of the occult, law, research, the secret service and politics.

Sagittarius - ruled by Jupiter, which also rules the first

With Sagittarius in the tenth you are a natural teacher, your work is very important to you. If Jupiter is also placed here it activates a powerful Hamsa yoga which gives added protection and strength. You need a career where you have power and your authority and wisdom are respected. Likely Sagittarian careers are: teaching, planning, administration, publishing, preaching, the civil service and charity work.

Capricorn - ruled by Saturn, which also rules the eleventh

Here Saturn is working towards creating karma for the future. Capricorn is not afraid to face the tougher issues of life and here it is usually the karma of responsibility that you have to deal with. As the ascendant is Aries and Mars and Saturn are natural enemies, the tenth house associations with career and channelling the Mars energy through Saturn becomes a challenge. Capricorn professions suit power and responsibility: management in industry, politics, or the armed forces. Sport is also indicated here. Saturn placed here creates a Sasha yoga which brings success through hard work.

Aquarius - ruled by Saturn, which also rules the ninth

Here Saturn rules both the ninth and tenth houses so becomes a raja yogakaraka for Taurus ascendants. Saturn has an extra special part to perform here. It can give a very good life for the individual and ensure that you achieve all you desire. Aquarius in the tenth shows the ability to put the welfare of others before your own - an idealism that can be misunderstood. Aquarian careers are humanitarian jobs including charitable work, working with the masses or anywhere you can help to make the world a better place for other people. Astrology and writing can also be good for you. Saturn placed here will create a champion of the less fortunate.

Pisces - ruled by Jupiter, which also rules the seventh

Pisces here shows the capacity to deal with material issues on a deeply spiritual level. Jupiter as a benefic ruling a cardinal sign can have a negative effect on you. As Jupiter rules the seventh house, your career will be intimately connected with the quality of your relationships. If the two are in harmony it will help you move towards the enlightenment your soul desires. Your spiritual idealism can conflict with your material ambitions in life. Pisces here brings clairvoyant abilities, healing and interest in astrology and the occult. Possible careers are: teaching, the navy, shipping, import and export businesses and foreign travel. Jupiter here will give rise to a Hamsa yoga which makes the individual successful and respected.

Labha Bhava - The Eleventh House

This is the house of gains and profits made from our own hard work. Whereas the tenth house reflects our career and the second our unearned wealth, the eleventh house will indicate the results of our efforts in monetary terms. A self-made person will have a strong eleventh house. Any connection between its rulers and the ninth, second and the tenth houses further improve the earning ability of an individual. This house shows only the ability to make money. To find out if you will be able to hang on to it you need to study the twelfth house of expenses and the second of banking. All planets are considered to be well placed in the eleventh as they become planets of gain, but the ruler is considered a negative planet with the ability to spoil the significations of the house where it is placed. As the eleventh house ruler is the sixth from the sixth, it reflects the dushtana house and so acts as a difficult planet which creates obstacles wherever it is placed. The eleventh house also represents the crown chakra, the highest pinnacle of your spiritual achievement in this life. It can give you an understanding of why you were born and the whole meaning of your life. Karaka planet: Jupiter - the fruits of our endeavours, both financial and spiritual, elder brothers.

The eleventh house ruler through the houses

In the **first** house, you profit through your own efforts and are very concerned about the correct results from your efforts, whether they are on a spiritual level or a material level.

In the **second** house it indicates material gain - the ability to make money and save it. The second house is the fourth from the eleventh, so in some way your home represents where you make your gains. Your earnings and ability to save are linked.

In the **third** house, it suggests you can make money from your own efforts.

In the **fourth** house it indicates working from home, or the ability to make money from real estate.

158

In the **fifth** house, it enhances the creative connections of your earnings. Here the eleventh house ruler will aspect its own house, further enhancing the qualities of gain and earning. This is a direct link with your creativity - insight with the ability to make money.

In the **sixth** house, the eleventh house ruler indicates success through hard work. Both the sixth and eleventh are upachaya houses, so they improve with time, but in the meantime they can put unexpected obstacles in the way of gain.

In the **seventh** house - the relationship with your partner can be financially profitable, whether on a personal level or through business. It can also indicate the ability to make money from efforts which are connected with partners. It is important to look at the tenth house as well. Here you can also consider the malefic aspect of the eleventh house, as this can create obstacles through difficulties or disease.

In the **eighth** house, money can come from research, astrology, history or past life work. The eleventh house ruler here can also show secret manipulation of money or profits, or money used for control of power.

In the **ninth** house this indicates luck. Its creates a Dhana yoga. Those who have amazing capacity to earn money and are extremely wealthy would have a connection between the ninth and the eleventh house - the ninth house being the eleventh house from the eleventh, further enhances the ability to earn.

In the **tenth** house - this is an excellent position, indicating that your earnings are directly connected to your career.

The **eleventh** house ruler placed in its own house shows a self-made person who has the knack of making money. It could also show a desire for spiritual progress, depending on the maturity of the soul.

In the **twelfth** house, it shows how we spend money. As this is the house of expenses, the eleventh house ruler placed here can indicate that you spend money as soon as you make it.

Signs in the eleventh house

Aries - ruled by Mars, which also rules the sixth
Mars ruling both the sixth and eleventh houses will create difficulties wherever it is placed. Aries in the eleventh shows earning comes from your own efforts. You can cope with obstacles on the path to material success. Social life can be very prominent.

Taurus - ruled by Venus, which also rules the fourth
Taurus ruling the eleventh house gives materialistic ambitions. You want to money but also feel the need to save your earnings for the future. You aim towards higher spiritual consciousness though you continue to work outwardly on the material level. There is idealism but also a practical approach to life and money.

Gemini - ruled by Mercury, which also rules the second
Mercury rules the second and eleventh houses, both connected with money, so it becomes the significator of both financial success and failure. Its position, strength and any connection with the tenth or eleventh house rulers can make you very rich. Gemini is a dual sign so this indicates more than one way of making money. Intellectual friends and a good social life are also indicated.

Cancer - ruled by the Moon
Cancer is ruled by the Moon so your ability to earn can be changeable. You may have an instinctive knack of making money, but that itself will not satisfy you. You are looking for a new way of expressing your spiritual side but there are material needs which also need to be satisfied. Your social life depends on whether your Moon is waxing or waning. The waxing Moon will be more social and outgoing, whereas the waning Moon would prefers fewer friends and wants to be alone sometimes.

Leo - ruled by the Sun

Leo in the eleventh house shows special status enjoyed in your social life. Leo will indicate looking to earn though ethical and straight means. There is an ability to make money from dealings with the government or those in authority, but that will not be the main focus in your life; there will be a part of you looking to fulfil a more spiritual aspect of your nature.

Virgo - ruled by Mercury, which also rules the eighth

Virgo ruling the eleventh house will make you very practical in the ways you go about earning money. As Mercury rules the dusthana eighth and the eleventh houses, its placement is very important for the Scorpio ascendant. It can create difficulties wherever it is placed.

Libra - ruled by Venus, which also rules the sixth

Libra ruling the eleventh house indicates social success, but it also shows you are trying to balance your life on two levels: the material and the spiritual. Libra is essentially a materialistic sign so there will be a strong need to have some monetary rewards for your efforts. As Venus is ruling both the sixth and the eleventh houses it becomes a difficult planet for Sagittarius ascendants, so its placement can create problems.

Scorpio - ruled by Mars, which also rules the sixth

This indicates the conflict between your need to follow a spiritual path and your desire for the good things that money can buy. You will have to have money but this in itself will never be enough. Here Mars rules the two difficult houses, so its placement can give problems.

Sagittarius - ruled by Jupiter, which also rules the first

Sagittarius here shows the moving of consciousness towards its spiritual objective. The money or financial indication can be strong, but there will always be a higher purpose for which the money will be used. Whether you are really using the money for spiritual means or not, you will be idealistic about the way you earn it. Here Jupiter rules both the second (money) and the eleventh houses (wealth) and is itself a karaka for wealth, so it has the ability to give abundantly.

Capricorn - ruled by Saturn, which also rules the eleventh

Capricorn ruling the eleventh shows you plan your finances carefully - you only earn as much as you need and there is no great desire to create wealth. Saturn rules the two houses which deal with the Sahsara chakra and merging the soul with the eternal forces, so there is usually some practical karma to be faced through Saturn's earthly restrictions before one can move towards fulfilment.

Aquarius - ruled by Saturn, which also rules the tenth

Aquarius here shows you are not bothered about earning for yourself but at the same time you want to be sure that your efforts are properly rewarded. You see yourself as unselfish but others would see you as self-obsessed. Saturn rules both the tenth and the eleventh houses, so career and the fruits of your actions are important. Money will come through hard work - Saturn's restrictions are the most difficult lesson for the Aries ascendant; understanding them will bring success both financially and in your career.

Pisces - ruled by Jupiter, which also rules the eighth

Pisces here shows a calm, easy-going approach to money making and financial gains, which can border on carelessness when associated with the rewards of your labour. You want to make the most of your life and express this on the highest possible dimension. Jupiter as the ruler of the eighth as well as eleventh can be a difficult planet for the Taurus ascendant, so there has to be a caution how the Jupiterian energies are expressed.

Vyaya Bhava - The Twelfth House

This is the house of loss or expenses and it is the most difficult house to understand. It represents the last part of life where we merge with the infinite; the loss is to with understanding how to give up our individual identity to the astral energies. This house deals with clairvoyance, intuition and the divisions between reality and dreams; the subtle energies which we experience but do not understand. By this stage we have lost touch with the subtleties of life, so we understand neither what our dreams tell us, nor the other astral messages our minds receive daily. Here we can develop these powers, but they are only found by self-imposed isolation or meditation - both of which are ruled by the twelfth house.

The twelfth house therefore signifies: sorrow and disappointments, resignation, retreat and imprisonment (both physical and emotional). It rules yoga and meditation, places where you are confined (either willingly or not) such as hospitals, monasteries, asylums and prisons, and those desires you indulge in secret; it also deals with 'pleasures of the bed' and sexual satisfaction. This house signifies karma accumulated in past lives, and after-death states. In a post-Freudian era, it rules your subconscious, and fantasy, including psychic, clairvoyant and dream experiences. The twelfth house represents **moksha** in your life - the process of breaking away from the cycles of life and death through renunciation. Karakas or significators: Saturn - sorrows; Ketu - moksha; Rahu - foreign travel.

The twelfth house ruler through the houses

In the **first** house, this indicates a lack of ego; also living away from your birth place or settling in a foreign country.

In the **second** house it indicates material loss. You can fritter away your inheritance, talents or innate abilities.

The **third** house connections with self-motivation, courage, writing, short journeys and brothers show loss or difficulties in these areas when the ruler of the twelfth house is placed here.

In the **fourth** house it indicates a change of residence. Also a difficult relationship with your mother, maybe through separation or loss.

In the **fifth** house it can indicate loss of children or separation from them. Here it could be through their living abroad or perhaps being sent to boarding school. On a more spiritual level it shows using your talents for the good of others although you can lack confidence yourself in these areas.

In the **sixth** house, you will work hard at your karmic issues and have the ability to face obstacles and enemies.

In the **seventh** house it suggests marriage to a foreigner. It can also create problems in marriages through separation or divorce.

In the **eighth** house it shows an aptitude with occult, hidden secrets, astrology, research, past-life connections; altogether a very secretive personality.

In the **ninth** house it will indicate searching for moksha or spiritual enlightenment. It can also create problems with your father.

In the **tenth** house it can bring sudden changes in your career. You can profit from dealing with foreign countries, but there is a feeling of sacrificing your career. It can also show work connected to hospitals and other kinds of institutions.

The **eleventh** house is the house of gains. The twelfth house ruler placed here would indicate you have the ability to spend. Your earnings are directly linked to your expenses. Also as the eleventh house is the twelfth house from the twelfth it further highlights the need for spiritual growth and merging with the eternal consciousness.

In the **twelfth** house, this makes a Vimala yoga which shows success abroad and the ability to control expenses. You are a special individual. In the strong house of isolation, it shows a strong personality which has difficulty in mixing with others.

Signs in the twelfth house

Aries - ruled by Mars, which also rules the seventh
Mars rules both the seventh and twelfth, which are both concerned with sex. If Mars is placed in either of these houses, or the fifth or the eighth house, it would indicate a strongly sexual nature. Aries in the twelfth will also show an idealism connected with the spiritual side of life; you have a thirst for new experiences connected with the taboo areas of life.

Taurus - ruled by Venus, which also rules the fifth
Taurus in the twelfth house will show expenses connected with the practical areas of life. There can be passionate desires and needs. Taurus as an earth sign ruling the house of spiritual enlightenment indicates that you have a pragmatic approach to inner needs. Here Venus rules the auspicious fifth house and the difficult twelfth house, but as its mooltrikona sign is Libra, it will give only good results wherever it is placed.

Gemini - ruled by Mercury, which also rules the third
Mercury rules two difficult houses - the third and the twelfth, therefore it has a capacity to create problems wherever it is placed. Mental energy has to be controlled and properly focused. Gemini ruling here will can double the size of expenses and you are likely to spend to fulfil both material and spiritual needs. The main thing to understand here is that you may still find yourself dissatisfied as you will not be able to find moksha or your spiritual self through spending.

Cancer - ruled by the Moon
Cancer is ruled by the Moon and it is said that the Moon does not have a dosha (affliction) of ruling difficult houses. But in practice the Moon will reflect it ownership of the twelfth house. It will create issues wherever it is placed. Cancer ruling here shows a desire to merge with the eternal forces, so there will be a strong sense of destiny towards developing your spiritual self. You will also learn to give up your ego through selfless tasks.

Leo - ruled by the Sun

Leo in the twelfth house shows a need to give up your individuality but at the same time practical considerations stop you from doing so. You could have heavy expenses. The Sun, like the Moon, is not supposed to have a dosha (affliction) in ruling the twelfth house, but it will create some kind of issue wherever it is placed.

Virgo - ruled by Mercury, which also rules the ninth

Virgo ruling the twelfth house shows a person who understands their spiritual restriction but feels frustrated by it. Mercury has its mooltrikona in Virgo, so wherever it is placed it will give strong sattvic tendencies. You will experience loss on a material level which helps you to grow on a soul level.

Libra - ruled by Venus, which also rules the seventh

Venus rules the seventh and the twelfth houses, both of which are concerned with sex. If Venus is placed in either of these houses or the fifth or the eighth house, it would indicate a strongly sexual nature. Libra in the twelfth also shows a balance being worked out internally between your spiritual and material needs.

Scorpio - ruled by Mars, which also rules the fifth

The mooltrikona sign for Mars is Aries, so the stronger influence will be from the fifth house, but it will not necessarily bring disruption. The fifth house of romance and twelfth house of sexual pleasures are linked by Mars and if there is a further link to the seventh and eighth houses it will show a strongly passionate nature. Scorpio ruling the twelfth house will also show the struggle of the soul in finding its true path; you have a strong sexual nature but the soul is reaching towards the higher self. You will be struggling with this dilemma until you can understand and reconcile the two.

Sagittarius - ruled by Jupiter which also rules the third

Sagittarius here shows you are moving towards your spiritual objective but are still learning to face karmic restrictions; there are issues which block your progress and as Jupiter rules two difficult houses here its placement will create problems.

Capricorn - ruled by Saturn, which also rules the first

Capricorn ruling the twelfth shows that Saturn is ruling both the houses of the self and self-undoing. You will need to develop an attitude of caring for others and work at letting go of your ego. If you do not understand this part of your nature, it will cause frustration. Saturn as the teacher of lessons which help the soul mature can be your friend or enemy, you will have to make the choice.

Aquarius - ruled by Saturn, which also rules the eleventh

Aquarius in the twelfth shows that part of your karma is the breaking up of your personal ego. Lessons in life will teach you to care for others and break away from thinking about the individual. Saturn here controls both your expenses and earning - you may always feel restricted with your spending. Saturn can cause problems for you wherever it is placed as it rules two difficult houses.

Pisces - ruled by Jupiter, which also rules the ninth

Pisces here shows an inner peace; you realise that the true aim of the soul is to experience moksha and whilst the Aries ascendant helps you to achieve on a material level you are always aware of a higher purpose in life. This could be a bit difficult for other people to understand. Jupiter ruling the ninth house will give very good results wherever it is placed as Sagittarius is its mooltrikona sign.

The Nakshatras -
The Indian Lunar Zodiac

When ancient peoples looked up into the sky they saw patterns in the way the stars were clustered together. They named particular groupings of stars after symbols that were dominant in their culture: that's how the different constellations were first named and it is on these ancient identifications astrology is now based. However, there are other ways of interpreting the night sky. Jyotish has the oldest system, the lunar nakshatra zodiac, which influenced the Chinese Mansions and Arab Manzils. It begins at 0° Aries and is based on the Moon's movement against the stars beyond it as it makes its way around the zodiac each lunar, or sidereal, month. This journey of 27 days, 7 hours, 43 minutes and 11.5 seconds brings the Moon back to the original position, with no reference to the Sun. So if at the start of a sidereal month the Moon was at 5° Aries, at the end of that sidereal month it will be in the same place again, and therefore the same nakshatra (5° Aries is in Ashwini). The sidereal month forms the basis of the lunar calendar still used by Vedic astrologers. The coming lunar month is ruled by the nakshatra that the current full Moon is in.

This way of considering the relationship between the planets and the stars divides up the ecliptic not into constellations but into sections of 13° 20', the distance travelled by the Moon in one solar day. The resultant 27 sections are known as the nakshatras. Their importance in Indian life is something that clock-based and urbanised westerners may find difficult to appreciate, but the nakshatras have been part of the bedrock of Vedic astrology for centuries.

The Nakshatras and the Soul

'**Naksha**' means 'to approach' and '**Tra**' means 'to guard'. The whole word also means 'a star'. Each nakshatra is associated with a particular star, usually the brightest in its constellation. In the mythology of the nakshatras the star is a god or goddess whose duty it is to watch over the cosmic evolution of the soul. 'Nakshatra' also means 'one that never decays': the protective watch of the nakshatras over the soul will continue through many human lifetimes. They are essentially a passive energy, however, and their influence will not be felt unless occupied by the ascendant or one of the grahas at birth. The nakshatras are the key to Vedic astrology as they combine the solar and the lunar zodiacs; they are referred to in nearly every Vedic technique.

The Nakshatras by the Day

As the nakshatras are a lunar zodiac, the position of the Moon is of prime importance, both natally and by transit. The Moon's passage through the nakshatras makes a difference to your life on a very personal level as well: each one has a slightly different relationship (makes a different aspect) to the nakshatra it was in on the day of your birth. This is known as **tarabala**, and by using the grid shown at the end of the chapter you will be able to work out your own cycle. As you become more familiar with the nakshatras you will be able to make use of this energy in a constructive way.

Mahurata - Electional Astrology

Mahurata chooses correct times for planned events such as a marriage or the foundation of a new business venture; by setting up a chart for them in advance one can make the best possible use of the planetary energies. Knowledge of the nakshatras is essential to this process.

Synastry - Relationship Astrology

Most marriages in India are still arranged by the families of the partners. The comparison of the charts of the likely bride and groom is an important part of the arrangements; the placement of the grahas, especially the Moon, in the nakshatras is considered when deciding whether the couple would be compatible on a sexual, romantic, practical and spiritual basis.

The Dashas
In Vedic astrology our lives are seen as a series of phases - the dashas - each one ruled by a particular planet. Calculation of which dashas you will experience in your life (it's not physically possible to live through them all) and their timing is taken from the exact nakshatra position of the Moon at birth. I'll go into this in more depth later in the book.

Rectification
Drawing up a correct natal chart requires an accurate and precise time of birth. Rectification is an astrological technique used to refine uncertain birth-times and it is particularly important in India, given the importance of electional astrology. A skilled astrologer can use the nakshatras to ascertain the birth-time with a high level of accuracy.

Interpretation of the Nakshatras
I've already mentioned that the nakshatras are only activated in any chart if they have a planet in them; the nakshatra of the planet that rules the ascendant is also studied, as discussed further on. Each of the zodiac signs with which we are already familiar is divided into two and a quarter nakshatras; this influences the energy of a planet in that sign, like a ray of light passing through a prism.

Rulership
In general, we interpret the lunar zodiac using the same rules as we would the twelve signs of the zodiac. When a particular nakshatra contains natal planets, your ascendant or Rahu Ketu, the interpretation starts with that nakshatra's ruling planet, looking at where in the natal chart the ruling planet is and which houses it rules. The ruler of the ascendant nakshatra acts as the final dispositor for the planets; that is to say, all other rulerships are referred to this one. For example, if you have the ascendant at 11° Taurus it will fall in the nakshatra

called Rohini, which is ruled by the Moon. However, as Taurus is ruled by Venus, your ascendant will be influenced by Venus **and** the Moon.

Beginning with number 1, at 0 Aries, rulership of the nakshatras is in this order: Ketu, Venus, Sun, Moon, Mars, Rahu, Jupiter, Saturn, Mercury; then starting again with Ketu and so on through to nakshatra number 27.

Further divisions give even greater accuracy in interpreting the chart: each nakshatra is subdivided into four parts known as **padas** or feet, representing the division of one solar day (24 hours) into quarters - sunrise, midday, sunset and midnight. Each pada has its own zodiac-sign ruler and therefore a strong relationship with the sign's ruling planet. So rulership of points on the natal chart will depend not only on which nakshatra they are in but also in which pada. Three people all born with Moon in Libra could have the Moon in three different nakshatras and thus nine different quarters. They will have very different personalities and lives; as will three people with Moon in Libra in the same nakshatra but in different padas. Such multi-level interpretation of the position of just one planet is very difficult for a beginner to cope with, but it does help explain why less focused interpretations of planets may not work for everyone. For example, take a client with the Moon in Virgo, ruled by Mercury. This person doesn't feel especially Mercurial; on the contrary, they have a strongly solar side to their emotional make-up. Using the nakshatras and padas can offer a solution to this apparent paradox, as in this particular case the nakshatra this person's Moon occupies is ruled by the Sun!

Pariyayas - the Cycle of the Nakshatras

The 27 nakshatras are subdivided into three groups of nine which can be seen as the symbolic journey of a soul. The three groups are associated with the different gunas or mental attitudes:

• **Nakshatras 1-9: associated with rajasic mental attitude**
These nakshatras emphasise newness, innovation and searching; in the material world, for achievement, or on a spiritual level, for a new dimension. If you have a majority of planets in the zodiac signs

Aries to Cancer or the Sun and/or Moon in these nakshatras, you will be like this.

•   **Nakshatras 10-18: associated with tamasic mental attitude**
This group emphasises worldliness - a necessary next step in any soul's progress but a trait it must leave behind if it is to find enlightenment. People with several planets in the signs Leo to Scorpio, or Sun and/or Moon in these nakshatras will relate to this.

•   **Nakshatras 19-27: associated with sattvic mental attitude**
The last group emphasises purity. Having rejected worldliness because it doesn't bring true fulfilment, the soul searches for the Truth; by the last nakshatra, ruled by Pisces, you may have some sense of what that Truth is. With a majority of planets in Sagittarius to Pisces, or Sun and/or Moon in these nakshatras, you will be like this.

Gandanta Points
These are the three places (of about 1 degree) where the end of each of the three pariyaya cycles coincides with the ending of one zodiac sign and the beginning of another: Pisces to Aries, Cancer to Leo and Scorpio to Sagittarius. We think of these three areas as having particular karmic significance: when the natal ascendant or Moon is located near them, it suggests that this lifetime is one of critical importance to the development of the soul.

Lagna Gandanta - where the **ascendant** at the time of birth was in one of these areas.

Nakshatra Gandanta - where the **Moon** at the time of birth was in one of these areas. (This placement of the natal Moon indicates an incarnation with a very special purpose.)

So, as you are beginning to see, each nakshatra has a wealth of mythology and symbolism all of its own, quite separate from the symbolism of the signs and grahas.

The Importance of the Nakshatras

Knowing the nakshatra placements of your ascendant and grahas is very important as prediction and the choosing of auspicious days cannot really be done without it. Although the concept may be hard to grasp at first it really is worth spending some time on this area; studying the nakshatras relevant to your chart will lead to a much deeper understanding of your inner motivation. The nakshatras are particularly personal, best reached through their symbols: meditate on them and on their meaning for you. Their study, even in your own chart, is the work of a lifetime. They work on many different levels and their full meaning will only be revealed over time.

Not much is written in English on this vast subject. The concept of a lunar zodiac has mostly gone from western culture so that even the astrologers are not familiar with the underlying principles. It is impossible to do the nakshatras full justice in this introductory book; to describe their rich symbolism and explain all the relevant techniques would take a book in itself. I do hope though, that the following section helps you to understand their importance and begin to appreciate their relevance in the chart.

The Nakshatras

1. Ashwini

0° - 13°20' Aries
Ashwini's symbol is the head of a horse
The ruling deity is the Ashwini Kumaras
The Sun exalted in Ashwini
It is ruled by Ketu

Ashwini, the first nakshatra, is ruled by Ketu and is in the sign of Aries. Kumara is a general name for a boy, youth or prince. Aries deals with birth, a new life, freshness of approach and start of a new cycle of life. Ashwini indicates the beginning of the soul's journey into the earthly life. Ketu, as the significator for moksha ruling the beginning of life (indicated by Aries), shows that the true reason of our manifestation on earth is to find moksha - spiritual liberation and the final release from the cycles of life and death. This is the stage where the mind is pure and we have not yet entangled ourselves into knots which represent the attachments to life. The Sun, the significator of the soul and our inner consciousness, is exalted in Ashwini.

Ketu acts like Mars, but on a psychological level, so the purity

174

of Martian action, courage and protection of humanity is powerfully indicated. The past life connection is very strong, specially if the Moon is placed here, as Ketu is the planet that keeps the secrets of past lives.

The Ashwins were twin sons of the Sun God. They represent the transition from darkness to light and herald a new dawn; a time when there is an intermingling of the dualities of day and night, past life and present, heaven and earth. They are the celestial physicians who have great healing powers. People born in Ashwini are great healers and they have the ability to prolong life. It is creative power in its latency. They can be successful on both the material and spiritual levels.

2.   Bharani

13°20' - 26°40' Aries
The symbol of Bharani is Yoni - the female sexual organ
The presiding deity is Yama - the god of death
Saturn is debilitated in Bharani
It is ruled by Venus

Bharani's basic principle is Shakti, the passive female power. It is this energy that incubates the soul and transports it from one realm of existence to another. Put another way it takes you from a spiritual manifestation to a more objective one.

The symbol for Bharani is Yoni - the female reproductive organ; this establishes Bharani as a channel for creation.

The ruling deity is Yama, the god of death, although this doesn't just mean physical death. It can mean the ending of one chapter of your life. Yama is also responsible for the seed of new life. He allows us to detach ourselves from previous lives so that we can be reborn to create fresh karma. In yoga practice, the disciplines of Yama (restraint) and Niyama (practice or observation) are used to channel physical energies. Whichever interpretation you take for Yama, Bharani directs the inner nature towards its highest intensity. The rulership of Bharani by Venus but within the energy of Mars makes the action very much on a material plain. Bharani people believe in excess; whether they are indulging in sex or doing yoga they do not know when to stop. They are idealistic, which can sometimes be misinterpreted

Saturn, the planet of karmic restriction, is debilitated here. Saturn wants the soul to focus on paying for its past karma. Bharani is about youthfulness, the opposite of Saturn's nature. It is also a **brahamchari**, which means a bachelor. The sexual nature of this nakshatra make it very difficult for the brahamchari Saturn to deal with its impulses.

3. Krittika

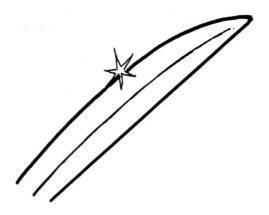

26°40' Aries - 10°00' Taurus
The symbol of Krittika is a razor
The presiding deity is Agni - the god of fire
The Moon is exalted in Krittika
It is ruled by the Sun

The first quarter of Krittika lies within Aries, ruled by Mars, and the other three-quarters in Taurus, ruled by Venus. It is ruled by Sun. You will remember the myth of the Krittikas - their role in the birth of Mars (and his ensuing destruction of the demon) links them to impossible feats. Power and war are the two main attributes. It is a malefic nakshatra as it has the capacity to nurture potentially destructive forces. Like a mother, Krittika has no choice regarding the seed she carries; the mother does not know how her progeny will turn out.

The Venusian earthiness of Taurus and the Solar fire of Krittika make planets very fiery, practical and sensuous. The Moon is exalted in Krittika at 3° Taurus. The mind, as signified by the Moon, has both constructive and destructive impulses, so its exaltation here shows the ability to control the destructive side of its nature.
Krittika has the capacity to create powerful people who are not afraid to confront difficult situations. Planets in Krittika need to be guided towards their positive nature as there is always a potential for destruction.

4. Rohini

10°00' - 23°20' Taurus
Its symbol is the chariot
The ruling deity is Brahma, the creator of the Universe
Rohini is ruled by the Moon

Rohini in Sanskrit means 'red', which relates to passion and sensuality. It is in the sign of Taurus ruled by Venus, and the nakshatra is ruled by the Moon. The combination of Venus and the Moon indicates great beauty, perfection, and a striving towards feminine essence. Rohini is considered the favourite wife of the Moon. (According to mythology, the 27 Nakshatras are the 27 wives of the Moon* each of whom he stayed with for one day a month.) The other wives, jealous of the Moon's infatuation with Rohini, complained to Brahma, the creator, who cursed the Moon to lose his power totally and then allowed him regain it - which in our terms has become waxing and waning cycles. The Moon becoming infatuated with Rohini reflects the soul's entanglement with matter. It is here that he becomes involved with the earthly illusions which directly lead to the of purity; here also is where and why the waxing and waning cycles of life and death begin. It directs the soul towards the physical world with its pleasures and pains. The Moon and Venus, which are essentially material planets, can become intensely involved

178

in Rohini's pleasures and attractions. Brahma, the ruling deity of Rohini, is the creator of the universe, which further indicates that procreation and life on earth are part of the bigger picture he has yet to reveal. At this stage he guides the soul into the first part of its involvement with the world of senses, an experience that is essential to the growth of the soul.

*The Moon is often regarded as a male deity in the Vedas.

5. Mrigasira

23°20' Taurus - 6°40' Gemini
Its symbol is the head of a deer
The ruling deity is Soma
Mrigasira is ruled by Mars.

Mriga means a deer and Sira means head. The head of the deer is also a symbol of the Moon. Mrigsira is situated half in Taurus (ruled by Venus) and half in Gemini (ruled by Mercury). It is ruled by Mars - the planet of action and courage, which here aids the consciousness to move onto a different level of manifestation. The splitting of Mrigasira between the creative and sensual instincts of Taurus and the mental, intellectual activity of Gemini needs the Mars energy to move towards individuality.

    To understand the impact of Mrigasira, we need to refer to Tara's Rahasya (secret) as told in the Vedas. As you will remember,

Tara was the wife of Jupiter and she had an affair the Moon which resulted in the birth of Mercury. In the context of this nakshatra, the myth illustrates that sense of dissatisfaction with the way things are - the desire to experience 'something more'. The intellect is considered to be just a fragment of the mind, so for it to be born there had to be a merging of Tara's godly impulses with the earthly impulses of the Moon - a duality which is reflected in the quality of Mercury.

Mrigasira essentially shows the beginning of the search to live life on a different level, the dissatisfaction with the present circumstances however good or pure they may seem. At Mrigasira, the soul loses its inherent purity as its journey finally takes it into the realms of worldliness.

6. Ardra

6°40' - 20°00' Gemini
Its symbol is the head or the jewel
The ruling deity is Rudra - the god of destruction
Ardra is ruled by Rahu - the North Node

Ardra means green, moist. It is situated entirely in Gemini, ruled by Mercury. Ardra itself is ruled by Rahu. This dual rulership of

Rahu and Mercury explains the field of operation for Ardra: Rahu as Vasuki drank the nectar which made him immortal, therefore as the ruler of Ardra he wants to achieve the highest ambitions. Mercury indicates that the sphere of activity is going to be intellectual. Rahu makes us want to achieve the impossible, reach for our highest aspirations. The search here is for intellectual perfection.

The symbol of the jewels gives the ability to absorb kinetic, mystical and spiritual energies from the Sun. Jewels are known to absorb energies around them and transmit them to the wearer. In the same way, Ardra has the capacity to absorb these powers, using them for higher or lower purposes.

The other symbol of Ardra is the head - obviously where the brain (and thus the mind) is biologically situated. The brain is formed by experiences from the past karma, but the mind can again work in either a positive or negative way. Ardra's symbols therefore represent ideas and the capacity to think.

The overall influence of Ardra indicates the duality of Gemini: the lust for immortality represented by Rahu, the duality of the mind and intellect by Mercury. Both can be used to enhance the world or destroy it. At the cosmic stage of Ardra, there is conflict on the outer level where we are dissatisfied with our present surroundings and start looking for answers. This can be through exploring and communicating with the occult.

Rudra, the god of destruction, is a form of Shiva and is the deity of Ardra. His mission is to destroy ignorance, so he directs the consciousness towards knowledge and finding the answers for ourselves about this manifestation. At Ardra we begin our studies in the Law of Nature. For the first time we become dissatisfied with the materialistic nature of our lives and start towards expanding the horizons of our spiritual selves.

7. Punarvasu

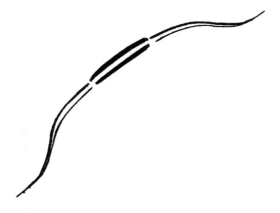

20°00' Gemini - 3°20' Cancer
Its symbol is the Bow
The ruling deity is Aditi
Punarvarsu is ruled by Jupiter

Punarvasu is situated towards the end of Gemini. It has three quarters in Gemini ruled by the Mercury and the final quarter in Cancer ruled by the Moon. The nakshatra itself is ruled by Jupiter - the celestial guru who is there to guide us to our righteous path. Punarvasu deals with the transfer of knowledge from the spiritual to the earthly, and Jupiter as the true teacher has the responsibility to guide this process. The Gemini part of the nakshatra gives the duality of purpose, the intellect being torn in two directions. The Cancer part of the nakshatra indicates transferring the spiritual knowledge into its earthly domain.

Punar Vasu translates into Punah as 'again', and Vasu, meaning 'brilliant', like rays of light. Punah also means to stay. The full meaning of the nakshatra is to live simultaneously at different levels of cosmic manifestation. Punarvasu also relates to the Vasus, the Vedic deities of whom there were eight: Apas, Dhruva, Soma, Dhara, Anila, Anala, Pratyusha and Prabhas. These deities have a strong connection with the Sun and appear at different stages of manifestation to guide the soul towards its true direction. They transform the messages from a higher realm into ideas to guide us in earthly life; like the rays of light from the Sun which bring the divine message to earth. Punar Vasu's ruling deity is Aditi who is the female principle as well as the representation of infinity.

The symbol of the bow indicates that this nakshatra is the link between the Archer and his objective. The Archer is the man who needs the link of the bow/Punarvasu to achieve his objective. Whether they are on a spiritual level or a material one, Punarvasu creates the situation where you can prepare to reach for your goals.

8. Pushya

3°20' - 16°20' Cancer
The symbols are a flower, an arrow and a circle
The ruling deity is Brihaspati
Jupiter exalted in Pushya
It is ruled by Saturn

Pushya is within the sign of Cancer (ruled by the Moon) and is ruled by Saturn. The word itself means holy, pure and auspicious. Pushya's presiding deity is Brihaspati, which is another name for Jupiter, the advisor to the gods. It is an expansive planet, increasing everything it touches, but Saturn, the planet that brings forth karmic restrictions is the ruler of the nakshatra; this dual influence on Pushya is what makes it so special. A balance between expansion and restriction is achieved under Pushya; the soul's restrictions as well as its knowledge are fully expressed here. At this stage, the soul understands that this life is but a part of the greater cycle, not the whole thing in itself; there is a limited destiny to be experienced which is connected to the growth and restrictions of this life. The soul matures through this incarnation.

The symbol of the flower (any flower) is usually the expression of latent faculties, the outward expression of inner ideas. That of an arrow shows ambition and directed activity. The circle is complete in itself; it focuses our attention on this lifetime in its entirety, not just the beginning or the end of it.

Jupiter is exalted in Pushya. It deals with knowledge, teaching, advising and expansion on a spiritual level and is placed in the nakshatra of its opposing force Saturn, which is tamasic and very much concerned with worldly affairs. Jupiter's exaltation here indicates that Saturnine restrictions are necessary for wisdom to dawn, for the harnessing of knowledge and creating strength.

9. Ashlesha

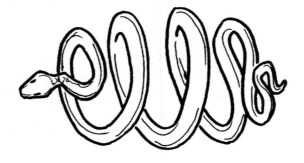

16°40' Cancer -   0°00' Leo
The symbol is the Serpent
Its presiding deity is the Nagas
Mars debilitated in Ashlesha
It is ruled by Mercury

Ashlesha is wholly in Cancer. The ending of Ashlesha and the ending of Cancer coincide - the Lunar and the Solar zodiac meet here, which makes this nakshatra extremely powerful on a spiritual level thus destiny plays an important part for those born in Ashlesha. Destiny is something you cannot control, it is borne from your own actions in previous lives. Ashlesha means alienation or discord. Here the soul separates itself from one level of manifestation to move towards another. This can create discord in the material aspects of one's life.

The ruler of Ashlesha is Mercury, which acts as the celestial bridge between higher forces and the earth. It is also the intellect that guides our rational thinking and the ego, which makes us different from other animals; the Moon, the ruler of the sign, represents the mind which controls us. Together these concentrate Ashlesha on the development of the mind and changes in the human psyche. Mars, the planet of action, is debilitated in Ashlesha, so its natural urge to take the initiative is somewhat dampened by the strongly psychic energies here.

The presiding deities of Ashlesha are the Nagas, snakes who have great occult powers. It would be wrong to think of them as merely poisonous snakes that kill. Ashlesha people are supposed to have incisive vision which enables them to look into the hidden secrets of nature and understand true wisdom. The snake carries his poison in a pouch so it's not actually in his body. It will only use this poison when forced to do so. Also, just as poison can be used for healing or for killing, so the Nagas have the capacity for both good or ill. Ashlesha can lead people to knowledge, wisdom, wealth and prosperity but it can also take them down the path of danger, self- destruction, sexual adventure and the unexpected. Snakes shed their skins periodically which serves to remind us of the cycle of rebirth and transformation. Ashlesha being at the junction of the Solar and Lunar zodiacs shows the ending of one cycle of life and the beginning of another. This process of shedding old skin is always painful; it relates to a change of the mind - emotional and intellectual and the evolving of human consciousness.

10. Magha

0°00' - 13°20' Leo
The symbol is a house or a palanquin
The presiding deity is Pitris - the forefathers
Magha is ruled by Ketu

Magha means mighty and great, and is the second nakshatra ruled by Ketu. It is in the sign of Leo and ruled by the Sun, so it isn't surprising that people born in this nakshatra aspire towards greatness. Magha is the beginning of the second cycle in the soul's journey; the signs Leo to Scorpio indicate the soul's full involvement in the pleasures and pains of earthly life. Ketu, as the significator of spiritual realisation rules the starting point of the journey into matter, which shows how important it is to experience the realities of life whilst still fulfilling the divine mission of the soul.

Magha's ruling deities are the Pitris, the fathers of humanity whose mission is to guide their children onto the right path in life; they only interfere if you deviate. Ketu and Pitris both guide the soul towards its special mission. Planets in Magha are idealistic even if their mission is to fulfil materialistic needs; this can create mis-understanding amongst friends who may suspect your honour and sincerity. Magha gives a lot materially, but the person ruled by Magha knows intuitively that happiness is but an experience; he still needs to follow the inner purpose of life and move towards moksha.

The symbols of Magha are a palanquin and a house. The house is a synonym for the body, which is the tool to carry out the spiritual mission in life. The palanquin is supported by a central rod made from a bamboo pole; the central rod represents the spinal cord and the knots in the pole are the chakra points; the people carrying the palanquin are the sense and action. This symbolism gives clear direction to Magha that the senses have to be conquered; they become like the servants carrying the palanquins and the chakras have to be activated to reach towards true understanding. At this stage however the direction is being given but not necessarily the answers.

11. Purva Phalguni

13°20' - 26°40' Leo
The symbols are a bed, fireplace and platform
Its ruling deity is Bhaga - the Vedic god of luck
It is ruled by Venus

Purva and Uttara Phalguni are two parts of a whole nakshatra of four stars, and the constellation resembles a bed. They indicate similar purposes with a very specific difference.

Purva Phalguni is entirely in the sign of Leo ruled by the Sun. It is ruled by Venus, which of course rules the good things in life. Phalguni means the nakshatra which gives the fruit of our endeavours and it has the capacity to fulfil our desires on a materialistic level.

The Sun and Venus combination gives abundant wealth and happiness. The Sun, representing the soul, takes time out in this nakshatra to relax a bit, to allow itself to be distracted by the Venusian pleasures of life.

The symbols of Purva Phalguni, the bed, the platform and the fireplace, are all places where we take time off from the main focus of life to enjoy earthly pleasures. The Upanishads tell how the people used to gather around the fire to listen to the tales of the gurus. This particular nakshatra indicates where the soul rests from its purpose of finding salvation and enjoys its Karma Phal, the fruits of its actions.

The ruling deity of Bhaga, the god of good fortune and luck, indicates that the fruits are usually highly auspicious. Bhaga also represents a woman's womb and procreation, as it is considered good luck for a woman to be able to bear children. Naturally this is where the area of life concerning children or creativity is very pronounced. Being a female nakshatra, Purva Phalguni needs other dynamic energy to activate it.

12. Uttara Phalguni

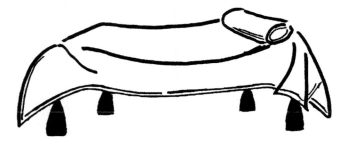

26°40' Leo - 10°00' Virgo
The symbol is four legs of the cot
The ruling deity is Aryaman
It is ruled by the Sun

Uttara Phalguni is the continuation of Purva Phalguni. It is the male energy to Purva's female and represents the other half of the picture.

Uttara Phalguni is a quarter in Leo and three quarters in Virgo; Leo is the sign for royalty, Virgo the sign for service, and these dramatically different qualities are represented by the signs. Uttara Phalguni is ruled by the Sun - the ruler of the universe, the significator of authority and power. The Sun signifies creation and carries within it the knowledge of individual karma. Uttara Phalguni allows the soul to recognise its own failings as well as restrictions imposed by its limited destiny in this life.

The four legs of the cot represent the sexual energy of the soul, the downward flow of the power. Each of the legs represent the sheaths in which the soul becomes entangled - the physical, the etheric, the astral and the mental. These sheaths surround the evolving soul during its stay in the Phalgunis. There is realisation that we are nothing more than a fragment of the whole universe, part of cosmic law; that our soul is rendered helpless in any attempt to reach for the sky by its connection to the earthly incarnation, a servant to its lower desires.

Aryaman, the ruling deity of Uttara Phalguni is famous for his leadership qualities. As a nakshatra it bestows those qualities on an incarnating soul as well as allowing it to recognise that its ambitions are limited by the enormity of the task ahead. It gives courage in the face of adversity, individual effort against all the odds. It creates isolation as one learns to shed the constraints created by past karma.

13. Hasta

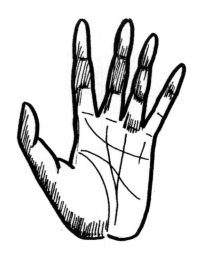

10°00' - 23°20' Virgo
The symbol is the hand or palm of the hand
The ruling deity is Savitar, the Sun God
Mercury is exalted in Hasta
It is ruled by Moon

Hasta is ruled by the Moon and is placed entirely in the sign of
Virgo (ruled by Mercury). The Moon controls the mind and Mercury
the intellect and ego, or the **ahamkar**, which develops with the
intellect. According to the Vedas, Mercury is the child of the Moon
(read the myth in the Mrigsira nakshatra); this nakshatra reflects
the entire mind.

Its symbol is the palm of the hand, where the complete destiny
of an individual is given. The right and the left hands are positive
and negative, male and female energies. The four fingers of the hand
show the four motivations - Artha, Kama, Dharma and Moksha,
the three digits on the fingers are the three gunas - Rajas, Tamas
and Sattva. The four fingers are also the four directions - North,
South, East and West. The fingers and the thumbs show the five
senses (sight, hearing, taste, smell and touch) and the five elements
(water, earth, sky, air and fire). The digits on the four fingers show
the twelve zodiac signs, and the digits of the thumbs and fingers
are the thirty days of the solar month. The hand reflects the solar

system and its planets. To write about all we can see from the hand is an entire field of knowledge - this all reflects the Hasta nakshatra. Mercury is exalted here.

Hasta has the quality for the individual to change, to grow in different directions. It provides immense opportunities for growth and expansion. The inner urge is to stride ahead but external forces restrict progress so the result is conflict and crisis. Souls are guided towards **nvritti marg** - renunciation, public service and becoming a sustaining power in the community.

The ruling deity of Hasta is Savitar which is a personification of the Sun, and therefore of the soul. Savitar deals with the healing regenerative energies.

14. Chitra

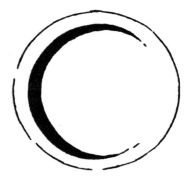

23°20' Virgo - 6°40' Libra
The symbol is a pearl
The ruling deity is Tvashtar
Venus is debilitated here
It is ruled by Mars

Chitra means a picture, or worldly illusion, something beautiful. People with their Moon in Chitra are usually very attractive and have a magnetic personality. It is placed half in Virgo, ruled by Mercury and half in Libra, ruled by Venus. The nakshatra is ruled by Mars, the significator for courage, action and leadership, but the combination of Mars and Mercury is a difficult one so in the Virgo part of the nakshatra there are negative energies to be dealt with. Chitra is a powerful nakshatra whose presiding deity, Tvashtar, is the celestial architect. The prime impulse of Chitra is to transform, to cut away the layers that hide our true self. Mars in such a powerful position will have tremendous capacity to break through barriers to give us what we desire. It breaks through the intellectual barriers in Virgo and in the sensual ones in Libra. In Chitra/Virgo, Venus is debilitated. Venus is the planet for love, romance, commitment, marriage, the luxuries of life, so the intellectual transformation which takes place in Chitra/Virgo becomes difficult to deal with. Therefore it acts contrary to its natural impulses and becomes a perfectionist and over-critical.

Chitra begins the process of unfolding the hidden nature of man. Tvashtar, the architect must cut away the rough edges; it is never an easy process.

The Chitra individual will find itself in situations that force it to reform. The process is painful: the ego has to be cut away so that the inner soul can break through. The symbol of the pearl for Chitra reminds us that in the same way as the shell has to be broken for the shining pearl to emerge - after many years of growth - so, after many lifetimes and many ordeals does the true personality of the individual shine through. This breaking of the shell is a difficult process and usually means an individual has to make immense changes over a long period to make progress.

The hidden perfection of a pearl can only be externalised by great insight and courage to fight and bear great ordeals. Mars does not accept defeat; any confrontation provides it with added incentive to fight and attain its goal.

15.   Swati

6°40' - 20°00' Libra
The symbol is coral
Its ruling deity is Vayu, the god of wind and life breath
The Sun is debilitated in Swati
It is ruled by Rahu

The second nakshatra ruled by Rahu is Swati, the name given to one of the wives of the Sun god. Planets in Swati indicate the depth of the soul's involvement in materialism and the indicator of the soul in our chart, the Sun, is debilitated here. Under Swati, the impulse is material gain. Venus rules the earthly needs in an individual; combining it with Rahu adds further to the desire for success, wealth and finance. Many millionaires are born with their Moon in Swati.

The location of this nakshatra in Libra indicates that the experience of full involvement in earthy, materialistic pleasures will bring with it dissatisfaction because the scales will be laden on one side. Once success is achieved we feel empty, alone and dissatisfied with our achievement. Many try for more success but the correct thing would be to look inwards. Libra is the stage when we start to think about spiritual meaning but only once the other urges have been fulfilled. The spirit is encased in outer physical sheaths, which restrict it, whilst further enhancement depends upon the development of its inherent potential. Equilibrium is reached when the tension of these opposing forces becomes equally balanced.

The presiding deity is Vayu, which rules the material world

along with Agni (fire) and Surya (the Sun). Its area of operation is Prana - the life breath without which we would perish. Our desires and the intellect are controlled by Vayu, which makes Swati essentially materialistic and involved in mundane pursuits.

The symbol is coral which has a hard outer sheath but is self propagating. It lives in a marine environment which it both affects and is affected by. This symbolises the human being, who lives in the world which influences his life, but in turn the human being makes an impact on the world around him.

16. Vishakha

20°00' Libra - 3°20' Scorpio
Its symbol is the potter's wheel and the archway
The ruling deities are : Agni, the god of Fire
                        Indra, the god of gods
Saturn is exalted and the Moon debilitated in Vishakha
Vishakha is ruled by Jupiter

Vishakha is three quarters in the sign of Libra ruled by Venus and a quarter in the sign of Scorpio ruled by Mars. Vishakha itself is ruled by Jupiter. Saturn is exalted in the Libra portion and the Moon is debilitated at 3° Scorpio in the Scorpio part; this shows the great duality of this nakshatra. Saturn's exaltation forces the soul to learn

194

from its experiences in life and change its outlook. The Moon, which is the reflection of the soul and the significator of the mind, is debilitated. The great churning of mind takes place in Vishakha between the lower self and its higher aspirations. The Moon does not want to change and is happy with its earthly inclinations, but at this stage of life, it is forced to recognise the ultimate purpose of life - moksha.

In the Libra part, Vishakha provides affluence, comfort and pleasant experiences in life. In Scorpio, it is full of trials and tribulations.

Vishakha is the only nakshatra to have two ruling deities: Agni and Indra. Agni is fire, which burns away all that is superfluous, while Indra enjoys sensual enjoyment and luxury. The two opposing deities cause turmoil and stress.

The symbol of potter's wheel shows the static inner core which is steeped in the tamas of worldly illusions. The clay fashioned by the potter is likened to life, which is shaped in different ways by the hands of destiny, the experiences of life help it to mature.
The archway represents the threshold of a new life. The change is yet to take place, as this is the soul looking from outward to within. It has reached the point in life where there is a desire to go towards the inner sanctum, the great unknown, which can bring up negative and positive issues. There is no guarantee of what awaits. Again, Jupiter, the advisor and teacher to the god as the ruler of this nakshatra, is at hand to steer the soul from its earthly responsibilities to more spiritual dimensions. (See Punarvasu nakshatra).

17. Anuradha

3°20' - 16°40' Scorpio
The symbol of Anuradha is a lotus
Its ruling deity is Mitra, the god of light
It is ruled by Saturn

Anuradha is placed entirely in the sign of Scorpio, ruled by Mars. The nakshatra is ruled by Saturn. Mars gives us the courage and confidence to face the spiritual trials and tribulations that are put in our path by Saturn. Mars wants to act and Saturn keeps bringing up karmic restrictions which the soul is forced to overcome. Saturn is rigid and inflexible; it has a specific purpose and will not allow anyone or anything to stand in the way of a karmic lesson. Mars is of course a natural warrior who will fight any such restrictions. This causes a great deal of trauma until these contrary energies are properly harnessed.

The symbol of Anuradha is the lotus which flourishes in stagnant waters and flowers in all its beauty in mud. The seeds are cast in the mud and the flowers grow towards the solar energy. Once the plant has flowered, it withers away and returns to the mud, where it will root again to repeat the whole process. The lotus is said to flower so that it can be laid at the feet of the gods - the soul is born so it breaks away from the process of life and death. These images together illustrate the evolutionary aspect of the soul. It reaches to the Sun (universal consciousness) from the mud (the soul concealed in matter) and the withering away shows death; rebirth is the process of the rooting and re-flowering of the lotus.

Mitra, the ruling deity of Anuradha, is the god which rules daylight. Mitra means friends which unites opposites. It unveils the experiences of the night. In Anuradha, it exposes the latent potential that has become hidden by a life engulfed in materialism.

18. Jyeshta

16°40' Scorpio - 0°00' Sagittarius
The symbol of Jyeshta is an umbrella and an earring
The ruling deity is Indra, the god of Gods
It is ruled by Mercury

The ending of Jyeshtha and the ending of Scorpio coincide - the Lunar and the Solar zodiac meet. This is an extremely powerful junction because here the soul breaks away from its materialistic course of life and moves towards the final part of the journey. The placement of the Moon or the ascendant in the final parts of Jyeshta give a person a strong sense of destiny where he has to struggle with his lower and higher desires. The ruler of Jyeshtha is Mercury, the celestial link between materialism and spiritualism. At Jyeshta the change starts, and if the soul is not ready, it struggles against the restrictions and creates unhappiness.

Jyeshta means elder sister, the middle finger or the holy river Ganges, and thus has some esteem attached to it. The elder sister is looked upon with great respect as she is like one's mother. The river Ganges is said to wash away all our negative karma. The middle finger is the finger of destiny and it is used in yoga during pranayama to control the flow of breath. At Jyeshta we are given the guidance to activate the kundalini and the seven chakras. In order for the kundalini to unfold, we have to master the lower nature; Jyeshta encourages us to master our desires through the practice of yoga, austerity and meditation. The control over breath which we undertake with pranayama is the ultimately control over life.

The earring and umbrella are status symbols. They are given to those who have passed tests of life and achieved the wisdom and knowledge which others can look up to. The soul goes through problems and difficulties on the material level so that it is ready for the initiation into higher knowledge which is going to follow. Indra, the ruling deity controls the pleasures of life. He achieved this status after hard toils and difficult lessons. It shows that at Jyeshta the soul struggles to achieve the high esteem which will allow it to be privy to the secrets of the universe; by gaining this knowledge it will then have the capacity to control the quality of its life.

19. Mula

0°00' - 13°20' Sagittarius
Its symbol is the tail of a lion or an elephant's goad
The ruling deity is Nritta
Mula is ruled by Ketu

Mula is the third nakshatra ruled by Ketu. In this final part of the soul's mission it is searching for a way to escape from the cycle of life and death. This is one of the most difficult nakshatras for planets to be situated in, especially the Moon. The deity that rules Mula is Nittriti, the goddess of death and destruction; she personifies the destruction of the material sheath and the foundation on which spiritual enfoldment can be undertaken. The pain experienced by the influence of Mula changes the personality. Attachment to the lower nature and material tendencies have to be severed so that a new spiritual beginning is possible. This is the nakshatra of initiation towards spiritual realisation. Ketu fulfils its role as Moksha karaka by arousing the soul towards its ultimate destination. Mula means root and it also is Muladhara chakra (the base chakra) where the kundalini power is activated.

The elephant's goad is used to guide the elephant in the correct direction. In terms of people this symbol represents the constant prodding or pain we have to suffer in our search for the spiritual pathway.

The lion uses his tail to express his anger and supremacy. These show two opposite sides of the Mula characteristic. There can be immense anger directed at others and power issues are strong here. Jupiter as ruler of the sign represents wisdom and Ketu is the past karma which we carry in the subconscious. If this is not being expressed or channelled properly, it can lead to abuse of power.

20. Purvashadha

13°20' - 26°40' Sagittarius
The symbol is the elephant's tusk
The presiding deity is Apas - the water god
Purvashadha is ruled by Venus

The nakshatra of Purvashada is in Sagittarius. Jupiter rules Sagittarius and the nakshatra ruler is Venus. The focus is on Jupiterian wisdom, expansion of ideas and beneficence with the Venusian idealism and justice. Both Jupiter and Venus are spiritual teachers. Venus advises the humans and the demons, while Jupiter is guru to the gods, so the message here is to do things in the right way. Purvashadha looks at universal issues and how we as individuals will deal with them. Purva and Uttara Ashada are one half of a whole nakshatra. Purva means first, indicating it is the former part of the Ashadha nakshatras. Ashada means invincible, and this is the first nakshatra where we recognise the invincibility of strength gained from wisdom.

Apas, the god of water, indicates the transforming nature of this nakshatra. Water is always used in rituals to cleanse and rejuvenate the inner soul as it symbolises purity and is sattvic - Ganga Jal or the water of the river Ganges is used on all auspicious occasions. At Purvaashada, the soul wants to cleanse its sins to prepare for the final journey. The heightened sensitivity which comes about from cleansing the outer karma is the most important condition of transformation, and ushers in the dawn of spirituality.

Water is also changeable and represents emotions. Those born under Purvaashadha can be unsettled, suddenly shifting the direction of their life. This makes them difficult to understand and partnerships with them can be tough because of their apparently fickle nature.

The symbol of the elephant's tusk shows the revelation of the inner faculties. The tusk is the most expensive part of the elephant, valued so much for its beauty that the elephant is killed for the sake of it. The knowledge which Purvaashadha uncovers is also valued by others but it can lead demonic forces trying to take away this new power. The elephant lives in constant danger of losing his most valuable asset; a person seeking his higher self has to face dangers from the world around him in pursuit of his chosen path. The tusk, if cut off, will grow again, showing that wisdom once gained cannot be taken away.

21. Uttarashadha

26°40' Sagittarius - 10°00' Capricorn
The symbol is the planks of a bed
The ruling deity are the Vishwedevas - the universal gods
Uttarashadha is ruled by the Sun

This is the second half of the Ashadas; Uttara means higher. The first quarter of Uttara Ashadha is in Sagittarius, ruled by Jupiter, and the remainder is in Capricorn, ruled by Saturn. Uttara Ashadha itself is ruled by the Sun. Consciousness is signified by the Sun and the combined influence of Saturn and Jupiter moves it in a wholly different direction. Jupiter teaches wisdom through knowledge while Saturn teaches knowledge through experience of life. They both guide us - one by expanding our intellectual horizons and the other by bringing about restrictions which lead ultimately to self-knowledge. The planks of the bed, the symbol of Uttarashadha, do not just indicate a place for sleeping and resting. The planks indicate an austere bed, not one of comfort. Sleep is a necessary requirement to open our minds to higher connections; rest is used in yoga to relax the muscles so that the next asana can be taken slightly further. In the same way, Uttarashadha creates conditions for the relaxation of the body so that the mind can move further along its path of enlightenment.

Jupiter, the planet of knowledge and wisdom, is debilitated here in the Capricorn part of Uttarashadha. New wisdom here has to be through life experiences, and Jupiter is no use in avoiding the harsh realities of karma.

The ruling deities the Vishwedevas, the universal gods, show that Uttarashadha has to concentrate on worldly issues. It shows a life lived in public with an inner desire to be alone. The Vishwedevas guide us towards social interaction but the inner self has to be detached. The responsibility of our past karmas have to be completed before we can move on to the final level of manifestation.

22. Shravana

10°00' - 23°20' Capricorn
The symbols are an ear and an arrow
The ruling deity is Vishnu, the preserver of the Universe
It is ruled by the Moon

Shravana is ruled by the Moon and the nakshatra is placed in Capricorn which has the rulership of Saturn. This Saturn/Moon combination makes for difficult situations. The Moon waxes and wanes, is emotional and changeable, Saturn is disciplined, rigid and inflexible. Saturn will teach us to control our emotions, be detached from the up and downs of life. Shravana forces us to take more responsibility for ourselves as we experience inner growth and move towards higher knowledge.

Shravana means listening and this is the nakshatra of total silence. To listen to the sounds of silence can only be done through self-discipline, yoga and the path of truth. This silence develops in us the ability to see through the illusions of life. The Moon in this nakshatra echoes the need for quietness and reflection. The silence that this total meditation brings in our hearts will lead to a better understanding within ourselves; to sit in silence we have to like ourselves; it forces us to recognise our own truths and not simply hide within the cacophony of life.

The symbol of the ear assigned to Shravana further enhances the listening quality. To hear the various sounds and know how to listen will bring you the essence of what you are hearing and learning. To listen is to learn.

Vishnu, the ruling deity supports the soul through its difficulties and tribulations as it matures. It teaches a person to distinguish between fact and fiction in life.

23. Dhanishta

23°20' Capricorn - 6°40' Aquarius
The symbol is the drum
The ruling deities are the Eight Vasus
Dhanishta is ruled by Mars

Dhanishta is placed half in Capricorn and half in Aquarius. Both are ruled by Saturn, representing restriction, but Dhanishta is ruled by the opposing energy Mars - which of course stands for bravery and action. When Mars and Saturn conjoin, it is usually considered a warlike formation. The war in this case is being fought between the material and the spiritual self. Saturn brings forth situations that enable past karma to be cleansed. Mars wants to break through spiritual barriers but Saturn restricts it because there are still areas of life to perfect before spiritual liberation can be achieved.

Dhanishta means a flute or a drum. Here it means the flute of Krishna or the drum of Shiva. The symbol of the drum implies it is beating to the rhythm of someone else - others are to play their song through this drum. It is essentially a lonely existence from a very early age. This can mean that you are fulfilling other people's expectations rather than your own. Both the drum and the flute are hollow from within; this means an emptiness within the Dhanishta person unless he finds something to fill it. Sometimes this can be fruitless chasing of dreams or illusions. Dhanishta shows musical talent.

Vasus are the eight personifications of the Sun and are known as Apas, Dhruva, Soma, Dhara, Anila, Anala, Pratyusha and Prabhas. These deities have a strong connection with the Sun and appear at different stages of manifestation to guide the soul towards its true direction.

24. Shatabhishak

6°40' - 20°00' Aquarius
The quarters are ruled by Jupiter, Saturn, Saturn and Jupiter
The symbols for Shatabhishak are a horse or a thousand flowers
Its ruling Deity is Varuna
It is ruled by Rahu

Shatabishak is entirely in the sign of Aquarius, ruled by Saturn. Rahu's rulership makes a very difficult combination where life has to have a purpose and the total direction is about learning lessons. Rahu gives results like Saturn but on a psychological level. This double Saturnine influence on planets placed here is difficult to handle unless our activities are directed towards service to humanity. Here both Rahu and Saturn are concerned with changing our life's purpose, giving us the final answers. Rahu on the internal level and Saturn on an external level offers restrictions, obstacles and transformation. The need to understand the final lessons of life as well as responsibility to others are two of the important aspects of Shatabishak.

Its symbol is the thousand petalled flower; Shatabishak is where the kundalini flowers and we reach towards the full awareness of our consciousness. This is the stage in life where we activate the Sahasara (Crown) chakra and Rahu brings forth its full power as the teacher of cosmic law. When the Moon is in Shatabishak its materialistic tendencies are shed completely and we move towards the next phase of spiritual development. Shat means a hundred and Bhishak means formidable, intimidating; together they indicate steep learning curves to be undergone by the soul in pursuit of its ultimate destiny.

The presiding deity, Varuna, bestows knowledge and wisdom on the person so that a ray of light shines through him. The ray of light is the perception of why we are here, the real purpose of the soul. This light guides the person under the direction of Varuna towards a new approach to life.

25. Purva Bhadra

20°00' Aquarius - 3°20' Pisces
The symbol is the sword
Its presiding deity is Aja Ekapada
Purva Bhadra is ruled by Jupiter

Purva Bhadra is three quarters in Aquarius, ruled by Saturn and a quarter in Pisces, ruled by Jupiter. The nakshatra is also ruled by Jupiter. Aquarius is the beginning, the dawn of new consciousness within ourselves and on the world stage. It stands for purification - transformation is a key word. Discarding the old life, so that new realities can emerge. Aquarius is ruled by Saturn, Purva Bhadra is ruled by Jupiter. Saturn transforms consciousness through restrictions, structures and obstacles whereas Jupiter expands and pushes through new frontiers. The mingling of the contrary energies of the two rulers brings about far-reaching changes in the individual psyche. At Pisces, it is the stage of merging individual consciousness with the universal one. Purva Bhadra stands for stability, courage and change. Idealism is the essence of this nakshatra. It wants to change the world, to merge with the cosmic ocean of eternity, and to fight for a cause regardless of the consequences.

Purva Bhadra and Uttara Bhadra are also different parts of the same nakshatra. Purva again means first and Bhadra means auspicious and blessed.

The ruling deity Aja Ekapada represents the unborn cosmic energy - where the seeds are being sown for the next stage in our evolution.

The symbol of the sword shows an instrument which can be used to attack as well as to defend. The sword cuts through any restrictions, but also symbolises a fight for universal causes.

26. Uttara Bhadra

3°20' - 16°40' Pisces
The symbol is twins
The ruling Deity is Ahir Budhyana
It is ruled by Saturn

Uttara Bhadra is in Pisces, which is ruled by Jupiter, but the nakshatra is ruled by Saturn. Saturn is linked to resistance, difficulties and opposition in the beginning but harmony by the end. Jupiter is the only planet which can balance the Saturnine energies (see Pushya Nakshatra). This nakshatra becomes very powerful when associated with any planet. Although it is passive and non-active, it is also highly dynamic when influenced by an active force. It enables an individual to comprehend wisdom concealed in different forms of manifestation. Whatever happens to the individual there is growth and expansion of consciousness. There is opportunity to preserve, protect and co-operate with the divine plan despite hardships. Mercury is debilitated here. It represents the search of an individual in the material realms and signifies intellect and individuality. At Uttara Bhadra, the individual voluntarily gives up both his personality and his ego to merge with universal consciousness.

Ahir Budhyana, its ruling deity, is the god associated with water and darkness. The passivity of darkness is the mysterious source from which all forms of creation have arisen. It signifies the merging of consciousness into the deep sea of eternity. Ahir Bhudiyana is also a serpent which represents wisdom; the snake sheds its skin showing the rebirth and cycles of life a soul passes through during its journey (see Ashlesha nakshatra).

27.   Revati

16°40' - 30°00' Pisces
The symbol is a fish
The ruling deity is Pushan
Revati is ruled by Mercury

Revati links the beginning with the end; Rev means to go, move, and Ati to go beyond, transcend. Together they mean transcending from one manifestation to another. Both the Solar and Lunar zodiac end here with the last nakshatra. Having an ascendant or the Moon placed in Revati indicates a soul who has to experience a very intense incarnation in this life. Events happen which are directly linked to the destiny of the soul in ending one cycle of manifestation and preparing for a new one; it is where the seeds are sown for fruition at a later date. Revati is ruled by the celestial messenger, Mercury, and its ruling deity is Pushan, which is another name for the Sun. The Sun nourishes the earth and as Pushan he also measures the skies, which means that he is privy to the ultimate truths. Being the last nakshatra of the zodiac, Revati is powerful in realising the ultimate truths about us; life, death, transformation, change - all come under the premise of this fixed star.

Venus is exalted in the last part of Revati. It symbolises sex and procreation, and Venus being at its most powerful here means that life is not all about endings. A seed is sown at this juncture for future growth.

The symbol of the fish is auspicious because it represents procreation and creativity.

Vimshottari Dashas - The System of Prediction

The vimshottari dasha is the planetary system of predicting events in our life, and it is unique to Vedic astrology. Vimshottari means '120' - the optimum life-span in the era in which the Vedas were written; dasha means 'direction'. Originating in the era when the Vedas were written, the system assumes an average life-span of 120 years! Those 120 years are divided into various phases, controlled by the nine planets: the Sun, the Moon, Mars, Mercury, Jupiter, Venus, Saturn, Rahu and Ketu. Moving out of one phase into another involves a change of life direction. Whilst the birth chart suggests the passive influences you have brought with you, and the past life karmic issues that form part of your character, it is the dasha system that indicates **when** these issues will become prominent. On analysis of your chart, you will be aware that certain areas of life will run smoothly, whilst others will prove troublesome; understanding your dasha pattern will help you to anticipate them and act accordingly. The usual questions of marriage, children, career, and house moves can all be given timings in this way.

The Dasha Patterns

The dasha pattern shows which planets will be ruling at particular times in your life; they fulfil three roles in the dasha periods:

- They will act according to their own energies

- Their role as rulers of the houses: the Sun and Moon rule one sign each, therefore they will rule one house each. Mars, Mercury, Jupiter, Venus and Saturn rule two signs - therefore two houses each

- Their role as karakas or significators (Sun - father; Jupiter - teacher etc.)

Sometimes the planetary placements in your chart are echoed by the dasha pattern, so you could be working on one issue for many years: for example a 19 year dasha of Saturn placed in the seventh house followed by a 17 year dasha of Mercury which rules the seventh house. It could also be that you have strong yogas, but the main dashas don't reflect the planets which form them. Maybe you have a strong chart but only experience the effects during sub- and sub-sub dashas. The dasha phases occur in the following order, and last for specific periods:

The Sun	6	years
The Moon	10	years
Mars	7	years
Rahu	18	years
Jupiter	16	years
Saturn	19	years
Mercury	17	years
Ketu	7	years
Venus	20	years

All of the information you are about to compile is available on computer software or by ordering it from the sources at the end of this book, but for those of you who would like to work it out for yourselves here it is:

The first dasha in the cycle is decided by the position of your natal Moon, and to work out your dasha pattern you need to find out the dasha period you were born into. We'll follow through an example, using the Moon at 8° 5' Leo. Looking at the **Vimshottari**

212

Dasha by Longitude of the Moon Table, we see that the column on the far left lists the longitude of the Moon for Aries, Leo and Sagittarius and starts with the Ketu dasha: the closest degree to our example is 8° - showing as 2 years 9 months and 18 days remaining of the Ketu dasha. However, we still have 5' to account for, so looking at the smaller grid (**Proportional Parts**) we see that 5' in the Ketu column is equal to 16 days. This amount must be **deducted** from the time remaining: this leaves 2 years, 9 months and 2 days of Ketu dasha left at the time of birth. (Note that if the closest value to your Moon degree on the Vimshottari chart was **larger** - rather than smaller as in our example - you would **add** the amount shown in the proportional amounts table.)

Now you can work out your entire cycle and the dates that the new dasha periods will begin, as they always follow the same pattern. As the list on the previous page shows, the Ketu dasha is followed by Venus, so the person in our example will move into their Venus dasha at 2 years, 9 months and 2 days of age; a period that will last for twenty years and be followed by a six year Sun dasha. Use this table to work out your own pattern, starting with your birth dasha against the first row and continuing down through the dasha cycle until you have dates or ages for every period.

	Dasha	From (date)	To	Placed in which sign	Rules which houses
1					
2					
3					
4					
5					
6					
7					
8					
9					

The first, third, fifth and seventh dashas are supposedly the more difficult times. Indian astrologers would also use this pattern to look at longevity. Childhood death is reflected by the first dasha; the length of a short life-span is indicated in the third dasha; a medium

Vimshottari Dasha by Longitude of the Moon

Long. of Moon °	'	Moon in Aries, Leo, Sagittarius		y	m	d	Moon in Taurus, Virgo, Capricorn		y	m	d	Moon in Gemini, Libra, Aquarius		y	m	d	Moon in Cancer, Scorpio, Pisces		y	m	d
0	0	Ketu		7	0	0	Sun		4	6	0	Mars		3	6	0	Jupiter		4	0	0
0	20			6	9	27			4	4	6			3	3	27			3	7	6
0	40			6	7	24			4	2	12			3	1	24			3	2	12
1	0			6	5	21			4	0	18			2	11	21			2	9	18
1	20			6	3	18			3	10	24			2	9	18			2	4	24
1	40			6	1	15			3	9	0			2	7	15			2	0	0
2	0			5	11	12			3	7	6			2	5	12			1	7	6
2	20			5	9	9			3	5	12			2	3	9			1	2	12
2	40			5	7	6			3	3	18			2	1	6			0	9	18
3	0			5	5	3			3	1	24			1	11	3			0	4	24
3	20			5	3	0			3	0	0			1	9	0	Saturn		19	0	0
3	40			5	0	27			2	10	6			1	6	27			18	6	9
4	0			4	10	24			2	8	12			1	4	24			18	0	18
4	20			4	8	21			2	6	18			1	2	21			17	6	27
4	40			4	6	18			2	4	24			1	0	18			17	1	6
5	0			4	4	15			2	3	0			0	10	15			16	7	15
5	20			4	2	12			2	1	6			0	8	12			16	1	24
5	40			4	0	9			1	11	12			0	6	9			15	8	3
6	0			3	10	6			1	9	18			0	4	6			15	2	12
6	20			3	8	3			1	7	24			0	2	3			14	8	21
6	40			3	6	0			1	6	0	Rahu		18	0	0			14	3	0
7	0			3	3	27			1	4	6			17	6	18			13	9	9
7	20			3	1	24			1	2	12			17	1	6			13	3	18
7	40			2	11	21			1	0	18			16	7	24			12	9	27
8	0			2	9	18			0	10	24			16	2	12			12	4	6
8	20			2	7	15			0	9	0			15	9	0			11	10	15
8	40			2	5	12			0	7	6			15	3	18			11	4	24
9	0			2	3	9			0	5	12			14	10	6			10	11	3
9	20			2	1	6			0	3	18			14	4	24			10	5	12
9	40			1	11	3			0	1	24			13	11	12			9	11	21
10	0			1	9	0	Moon		10	0	0			13	6	0			9	6	0
10	20			1	6	27			9	9	0			13	0	18			9	0	9
10	40			1	4	24			9	6	0			12	7	6			8	6	18
11	0			1	2	21			9	3	0			12	1	24			8	0	27
11	20			1	0	18			9	0	0			11	8	12			7	7	6
11	40			0	10	15			8	9	0			11	3	0			7	1	15
12	0			0	8	12			8	6	0			10	9	18			6	7	24
12	20			0	6	9			8	3	0			10	4	6			6	2	3
12	40			0	4	6			8	0	0			9	10	24			5	8	12
13	0			0	2	3			7	9	0			9	5	12			5	2	21
13	20	Venus		20	0	0			7	6	0			9	0	0			4	9	0
13	40			19	6	0			7	3	0			8	6	18			4	3	9
14	0			19	0	0			7	0	0			8	1	6			3	9	18
14	20			18	6	0			6	9	0			7	7	24			3	3	27
14	40			18	0	0			6	6	0			7	2	12			2	10	6
15	0			17	6	0			6	3	0			6	9	0			2	4	15
15	20			17	0	0			6	0	0			6	3	18			1	10	24
15	40			16	6	0			5	9	0			5	10	6			1	5	3
16	0			16	0	0			5	6	0			5	4	24			0	11	12
16	20			15	6	0			5	3	0			4	11	12			0	5	21
16	40			15	0	0			5	0	0			4	6	0	Mercury		17	0	0
17	0			14	6	0			4	9	0			4	0	18			16	6	27
17	20			14	0	0			4	6	0			3	7	6			16	1	24
17	40			13	6	0			4	3	0			3	1	24			15	8	21
18	0			13	0	0			4	0	0			2	8	12			15	3	18
18	20			12	6	0			3	9	0			2	3	0			14	10	15
18	40			12	0	0			3	6	0			1	9	18			14	5	12
19	0			11	6	0			3	3	0			1	4	6			14	0	9

Vimshottari Dasha by Longitude of the Moon

Long. of Moon		Moon in Aries, Leo, Sagittarius			Moon in Taurus, Virgo, Capricorn			Moon in Gemini, Libra, Aquarius			Moon in Cancer, Scorpio, Pisces		
°	'		y	m	d		y	m	d		y	m	d		y	m	d

°	'		y	m	d		y	m	d		y	m	d		y	m	d
19	0	Venus	11	6	0	Moon	3	3	0	Rahu	1	4	6	Merc.	14	0	9
19	20		11	0	0		3	0	0		0	10	24		13	7	6
19	40		10	6	0		2	9	0		0	5	12		13	2	3
20	0		10	0	0		2	6	0	Jupiter	16	0	0		12	9	0
20	20		9	6	0		2	3	0		15	7	6		12	3	27
20	40		9	0	0		2	0	0		15	2	12		11	10	24
21	0		8	6	0		1	9	0		14	9	18		11	5	21
21	20		8	0	0		1	6	0		14	4	24		11	0	18
21	40		7	6	0		1	3	0		14	0	0		10	7	15
22	0		7	0	0		1	0	0		13	7	6		10	2	12
22	20		6	6	0		0	9	0		13	2	12		9	9	9
22	40		6	0	0		0	6	0		12	9	18		9	4	6
23	0		5	6	0		0	3	0		12	4	24		8	11	3
23	20		5	0	0	Mars	7	0	0		12	0	0		8	6	0
23	40		4	6	0		6	9	27		11	7	6		8	0	27
24	0		4	0	0		6	7	24		11	2	12		7	7	24
24	20		3	6	0		6	5	21		10	9	18		7	2	21
24	40		3	0	0		6	3	18		10	4	24		6	9	18
25	0		2	6	0		6	1	15		10	0	0		6	4	15
25	20		2	0	0		5	11	12		9	7	6		5	11	12
25	40		1	6	0		5	9	9		9	2	12		5	6	9
26	0		1	0	0		5	7	6		8	9	18		5	1	6
26	20		0	6	0		5	5	3		8	4	24		4	8	3
26	40	Sun	6	0	0		5	3	0		8	0	0		4	3	0
27	0		5	10	6		5	0	27		7	7	6		3	9	27
27	20		5	8	12		4	10	24		7	2	12		3	4	24
27	40		5	6	18		4	8	21		6	9	18		2	11	21
28	0		5	4	24		4	6	18		6	4	24		2	6	18
28	20		5	3	0		4	4	15		6	0	0		2	1	15
28	40		5	1	6		4	2	12		5	7	6		1	8	12
29	0		4	11	12		4	0	9		5	2	12		1	3	9
29	20		4	9	18		3	10	6		4	9	18		0	10	6
29	40		4	7	24		3	8	3		4	4	24		0	5	3
30	0		4	6	0		3	6	0		4	0	0		0	0	0

Proportional Parts

	Ketu 7 yr		Venus 20 yr		Sun 6 yr		Moon 10 yr		Mars 7 yr		Rahu 18 yr		Jupiter 16 yr		Saturn 19 yr		Merc. 17 yr		
	m	d	m	d	m	d	m	d	m	d	m	d	m	d	m	d	m	d	
1	0	3	0	9	0	3	0	5	0	3	0	8	0	7	0	9	0	8	1
2	0	6	0	18	0	5	0	9	0	6	0	16	0	14	0	17	0	15	2
3	0	9	0	27	0	8	0	14	0	9	0	24	0	22	0	26	0	23	3
4	0	13	1	6	0	11	0	18	0	13	1	2	0	29	1	4	1	1	4
5	0	16	1	15	0	14	0	23	0	16	1	11	1	6	1	13	1	8	5
6	0	19	1	24	0	16	0	27	0	19	1	19	1	13	1	21	1	16	6
7	0	22	2	3	0	19	1	2	0	22	1	27	1	20	2	0	1	24	7
8	0	25	2	12	0	22	1	6	0	25	2	5	1	28	2	8	2	1	8
9	0	28	2	21	0	24	1	11	0	28	2	13	2	5	2	17	2	9	9
10	1	1	3	0	0	27	1	15	1	1	2	21	2	12	2	26	2	17	10
15	1	17	4	15	1	11	2	8	1	17	4	2	3	18	4	8	3	25	15
20	2	3	6	0	1	24	3	0	2	3	5	12	4	24	5	21	5	3	20

Antar dasha table

Antardasa	Sun 6 yrs Sub Periods			Total			Moon 10 yrs Sub Periods			Total			Mars 7 yrs Sub Periods			Total		
	y	m	d	y	m	d	y	m	d	y	m	d	y	m	d	y	m	d
Sun	0	3	18	0	3	18							—			—		
Moon	0	6	0	0	9	18	0	10	0	0	10	0	—			—		
Mars	0	4	6	1	1	24	0	7	0	1	5	0	0	4	27	0	4	27
Rahu	0	10	24	2	0	18	1	6	0	2	11	0	1	0	18	1	5	15
Jupiter	0	9	18	2	10	6	1	4	0	4	3	0	0	11	6	2	4	21
Saturn	0	11	12	3	9	18	1	7	0	5	10	0	1	1	9	3	6	0
Mercury	0	10	6	4	7	24	1	5	0	7	3	0	0	11	27	4	5	27
Ketu	0	4	6	5	0	0	1	5	0	7	10	0	0	4	27	4	10	24
Venus	1	0	0	6	0	0	0	7	0	9	6	0	1	2	0	6	0	24
Sun	—			—			1	8	0	10	0	0	0	4	6	6	5	0
Moon	—			—			0	6	0	10	0	0	0	7	0	7	0	0

Antardasa	Rahu 18 yrs Sub Periods			Total			Jupiter 16 yrs Sub Periods			Total			Satum 19 yrs Sub Periods			Total		
	y	m	d	y	m	d	y	m	d	y	m	d	y	m	d	y	m	d
Rahu	2	8	12	2	8	12	—			—			—			—		
Juptier	2	4	24	5	1	6	2	1	18	2	1	18	—			—		
Satum	2	10	6	7	11	12	2	6	12	4	8	0	3	0	3	3	0	3
Mercury	2	6	18	10	6	0	2	3	6	6	11	6	2	8	9	5	8	12
Ketu	1	0	18	11	6	18	0	11	6	7	10	12	1	1	9	6	9	21
Venus	3	0	0	14	6	18	2	8	0	10	6	12	3	2	0	9	11	21
Sun	0	10	24	15	5	12	0	9	18	11	4	0	0	11	12	10	11	3
Moon	1	6	0	16	11	12	1	4	0	12	8	0	1	7	0	12	6	3
Mars	1	0	18	18	0	0	0	11	6	13	7	6	1	1	9	13	7	12
Rahu	—			—			2	4	24	16	0	0	2	10	6	16	5	18
Jupiter	—			—			—			—			2	6	12	19	0	0

Antardasa	Mercury 17 yrs Sub Periods			Total			Ketu 7 yrs Sub Periods			Total			Venus 20 yrs Sub Periods			Total		
	y	m	d	y	m	d	y	m	d	y	m	d	y	m	d	y	m	d
Mercury	2	4	27	2	4	27	—			—			—			—		
Ketu	0	11	27	3	4	24	0	4	27	0	4	27	—			—		
Venus	2	10	0	6	2	24	1	2	0	1	6	27	3	4	0	3	4	0
Sun	0	10	6	7	1	0	0	4	6	1	11	3	1	0	0	4	4	0
Moon	1	5	0	8	6	0	0	7	0	2	6	3	1	8	0	6	0	0
Mars	0	11	27	9	5	27	0	4	27	2	11	0	1	2	0	7	2	0
Rahu	2	6	18	12	0	15	1	0	18	3	11	18	3	0	0	10	2	0
Jupiter	2	3	6	14	3	21	0	11	6	4	10	24	2	8	0	12	10	0
Satum	2	8	9	17	0	0	1	1	9	6	0	3	3	2	0	16	0	0
Mereury	—			—			0	11	27	7	0	0	2	10	0	18	10	0
Ketu	—			—			—			—			1	2	0	20	0	0

one in the fifth and a long one in the seventh. However, this is only a broad outline and many other factors are taken into consideration.

The First Dasha
The first dasha of your life indicates what you will experience later on and it is the most important dasha to study. It shows the connection between this incarnation and your previous lives. You will need to study the house position of the first dasha ruler; a planet ruling the dusthana houses (6, 8 or 12) shows that you may face difficulties on the more mundane level which will focus your energies in a different spiritual direction. Next check the navamsha position of your dasha ruler; this will indicate the inner quality of the dasha and which issues are likely to dominate. What is the strength of the planet in the navamsha chart?

Finally and most importantly: look at the nakshatra for the position of the dasha ruler. Studying the deeper subtleties of the nakshatra will help you to understand your soul's purpose in this incarnation. Here again you need to see the relationship between your first dasha ruler and its nakshatra dispositor.

Antar Dashas or Bhuktis
We've now considered the **maha dashas,** the major dasha phases in some detail. To further clarify the picture in terms of **when** events are likely to occur we also need to study the **antar dasha** or **bhuktis:** each maha dasha has nine subdivisions called antar dasha. There are further divisions from this point but we won't be covering them in this book.

The first antardasha is ruled by the planet whose maha dasha it is: in a Jupiter maha dasha, the first antar dasha will be ruled by Jupiter, the next by Saturn, the third by Mercury and so on as in the list we've already seen. Using the previous example we'll work out the sub-dasha at the time of birth - this person was born with 2 years 9 months and 2 days remaining of a Ketu dasha. Looking at the antar dasha table in the Ketu section, we see that the Ketu cycle is seven years, so deduct one from the other, leaving 4 years, 2 months and 28 days. This value is greater than the end of the Rahu period shown in the table (3 - 11 - 18) but less than the end of the Jupiter (4 - 10 - 24) so the sub-dasha will be Jupiter; the next period will be Ketu-Saturn then Ketu-Mercury to the end of the dasha, which then changes to Venus maha dasha. During the whole period of a Ketu maha dasha, Ketu itself will be the major influence, but the planets involved in the different antar- dasha sub-phases will add their influence as well, helpful or not.

It's important to analyse the relationship between the rulers of the dasha and antardasha at the time of birth: are they friends, enemies or neutral with each other ? If the two were enemies it would show an inner conflict that would affect you throughout your life. On the other hand, friends would give you a good start and to some extent smooth the way ahead.

Key points in Judging the Dashas

Unlike in the times of the Vedas, nowadays very few people live through all nine dashas! Most of us have to be content with six or perhaps seven in a lifetime. The planet that rules your current maha dasha is a major influence on your life throughout this phase. If you are working with clients, the current maha dasha is a good place to begin an assessment of their present situation.

Keep these important points in mind when considering your current maha dasha ruler:

• **What is the graha's nature and purpose - and is it benefic or malefic in your natal chart?**
Each graha has its own purpose, and during its maha dasha that purpose will be an important motivation in your life. During your Saturn maha dasha you will experience the restrictions inherent in your karma. Saturn's maha dasha is also known as the one where you work hard! But Venus' purpose is to enjoy. Jupiter's is 'the getting of wisdom' - things come easier during its maha dasha and you may not have to work as hard as usual to get the same results. During the Sun's maha dasha your soul begins a new phase; issues of authority may arise. Mercury is very changeable; its maha dasha may see you tackling life's practicalities (it might be a good time for people in business) or learning new skills.
The current maha dasha will affect your life differently according to whether its ruler's influence tends to the benefic or to the malefic

in your natal chart. For example, in principle Saturn and Mercury are friends; but what relationship if any do they have in your natal chart? It is this specific relationship you will experience during your Saturn Mercury dasha.

- ### Which houses does it rule?

The grahas will rule different natal houses according to your rising sign, so Saturn dasha and Mercury antar dasha will mean different things to different people. For example: if your lagna was in Taurus, Saturn will rule your auspicious ninth and tenth houses while Mercury will rule the second house (wealth) and the fifth (creativity). Saturn-Mercury, therefore, will bring excellent results. However, if your lagna is in Cancer, Saturn will rule your seventh and eighth houses and Mercury the third and twelfth, so Saturn-Mercury will be a period of difficulty.

Look at the house position of the ruler of your current maha dasha. In general is its house placement weak or strong and is it in its own house? Which graha rules the house and is it friend or foe? These considerations can influence whether the dasha will be straightforward or traumatic for you.

- ### What is the ruler's position in your natal chart?

During a Saturn Mercury phase, the natal sign and natal house Saturn and Mercury are placed in will become important. If both planets are exalted in your natal chart (Saturn in Libra, Mercury in Virgo) you will experience Saturn-Mercury very differently from the way you would if they were debilitated (Saturn in Aries, Mercury in Pisces). Similarly, if Saturn and Mercury are well-placed by house (Saturn in the third, sixth, tenth or eleventh houses, Mercury in the first, fifth, ninth and tenth houses) you will experience Saturn-Mercury more easily than if they are poorly placed (Mercury in the eighth house, Saturn in the fourth). If Saturn is in the fourth house in your natal chart, happiness, your home, your private self will be the primary concerns, but with Mercury in your eighth house these areas will be a difficult feature of your Saturn-Mercury dasha phase.

- ## Relative placements from each other and the signs they rule

Grahas placed in the sixth, eighth or twelfth houses from the signs they rule will be difficult during their maha dasha phase. Taking our Saturn-Mercury example again: if Saturn was in Leo it would be in the eighth house from its own sign of Capricorn, and so would create problems in whichever house was ruled by Capricorn in your natal chart.

If Mercury in Libra was in the fifth house from its own sign of Gemini, it would enhance the prospects of the house ruled by Gemini in the natal chart. Virgo would be in the twelfth house from it however, so some difficult issues might arise there. Also if Saturn was in Scorpio and Mercury in Aries, Mercury would be in the sixth house from Saturn; this is a difficult position for them. But if instead Saturn was in Taurus and Mercury in Virgo, Mercury would be in the fifth house from Saturn and would produce a great antar dasha; they would be in trikona from each other.

- ## What relationships does it have with other planets in your natal chart?

The ruler of your current maha dasha will interact with all the grahas in your natal chart, so if it has a difficult relationship with any particular graha, when that planet's antar dasha comes along you are likely to experience a period of difficulty. Here's a reminder of the 'friends and enemies' list.

Saturn is friends and works well with	Venus, Mercury and Rahu
Saturn is the enemy of and works badly with	Jupiter, Sun, Moon and Mars

The Saturn-Mercury of our example in this section should be an easier phase than, say Saturn-Jupiter or Saturn-Sun.

The kind of problems that will arise when your maha dasha and antar dasha rulers are not friendly will be indicated by the natal house or houses ruled by the ruler of the antar dasha.

The Nakshatras of the Dasha Rulers

Understanding the nakshatras of your dasha rulers is the key to the subtle analysis of your dashas. The relationship between the dasha ruler and the nakshatra dispositor (friends, enemies or neutral) will show whether you are happy or in conflict with the energies indicated by the nakshatra; also, each one has its own energy, direction, deities and rulers, which give further clues as to how it will manifest in your life.

Some of the nakshatras are ruled by Rahu (Ardra, Swati and Shatabhishak) and Ketu (Ashwini, Magha and Mula). During the dashas of planets placed in the Ketu nakshatras the karmic aspects are further highlighted (see chapter on the Karmic Axis); there is often an accentuated feeling of striving for spiritual salvation and on a practical level, the desire to give up everything and move on. During dashas of the planets placed in the Rahu nakshatras you are likely to become ambitious, dissatisfied and feel the need to explore beyond established boundaries. This will again be on the mental plane and therefore difficult to pinpoint. Studying the nakshatras involved and the relationships between Rahu and Ketu and the planets will help you to get the most out of these particular dashas.

Interpreting the dashas

The Sun Dasha

The Sun dasha is connected to your self, personal ambitions, father, authority and your soul. Look at where your sun is placed and which house it rules. The house it is placed in will indicate the focus of your life; obviously there will be a different emphasis if the Sun is placed in the tenth house of career rather than in the seventh house of relationships.

If the Sun is exalted (Aries), you can expect to have a wonderful dasha. But beware here, an exalted Sun sometimes rest on its laurels, ready to bask in glory and not willing to get work done. You may find that you are not making any effort on your own behalf. A debilitated Sun dasha (Libra) can be a time where you are looking for inner light. It may highlight lack of confidence and vitality. You will have to work with it. If the Sun is placed in an enemy's house, you may find your hopes and dreams in conflict with your vocation. In a friend's house, the Sun would be comfortable and dasha is likely to be positive.

On a subtle level, we look at the nakshatra of the Sun, which gives a further indication of the effects of the Sun dasha. Always check the relationship of the Sun with the ruler of its nakshatra.

Moon Dasha

All the familiar lunar issues will be highlighted for you during the Moon dasha. You should try to keep in touch with the phases of the Moon, because as it waxes and wanes, you may find yourself picking up these traits - being changeable, fickle and unable to make up your mind. Also as the Moon is a passive planet needing the Sun's light, it will be a time when you need other people's energy to get you motivated. The Moon is fast moving and it signifies activity, so during a Moon dasha it important for you to keep moving. The Moon's passage through the different nakshatras will also be pertinent; now would be a good time to make use of the tarabala table in the Gochara chapter.

If the Moon in your chart is exalted, you can expect a wonderful time during its dasha. Check its strength - a full, waxing Moon which is exalted will have different impact in its dasha than a new or waning exalted Moon. A debilitated Moon dasha can create intense emotion, in which case you need to try and stay positive. As an example, a Scorpio Moon would want to use this time to explore the deeper aspects of life and here again you would check the phase and strength of the Moon.

The Moon in an enemy's house usually will create unsettled conditions, unless you learn to deal with them, while in a friend's house can be very sensual and pleasure-seeking which will be reflected in its dasha.

Mars Dasha

Mars is the planet of action so its dasha will coincide with a lot of coming and going. Courage, impulsiveness, passion, action-orientated activities will surface. You will need to be careful you do not become over-dominating and aggressive; keep yourself occupied. The greatest problem that Mars can face is inactivity. With a Mars dasha the temptation is to take on too much; temper could also be a problem. The end of a Mars dasha is usually difficult as it is moving towards the Rahu dasha. One should always treat this period with caution and patience.

If Mars is exalted, it will reinforce your ambitions and the ability to be a leader. This will focus your energy in a specific direction. A strong Mars can be too aggressive and will attempt to control others. Mars in debilitation will diffuse your energy, but this is not necessarily negative; just make sure you don't race around wasting energy. Mars in an enemy house could be uncomfortable time because of anger or frustration. Mars in its own house will be positive. In Aries the spirit of adventure tinged with idealism will be strong. In Scorpio, it will seek its higher spiritual life direction.

The relationship between Mars and its nakshatra ruler is of vital importance. The nakshatra itself will guide your spiritual direction but the relationship between the two will show whether you are comfortable with it or not. For example, if Mars is placed in any of the nakshatras ruled by Saturn (Pushya, Anuradha and Uttarabhadra pada), then during its dasha you will feel a conflict at the deepest level concerning the events of the period.

Mercury Dasha

Mercury is the planet of intellect and reasoning. It is essentially a planet which seeks reasons for the life we are experiencing now. It is a time for reasoned debate and expansion intellectually. Mercury is very changeable and therefore will naturally reflect its temperament in the form of you changing your mind frequently! A Mercury dasha leads to greater freedom of expression, especially coming after 19 years of the restrictive Saturn dasha.

If Mercury is exalted, it will make for a strong intellect which is very rational and focused. Mercury in debilitation will cause you to react emotionally, leading to mood swings and the knowledge that you are not thinking things through logically. A debilitated Mercury in its dasha can also indicate a tendency to depression and lack of mental stability.

Mercury in an enemy's house you can expect some internal conflict. Mercury in its own house will be positive. In Gemini, sometimes you find yourself doing two jobs, following two vocations in life and feeling very comfortable with it.

As before, study the nakshatra Mercury occupies and the relationship with its ruler to understand the deeper meaning of the dasha.

Jupiter Dasha

Jupiter rules all good things in life and during it dasha you will find expansion and happiness. If Jupiter is not a good planet for you, there may be the temptation to take unnecessary risks, which can create problems. The feel-good factor during a Jupiter dasha is strong and sometimes you take the easy way out; consequently you may find you haven't achieved much by the end of it.

Jupiter is the karaka of sons, your husband, wealth, gurus and teaching, so all these aspects will be highlighted. A Jupiter dasha/antar dasha will usually be the time you have children, get married or meet the love of your life (for women only).

If Jupiter is exalted, you are sure to be granted your desires - this period will be full of promise. Marriage, children, happiness can all be predicted. Jupiter in debilitation shows a strong inclination towards financial gains and practical rather than spiritual life direction. Here you may well meet a partner who is not so spiritually connected. Jupiter in an enemy's house will not be completely happy, so the dasha may not bring the bountiful results you expect. In this case it can lead you in the wrong direction or make errors of judgment. Jupiter in its own sign will give very good results. In Sagittarius, the focus will be towards teaching, growing from within, becoming recognised as an authority. In Pisces, there is a more profound aspect to Jupiter. Here the desire will be to merge with the eternal; in practical terms that means having an idealistic way of looking at life.

Venus Dasha

Venus rules the fine things in life like beauty, music, dance, pleasures, jewellery and finances and during its dasha you are likely to be attracted by any of them. Marriage is quite possible in this dasha. It strengthens existing relationships and shows just how much we want quality in our lives; Venus desires the best and it is here that we seek it. Try to remember throughout this dasha that, as in the mythological story, Venus can satisfy our material needs but it does not promise happiness.

If Venus is exalted, expect a wonderful Venus dasha. All your material desires will be granted. It is a time for success. Venus in debilitation shows a difficult period in your relationships. For men, this could be a trying time with your wife, or you may find yourself being over critical with others. Venus in an enemy's house will not be totally happy, so during its dasha you may get into a relationship which creates conflict either within yourself or with others. Financially, you may be making money from something you are not totally happy with. Venus in its own sign will give very good results. In Taurus, the focus will be towards more practical desires. Hard work, practical financial considerations and indulging your passions will be very strong. Passions can be for money, relationships, women, food and anything you relate to good times. This will be a good dasha where achievement from own efforts is also indicated.

Saturn Dasha

Saturn is regarded as the most difficult dasha. Here it is important to remember that it can be your greatest friend if you understand its dictates. With a bit of discipline a Saturn dasha can be very positive; it can give rewards which are long-lasting and permanent but only to those who work for them. A Saturn dasha during childhood can be tough as its lessons are difficult to deal with at a young age. If Saturn is in exaltation, it will give you excellent results. You will be naturally hard-working and responsible, but if it is debilitated, it will be a battle to achieve anything. The dasha can be one where you will find yourself acting contrary to the Saturnine restrictions and this can create problems.

Saturn in an enemy sign will make it hard for you to understand its power. It can lead to a difficult dasha which will need wisdom and patience to deal with. Saturn here can also create problems with health. In its own house it gives a strong sense of duty. In Capricorn, the approach will be pragmatic whereas in Aquarius you will be trying to sublimate your own needs and work for others.

Rahu Dasha

The effects of a Rahu dasha largely depend on its dispositor and the house placement. Rahu is always about experiencing life. During this dasha you must consciously try to control your ambitions; Rahu recognises no boundaries so it can create unrealistic expectations which are be frustrating if you can't achieve them. Rahu is the mouth of the snake so its venom is felt at the beginning of the dasha. I find the beginning and end of a Rahu dasha have to be handled with care when karmic influences dominate; how it will play out later in your life becomes difficult to judge.

During a Rahu dasha you also have a sub-dasha of Ketu. Here the karmic axis of your life becomes activated you can progress spiritually; its revelations can lead to the discovery of your spiritual self, thus changing the whole course of your life. It can also help you to recognise karmic limitations or become aware of your destiny.

Ketu Dasha

Ketu differs from Rahu here as you feel like giving up things rather than experiencing them. You may feel like changing jobs, giving up your old lifestyle or even moving into a retreat. Most people experience very powerful life issues over which they have no control. A Ketu dasha will lead to a spiritualising process, the soul is ready for it; there can also be immense success. It's important to realise though, that the end of the dasha usually takes away whatever has been given at the beginning; as always, check which houses are involved in the Rahu Ketu axis as they will indicate the areas of your life that will be affected by this dasha. Most people will experience this axis only once in their lives and find it can bring with it intense experiences.

Gochara - Transits

A natal chart indicates the actual position of the planets and the notional position of the axis Rahu/Ketu, at the moment of someone's birth. Since that moment they have continued to move around the zodiac. They still interact with natal charts at times; a period of interaction is called a gochara or transit. Transits may only last a relatively short time but they can be powerful and they are always considered in conjunction with the dashas: any transit by the ruler of your current maha dasha will be important. Most transits are looked at from the position of the Moon as the indicator of the mind; I also look at transits from the ascendant. If both are showing a similar transit and are backed up by the trend of the dasha, I know the influence will be undeniable. There are brief transits from the fast moving planets, like the Sun, Mercury, Mars and Venus, which can highlight short term issues - like meeting a romantic partner when Venus transits the seventh house (as it does once a year). This transit won't have a permanent effect as Venus will only stay there for about 25 days before it moves on. It can indicate a pleasant interlude rather than far-reaching events.

The planetary orbits through each sign of the zodiac is shown as follows:

	One zodiac sign (30°)	Whole zodiac (360°)
Sun	one calendar month	one calendar year
Moon	2½ days	27 days
	(it travels through one nakshatra each day)	
Mars	2 months	2 years
Mercury	25 days	11 months
Jupiter	one year	12 years
Venus	25 days	10 months
Saturn	2½ years	29 years 10 months
Rahu and Ketu	1½ years	18-19 years

How a New Transit will Affect you

Making a chart for the moment at which a planet enters a new sign will help you prepare for the transit ahead, by indicating where and how the transiting planet will make its impact on your natal chart. Use the natal chart with natal Moon on the ascendant. The position of the Moon on the chart for the entry into the new sign will show the transit's focus.

A transit by any planet continues from the moment that it enters a particular zodiac sign to the moment it leaves it. Transits of the Sun, Mars, Venus and Mercury through a sign are relatively fast. Jyotish considers the major transits to be those of Saturn and Jupiter, because they are much longer. By and large, transiting Saturn brings struggle and negativity and shows you where there is a problem in your life; Jupiter brings good luck and shows how the problem will be sorted out. The Moon's transits are vital in planning your daily life.

Transits of the Moon

We should continually be aware of the waxing and waning cycles of the Moon, and its position in different nakshatras, as they affect us in so many ways. In India no one begins a new project during a waning phase. Here again, the nakshatras are important: if you want to plan your life to go with the ebb and flow of the Moon's cycle (as we still do in India), you will need an ephemeris showing which nakshatra the Moon is in from day to day.

A quick way to check is to count from the nakshatra of your natal Moon to the nakshatra of the day and divide the number by nine (if divisible). The remaining number indicates the type of day you are going to face:

1. **Janma** - birth nakshatra.
   Physical danger - not a good day to begin journeys or start any activity that might be considered risky, but normal travel or day-to-day activities can be carried on as usual.
2. **Sampat** - wealth and prosperity.
   You will achieve what you are planning to do - this is a positive day.
3. **Vipat** - danger, losses and accidents.
4. **Kshema** - prosperity.
5. **Pratyak** - obstacles.
6. **Sadhana** - a day for realising ambitions.
7. **Naidhana** - dangers and difficulties.
8. **Mitra** - a good day.
9. **Param mitra** - a very good day.

Waxing and the Waning Phases of the Moon

The Moon's transits are seen by Vedic astrologers as a catalyst for events involving slower-moving planets. The waxing Moon cycle is also used in mahurata (electional astrology) to establish exact auspicious timing for events involving the starting up of anything. Similarly, the waning cycle is suitable for closing down and for processes of assimilation, but never for new projects. It doesn't matter whether the task you want to accomplish is great or small; plan your month ahead looking at the phases of the Moon and organise events for the days when the energy involved is at its best. It will give you a very good idea of how your days are going to turn out. For important events in your life, it is advisable to have the time properly elected by a professional Vedic astrologer.

Tarabala Grid - The Nakshatras by the Day

	1st Pariyaya	2nd Pariyaya	3rd Pariyaya
1. Janma			
2. Sampat			
3. Vipat			
4. Kshema			
5. Prayatak			
6. Sadhana			
7. Naidhana			
8. Mitra			
9. Param Mitra			

Write the name of your natal Moon nakshatra next to Janma, at the top of the first column; then continue adding the nakshatras in order, starting at the top of the following row when you have filled the first column, and so on until the chart is complete. The nakshatras falling into rows 1, 3, 5 and 7 do not vibrate well with your natal nakshatra; it's useful to note when the Moon transits these and plan accordingly. In general terms, if the transiting Moon is not in a favourable nakshatra it is probably a good idea to have a quiet day! Keeping a diary is a really effective way of understanding how much you are in tune with the lunar energy - see what the effect is when you 'go against' the trend for the day.

You can also use this table to check which of your natal planets fall into difficult nakshatras. These are the ones that are likely to give troublesome dashas.

Transits of Saturn

This is the planet of difficulties, obstruction and unwilling change. It is slow-moving and its purpose is to make us understand the limitations imposed upon us in life. It destroys our illusions and makes us face up to reality. By understanding the difficulties of a Saturn transit, you will be able plan accordingly. This transit does not have to be negative if you understand the role of Saturn and its potential. At the end of a Saturn transit, we are older and (hopefully) wiser. It teaches us patience and endurance. Remember: you cannot escape Saturn's restrictions. You have to learn to live with them and the best way to cope is through study, knowledge (Jupiter) and patience (Saturn).

Here are some very general guidelines on what to expect from the major transits of Saturn to your natal chart. Of course, each of us will experience them differently, according to the particular strengths and vulnerable points of our charts, and Saturn's influence in them.

Saturn's Transits of Your Natal Moon

• **Sade Sati**

Sade sati is the most important of Saturn's transits and I really can't emphasise this enough. It takes seven and a half years and is based on the natal chart with Moon ascending, beginning when Saturn enters the twelfth house and ending when it leaves the second house. Its most intense phase is the period when Saturn is 2-3° either side of the natal Moon. If Saturn is in Aries all those with natal Moon in Pisces, Aries and Taurus are affected. Those with Moons in Pisces will be in the last phase of it; when Saturn moves into Taurus, their sade sati will be over and that of people with natal Moon in Gemini will begin. The beginning of the transit will give an indication of the issues that will have to be faced. Sade sati results in a complete personal transformation, with changed priorities and usually a change in career or life direction. It is likely that you will have sade sati three times in your life, about every 24 years.

This is the most important transit you will look for when you study your birth chart. Periods of sade sati are crucial points in life when changes take place that require patience and wisdom to deal with; I know this sounds daunting but you must not worry unduly about this period. It is a time that can bring about immense growth if the energies are used properly. It will only be stressful if we try to avoid the issues that come up.

When Saturn moves into the twelfth house from the Moon it indicates the beginning of the end of a phase of life. To determine which phase this is you need to consider the house position of the Moon, and the dasha you are experiencing.

If the Moon is placed in the tenth house from the ascendant, the sade sati will affect the ninth house (father or higher education), tenth house (career), and eleventh house (gains and earnings) as counted from the ascendant.

Counting the transit from the Moon it would affect the twelfth house (loss and endings), first house (self) and second house (personal wealth). The second is also a maraka house so a Saturn transit through here leads to some unexpected ending in your life.

To cope with sade sati you have to see the bigger picture. As it is a long transit it is unlikely that every day will be difficult. Imagine it to be like a long winter - you need to be prepared! With a sade sati, recognising the difficult times of life actually makes them easier to deal with.

The dasha at the time of the sade sati is important. If you are experiencing a dasha of a sixth, eighth or twelfth house ruler then the general trend of your life is also suggesting change, trans-formation and difficulties (similar things to sade sati) so its effect could be extremely intense. If however, your dashas are of the auspicious fifth or ninth house rulers they will balance the restrictions of sade sati.

- **Kantaka Shani**

This happens when Saturn transits the house four ahead of where the natal Moon is placed: for example while Saturn is in Aries, it will be experienced by people with their natal Moon in Capricorn and will last for about two and a half years. When Saturn moves into Taurus, it will be the turn of those whose natal Moon is in Aquarius to have kantaka shani. Highlighting fourth house issues, this is usually a difficult period for home affairs, children and relationships. People often get divorced or move house at this time but be warned - you can't dodge Saturn's influence by changing partners or homes in advance!

- ## Ashtama Shani

Again of two and a half years' duration, this transit of Saturn affects the eighth house from the natal Moon: while Saturn is in Aries, people with natal Moon in Virgo will be having ashtama shani; when it goes into Taurus it will be the turn of natal Moons in Libra. Eighth house issues are very intense and difficult ones anyway and this transit can lead to the traumatic break-up of close relationships. It is usually a time to renegotiate partnerships but not a good time to enter into new ones.

Transits of Saturn to the Natal Sun

In general, Saturn's transits of the Sun indicate the culmination of something connected with the Sun: your career, your father or with regard to authority (your own or other people's). Of course, the only way to go from the heights is downwards!

When Saturn transits the seventh house from your natal Sun it is in the sign opposite it. With Saturn currently in Aries, those with natal Sun in Libra are affected by this at present. This transit can be good for your career - but very bad for your marriage!

A transit of Saturn through the fourth house from your natal Sun indicates a new beginning in your life but also a period of emotional turmoil. When Saturn goes into Aries, those with natal Sun in Capricorn will have this transit, which can also manifest itself as a change of residence.

The best of the 'Saturn to natal Sun' transits is where Saturn is in the tenth house from the Sun. While Saturn is in Aries, those with natal Sun in Cancer will have this transit. Concerned with tenth house issues, this transit can bring power and success and is considered to be a good one.

Saturn Conjunct Natal Saturn

This major transit occurs every 29 years and 10 months, when transiting Saturn returns to the degree and minute of the sign it was in at the time of your birth. At this point there is an erasing of past karma and you have the chance of a fresh start in life: you can look towards the future in a new way. It is likely that you will experience two Saturn returns in your life, perhaps three; the first in particular is seen as a coming-of-age.

Saturn Opposite Natal Saturn

This is the halfway point of the return cycle outlined above. It is the climax of the hard, Saturnian work begun 14 years before, when it was in its natal place. It can be looked at as a personal exaltation for your Saturnian aims.

Saturn's Ingress into the Signs

This should help you to work out exactly when Saturn's influence will be felt:

Sign	Date		Aspects
Aries	18/04/1998	(Debilitated)	Gem, Li, Cap
Taurus	06/06/2000		Can, Sco, Aq
Gemini	23/07/2002		Leo, Sag, Pi
	07/04/2003		
Cancer	05/09/2004		Vi, Cap, Aries
	26/05/2005		
Leo	02/11/2006		Li, Aq, Tau
	16/07/2007		
Virgo	09/09/2009		Sco, Pi, Gem
Libra	15/11/2001	(Exalted)	Sag, Aries, Can
	04/08/2012	(Exalted)	
Scorpio	02/11/2014		Cap, Tau, Leo
Sagittarius	26/01/2017		Aq, Gem, Vi
	20/10/2017		
Capricorn	24/01/2020		Pi, Can, Li
Aquarius	29/04/2022		Aries, Leo, Sco
	17/01/2023		
Pisces	29/03/2025		Tau, Vi, Sag

When there are two dates shown for Saturn's ingress into a particular sign, it indicates that Saturn has moved into the sign, retrograded backwards into the previous sign, then moved forwards again.

Transits of Jupiter - enjoy the good karma!

These are much more pleasant than transits of Saturn! Whatever the state of your natal chart, Jupiter transits are good! Jupiter is the great benefic: expansive and giving. The only place it may not give so much the feel-good factor is in Capricorn. As it creates a balance for Saturnian energy, the combination of a difficult Saturn transit and Jupiter in a debilitated sign might be a little tough. In India, people avoid doing anything during Jupiter's debilitation that can be left for a more auspicious day. Its escape into Aquarius is celebrated at the **Kumbha Mela** festival which begins as soon as the Sun has moved into Aquarius to join Jupiter.

Jupiter usually stays in a sign for about one year (though the length of time does vary) so each year different areas of your life will be highlighted according to which house is being occupied. Transits of Jupiter highlight the sign opposite and the fifth, ninth and seventh houses from its current position. While Jupiter is moving through Pisces it will be aspecting Cancer, Virgo and Scorpio. Its contact with Venus or the ruler of the seventh house always indicates a romance, while a transit of Jupiter opposite the natal Moon or Lagna indicates a good time to get married or a happy phase in an existing one. One of my clients experiencing a seventh house transit of Jupiter found her husband had booked them onto a romantic cruise!

A Jupiter transit to:

The Sun	-	brings success, perhaps promotion in your career.
Moon	-	brings peace of mind.
Mercury	-	enhances your intellect and improves your finances.
Venus	-	is similar to a transit of the seventh house as it brings romance into your life and improves existing romantic relationships. It is an auspicious time to get married.

Mars   -   gives you initiative and the courage to make changes.

Saturn   -   eases its heavy influence and makes the lessons of Saturn easier to deal with.

Rahu   -   can move you towards a spiritual direction different from that which is socially acceptable. It can highlight dealings with foreigners and also foreign travel.

Ketu   -   also indicates a change of spiritual direction, stemming from a sudden dissatisfaction with your life's present path.

A Jupiter return to the position it was in on your natal chart is the ending of one cycle and the beginning of another. This is particularly so for those of us who have lagna or natal Moon in the signs Jupiter rules, Sagittarius and Pisces. This transit can be a very positive experience. If you draw up a chart for the exact time of the return it will give you clear indications of what the next 12-year Jupiter cycle will be about. The list of dates for Jupiter's ingress into the signs is shown on the next page.

The positive and negative energies of Jupiter and Saturn are meant to balance each other out in the overall scheme of things. A good Jupiter transit can mitigate the effects of a rough Saturn one.

Jupiter's Ingress into the Signs - The Next Twelve Years

Sign	Date	Aspects
Pisces	12/01/1999	Cancer, Virgo, Scorpio
Aries	27/05/1999	Leo, Libra, Sagittarius
Taurus	03/06/2000	Virgo, Scorpio, Capricorn
Gemini	17/06/2001	Libra, Sagittarius, Aquarius
Cancer	06/07/2002 Exalted	Scorpio, Capricorn, Pisces
Leo	31/07/2003	Sagittarius, Aquarius, Aries
Virgo	28/08/2004	Capricorn, Pisces, Taurus
Libra	29/09/2005	Gemini, Libra, Aquarius
Scorpio	28/10/2006	Pisces, Taurus, Cancer
Sagittarius	22/11/2007	Aries, Gemini, Leo
Capricorn	10/12/2008 Debilitated	Taurus, Cancer, Virgo
Aquarius	20/12/2009	Gemini, Leo, Libra.

Transits of the Rahu Ketu axis

The real importance of these is that they bring eclipses, seen as opportunities for rebirth and transformation. Unless an eclipse makes a major impact on your natal chart, the transits of Rahu Ketu are not as important as those of Saturn and Jupiter. For an eclipse to have a major effect on your life it must take place within 1-2° of your lagna, natal Sun or natal Moon or 1-2° of being opposite them; then it will indicate a major change of direction in your life.

Vargas - The Divisional Charts

The word **varga** means a part or division. Vargas are used in a specialised but essential area of Vedic astrology which assesses a variety of charts arrived at by dividing the usual 30° per zodiac sign by different numbers. There are sixteen varga charts in all, but most astrologers use combinations of just six or seven. The **rasi** chart (natal chart) is also a varga chart: the 30° divided by one. If your rasi chart represents your whole outer personality in all its complexity, each varga chart represents one particular area of your life (house) writ large: it takes a theme already present in the rashi chart and magnifies it for closer study. The varga charts are often studied in groups so that recurrent themes can be followed through. A list of these is shown at the end of the chapter.

As a student it is important to know about these charts as in time you will want to use them to fine-tune interpretations and deepen your understanding. The real strength of the planets is revealed in the way they are enhanced or reduced by their position in the varga charts. Most Vedic astrologers in India will look at the **shadvarga** (6 divisional charts) or **saptavarga** (7 divisional charts) combination, but as beginners the most important varga to consider is the **navamsha** chart - it is like the foundation of the rasi (natal) chart.

For varga charts to be correct, it is important to have the exact time of birth: some of the vargas subdivide the 30° whole sign so minutely that a slight error in the time of birth can completely throw out the calculations - like the **shastiamsha** chart which divides each sign into 60 parts. It will be different for births only seconds apart and is an important tool in differentiating between twins who are born close together. The positions of the ascendant, Rahu and Ketu, and the planets in the divisional charts are all calculated using their original positions in the rasi chart as a starting point, but the resulting varga charts don't show degrees - only signs. Different rules apply for each varga; the calculation can become involved but it is included here for information so you can see how the charts are produced. Tables are given at the end of the chapter where required; all you need to do is transfer this information onto a new chart. The varga charts are also a standard feature of most Vedic astrology software packages. Generally transits are only applicable to the rasi chart.

The Varga Charts in More Detail

- **The rasi chart - the 30° zodiac sign divided by one**

This is the usual natal chart that uses your birth time to calculate the ascendant: the one that contains your outer personality, past and future, and from which all the varga charts are derived - both as regards calculations and interpretation. If the rasi chart does not suggest a character trait or an event, any indications of such a thing in another divisional chart will have to be weighed and assessed very carefully. The other varga charts can modify the rasi chart but they never replace it. This is also the chart used to consider your physical health.

- **The hora chart - two divisions of 15° each**

This simple division represents the male and female energies. Jyotish has always seen that a combination of these exists in everyone and what this chart shows is exactly how the planets work within the combination. The lists on the next page show you how to divide the planets into male (Sun) and female (Moon) energies, which can then be drawn onto a chart in the signs of Leo and Cancer respectively.

To see which hora your planet or ascendant falls into check the following list:

Sun 0 - 15°	**Sun** 15 - 30°	**Moon** 0 - 15°	**Moon** 15 - 30°
Aries	Taurus	Taurus	Aries
Gemini	Cancer	Cancer	Gemini
Leo	Virgo	Virgo	Leo
Libra	Scorpio	Scorpio	Libra
Sagittarius	Capricorn	Capricorn	Sagittarius
Aquarius	Pisces	Pisces	Aquarius

The hora chart has two main uses which focus on the issues indicated in the second house of the rasi chart. It can provide further information on your overall personality - whether, in general, you will be an active or a passive person, and how easy it will be for you to accumulate wealth. People with a majority of planets placed in the Sun's hora are active, very willing to take the initiative. However, they will need to work to achieve results; any money they come by will have been earned. If your lagna is in the Sun's hora you will need to work doubly hard! People with a majority of planets placed in the Moon's hora will not have to work so hard to get results - they may acquire wealth actually created by someone else. However, people with a strong female hora will have rather a passive temperament, needing someone else's energy to motivate them. If the lagna is placed in the Moon's hora, this indicates wealth will come to you without much effort.

The hora chart also shows how the male and female energies manifest. A masculine planet in Cancer causes inner tension, whilst a female planet in Leo will be given a more masculine expression. However, the malefic planets (Sun, Mars and Saturn) will be easier to cope with if they are in the male hora.

• **The drekkana chart - three divisions of 10° each**
The drekkana chart is calculated in the same way as the hora chart, but with three groups of signs rather than two. In this varga signs in the same elements are linked: the first 10° subdivision of any sign is ruled by its own ruler, the second 10° by the ruler of the

sign five signs from it and the final 10° of the chart are ruled by the ruler of the sign nine signs away. So the lagna or any planets in the subdivision 0 -10° Leo will be ruled by Leo's ruler the Sun; anything in 10 - 20° Leo will be ruled by Sagittarius' ruler Jupiter; and anything in 20 - 30° Leo will be ruled by Aries' ruler Mars. The table for the drekkana varga is given at the end of the chapter.

The drekkana chart can be used to fine-tune the issues of the third house of your rasi chart: your siblings - a relationship which in Indian society is not to be set aside lightly; your friends, the alliances you might make, your courage, ability and motivation. The position of Mars is paramount - a debilitated Mars would suggest lowered vitality, low self-confidence, and a general lack of direction.

- **The chaturtamsha chart - four divisions of 7°30' each**

The four subdivisions of this chart are ruled by the first, fourth, seventh and tenth sign from the sign whose divisions are being calculated, linking signs in the same mode. So, if the sign being divided is Aries, the four divisions will be ruled respectively by the rulers of Aries, Cancer, Libra and Capricorn. If Gemini is being divided this way, the rulers of the subdivisions will be the rulers of Gemini, Virgo, Sagittarius and Pisces. A chaturtamsha chart fine-tunes the fourth house of the rasi chart and is used to study material comforts and pleasures, and your relationship with your mother. It also shows what efforts will be needed to achieve your various objectives. The chart can also focus on your inner emotions and happiness and your attitude towards comfort and your home. The chaturtamsha table is shown at the end of the chapter.

- **The trimshamsha chart - five divisions of about 6° each**

This varga is important in consultations as it focuses on the issues of the sixth house and the obstacles we will meet. The Sun, Moon, Rahu and Ketu are not taken into account in its interpretation. Rulership is as follows: in the odd numbered signs the first 5° are ruled by Mars (Aries), the next 5° by Saturn (Aquarius), the next 8° by Jupiter (Sagittarius), the next 7° by Mercury (Gemini) and the last 5° by Venus (Libra). In even signs this is reversed: the first 5° are ruled by Venus (Taurus), the next 7° by Mercury (Virgo), the following 8° by Jupiter (Pisces), the next 5° by Saturn (Capricorn) and the last 5° by Mars (Scorpio).

Interpretation focuses on Saturn as its position in the trimshamsha chart will indicate where you will face challenges. The ascendant in this chart indicates how you will deal with them.

• **The saptamsha chart - seven divisions of 4°17' each**

The subdivisions of a sign are ruled thus: if the sign being divided is an odd-numbered one - Aries, Gemini, Leo, Libra, Sagittarius or Aquarius - then rulership will begin with that sign. Thus 0 - 4°17' Libra is ruled by Venus, ruler of Libra.

If the sign being divided is an even-numbered one - Taurus, Cancer, Virgo, Scorpio, Capricorn or Pisces - the rulership sequence begins with the ruling planet of the opposite sign. So 0 - 4°17' of Scorpio will be ruled by Venus, ruler of Taurus, the next division will be ruled by Mercury, ruler of Gemini, the next by the Moon, ruler of Cancer and so on.

The saptamsha chart focuses on the issues of the rasi chart's fifth house. In Indian terms it is very much about children and grandchildren: how many you will have and how good your relationship with them will be. A broader and perhaps more westernised interpretation would cover other forms of creativity. A strongly placed lagna in the saptamsha chart indicates a very creative person and/ or children and a good relationship with them. Check the fifth house ruler - if it is in either the sixth, eighth or twelfth house there could problems relating to children. The position of the fifth house karaka planet, Jupiter, should also be noted.

• **The navamsha chart - nine divisions of 3°20' each**

This is the one varga chart that a Vedic astrologer would automatically use when preparing for a consultation with a client, and it is the foundation chart of the rasi chakras. Most astrologers in India will automatically know the navamsha positions from the degrees of the ascendant and planets - something a student should aspire to.
The navamsha chart is particularly helpful in relationship astrology. It highlights the issues of the auspicious ninth house: the positive karma you will be able to call on during this lifetime, the level of happiness you might expect, and what sort of future is indicated for you. The navamsha chart reflects how the resources of the inner

self copes with the ups and downs of everyday life and the spiritual challenges encountered by the outer self, and whether there will be a conflict between the two. It also shows those parts of your personality which you may be reaching towards in your life, but which may still be causing you some stress at present because progress is slow. We seem to grow into our navamsha charts as we get older. They are calculated in two steps:

- find which division of 3° 20' the planet (or ascendant) is in on the rasi chart and note its navamsha number

- find the cardinal sign in the same element; this is where you will count from.

The 30° are divided into 9 as follows:

00° 00' - 03° 20'	1st navamsha
03° 20' - 06° 40'	2nd
06° 40' - 10° 00'	3rd
10° 00' - 13° 20'	4th
13° 20' - 16° 40'	5th
16° 40' - 20° 00'	6th
20° 00' - 23° 20'	7th
23° 20' - 26° 40'	8th
26° 40' - 30° 00'	9th

Rulerships begin with the ruler of the cardinal sign in the same element:

sign being sub-divided	start counting at..
Aries, Leo, Sagittarius	Aries
Taurus, Virgo, Capricorn	Capricorn
Gemini, Libra, Aquarius	Libra
Cancer, Scorpio, Pisces	Cancer

As an example, consider Venus at 10° 20' Aquarius. From the first table we see that it falls into the 4th navamsha section. Aquarius is an air sign, and we find from the second table that the cardinal air sign is Libra. Count four signs on starting from Libra which takes us to Capricorn - so in the navamsha chart Venus has moved to Capricorn.

The placements of Venus (for men) and Jupiter (for women) in the navamsha chart are the important ones for relationship astrology: studying them will add depth and subtlety to the rasi chart's indications of whether the person will be able to form good relationships, and with whom. Actual interpretation is the same as for the rasi chart. If Venus or Jupiter is in the 6th, 8th or 12th house this will create problems for the person in their relationships. Placements in the navamsha chart can throw light on problems already showing in the rasi chart; or alleviate them. A woman with Jupiter conjunct Rahu in the seventh house of her rasi chart might have always had problems in relationships. In the navamsha chart her Jupiter might be in Aries. Aries is ruled by Mars and Mars and Jupiter are friends. Together, they indicate the possibility of improvement through understanding: the woman could take action (Mars) and learn (Jupiter) to become wiser (Jupiter) in her dealings with her partners.

Planets which are poorly placed in the rasi chart will become weakened in the navamsha, while well-placed ones will have their strength enhanced.

Navamsha position of the dasha ruler

The position of the dasha ruler in the navamsha chart is very important; it indicates the inner quality of the dasha period. If it is well placed by exaltation or mooltrikona (you need to refer to planetary strengths here too) the quality of the dasha will be enhanced. The opposite will create difficulties. With practice you will see the navamsha chart gives the underlying foundation and therefore more understanding of the dasha period too. The house where the dasha ruler is placed will also indicate which issues will come to the fore. If it is placed in the tenth house of career in the rasi chart, but the seventh in the navamsha, the dasha will affect both the career and relationships during its period.

Vargottama

A planet is vargottama when it is placed in the same sign in the rasi and the navamsha charts. This is considered the perfect position in the zodiac and is supposed to make the planet as strong as if it were in exaltation. Even if the planet is debilitated this position will strengthen it enormously.

The vargottama positions for rasi/navamsha charts are:

Aries, Cancer, Libra, Capricorn	00° - 03°20'
Taurus, Leo, Scorpio, Aquarius	13°20' - 16°00'
Gemini, Virgo, Sagittarius, Pisces	26°40' - 30°00'

- **The dashamsha chart - 10 divisions of 3° each**

The dashamsha chart focuses on the issues of the tenth house: career, ambition, status and life direction, and is one of the most frequently used varga charts. Calculation is not dissimilar to that for the navamsha chart - the 30 degrees are divided into segments of 3 degrees each:

00° - 03°	1st part
03° - 06°	2nd
06° - 09°	3rd
09° - 12°	4th
12° - 15°	5th
15° - 18°	6th
18° - 21°	7th
21° - 24°	8th
24° - 27°	9th
27° - 30°	10th

With odd-numbered signs the ten subdivisions of each sign begin with the sign being divided; with even-numbered signs they begin with the sign nine signs further round the zodiac from the one being divided.

The sub-divisions of:

Aries begin with	-	Aries	Libra with	- Libra
Taurus	-	Capricorn	Scorpio	- Cancer
Gemini	-	Gemini	Sagittarius	- Sagittarius
Cancer	-	Pisces	Capricorn	- Virgo
Leo	-	Leo	Aquarius	- Aquarius
Virgo	-	Taurus	Pisces	- Scorpio

Taking the example of Venus at 10° 20' Aquarius again, it falls in the fourth part of the first table and as Aquarius is an odd numbered sign, we count four signs on starting from there; the dashamsha position of Venus is Taurus.

The position of the planet which rules the tenth house of the rasi chart is the most important one in the dashamsha and the subdivision it is in will shed further light on your career. The position of the Sun is also important as it signifies status. If the ruler of the ascendant of the rasi chart is in the tenth subdivision of the dashamsha chart, career and status issues will be a very important influence on your life.

- **The dwadashamsha chart - 12 divisions of 2°30' each**

Giving further information on the issues of the twelfth house in the rasi chart, this is the past life varga. In it you can see something of your previous incarnation; it gives indications of the karma you bring forward into this life. You can take this process into lives further back with the **Chaturvimsha** chart, also called the **Siddhamsha** (see further on). Rulerships within the dwadashamsha chart start from the sign itself: an ascendant on the rasi chart at 1° Sagittarius will remain in Sagittarius in the dwadashamsha chart, ruled by Jupiter.

This chart is often thought of as the 'mother and father' chart - because your choice of mother and father in this life is part of your karma from past incarnations. Being born into a difficult relationship with one or both parents is seen as an attempt to become a more mature soul. However, this chart is not just about the past; as well as highlighting past-life issues likely to be prominent again in this one, it can be a powerful tool in helping you recognise your potential in this incarnation. It is interpreted in the same way as the rasi chart; grahas, house positions, rulerships and all meanings are the same; you can also make a chart showing the Sun or Moon on the ascendant just as you can with the rasi chart. The most important planets to assess are, of course, the Sun and Moon. The Sun represents the soul's path to the future - in a dwadashamsha chart, that is this present life, so it can throw light on current situations. For example, someone with Sun in Capricorn in the rasi chart but in Aquarius in the dwadashamsha chart indicates that, although in a past life they were learning to shed their ego and live more spiritually, in this one they need a more 'feet firmly on the ground' kind of existence. The Moon in a dwadashamsha chart represents the life before - in a dwadashamsha chart that is the life before last. As Rahu and Ketu have the same meanings in a dwadashamsha chart as in a rasi chart, Moon conjunct Ketu in the dwadashamsha chart indicates heavy-duty karma in the life before this one, from the life before that. The sign and rulership of the ascendant describes your physical being and personality in your last life. Every area of your life is covered by the dwadashamsha chart, mostly issues that you have already worked out. Here are details of other varga charts:

Shodhashamsha - 16 parts of 1°52'30" each
This varga chart emphasises fourth house issues like transport, the home, assets and your inner emotions.

Vimshamsha - 20 parts of 1°30' each
This varga chart looks at religious issues.

Chaturvimsha or Siddhamsha - 24 parts of 1°15' each
This varga chart looks more closely at the past life already highlighted in the **dwadashamsha** chart, but with a particular purpose in mind. It assesses your spiritual capabilities in this lifetime; your ability and willingness to pursue the spiritual life comes from the experience accumulated in your past lives.

Saptavimshamsha or Bhamsha - 27 parts of 1°6' each
Whereas the nakshatras divide the whole zodiac into 27 equal parts, this calculation does the same for one zodiac sign, and it is used to highlight your personal strengths and weaknesses.

Khavedamsha - 40 parts of 0°45' each
This varga focuses on your quality of life.

Akshavedamsha - 45 parts of 0°40' each
This varga chart is essentially like the rasi chart, but pinpointing the effects of the exact degree of the planet placements.

Shastiamsha - 60 parts of 0°30' each

The shastiamsha chart is frequently used in electional astrology in India. It is also used to differentiate between twins, whose shastiamsha charts will be different, but of course exact birth times are a necessity here. (In India the first breath is taken as the moment of birth.) Interpretation of the shastiamsha and the rasi charts are not the same - planets placed in benefic shashtiamsha are enhanced and planets in malefic shastiamsha are obstructed.

Using groups of varga charts

Specialised computer software produces the varga charts very quickly, although most astrologers only use the **shadvarga** or **saptavarga** vimshopak (planetary strength) groups. The great importance of the vimshopak calculations is that they are used to work out the dashas: when they will occur and whether they will be good or bad. Weak planets (low vimshopak totals) will create difficulties and the strong ones will enhance the dashas. Planetary strengths are covered in detail in the Graha chapter. There are four groupings of vargas :

Shodasavarga - all 16 divisional charts taken into consideration

Dashavarga - 10 vargas: rasi, hora, drekkana, navamsha, dwadashamsha, trimshamsha, saptamsha, dashamsha, shodhamsha, and shastiamsha

Saptavarga - 7 vargas: rasi, hora, drekkana, navamsha, dwadashamsha, trimshamsha and saptamsha

Shadvarga - 6 vargas: rasi, hora, drekkana, navamsha, dwadashamsha and trimshamsha.

Drekkana Table

Long up to	AR	TAU	GEM	CAN	LEO	VI	LI	SCO	SAG	CAP	AQ	PI
0 - 10°	Ar	Tau	Gem	Can	Leo	Vi	Li	Sco	Sag	Cap	Aq	Pi
10 - 20°	Leo	Vi	Li	Sco	Sag	Cap	Aq	Pi	Ar	Tau	Gem	Can
20 - 30°	Sag	Cap	Aq	Pi	Ar	Tau	Gem	Can	Leo	Vi	Li	Sco

Navamsha Table

Long up to	AR	TAU	GEM	CAN	LEO	VI	LI	SCO	SAG	CAP	AQ	PI
3°20'	Ar	Cap	Li	Can	Ar	Cap	Li	Can	Ar	Cap	Li	Can
6°40'	Tau	Aq	Sco	Leo	Tau	Aq	Sco	Leo	Tau	Aq	Sco	Leo
10°	Gem	Pi	Sag	Vi	Gem	Pi	Sag	Vi	Gem	Pi	Sag	Vi
13°20'	Can	Ar	Cap	Li	Can	Ar	Cap	Li	Can	Ar	Cap	Li
16°40'	Leo	Tau	Aq	Sco	Leo	Tau	Aq	Sco	Leo	Tau	Aq	Sco
20°	Vi	Gem	Pi	Sag	Vi	Gem	Pi	Sag	Vi	Gem	Pi	Sag
23°20'	Li	Can	Ar	Cap	Li	Can	Ar	Cap	Li	Can	Ar	Cap
26°40'	Sco	Leo	Tau	Aq	Sco	Leo	Tau	Aq	Sco	Leo	Tau	Aq
30°	Sag	Vi	Gem	Pi	Sag	Vi	Gem	Pi	Sag	Vi	Gem	Pi

Chaturtamsha Table

Long of planet	AR	TAU	GEM	CAN	LEO	VI	LI	SCO	SAG	CAP	AQ	PI
0 - 7°30'	Ar	Tau	Gem	Can	Leo	Vi	Li	Sco	Sag	Cap	Aq	Pi
7°30' - 15°	Can	Leo	Vi	Li	Sco	Sag	Cap	Aq	Pi	Ar	Tau	Gem
15° - 22°30'	Li	Sco	Sag	Cap	Aq	Pi	Ar	Tau	Gem	Can	Leo	Vi
22°30' - 30°	Cap	Aq	Pi	Ar	Tau	Gem	Can	Leo	Vi	Li	Sco	Sag

Saptamsha Table

Long up to	AR	TAU	GEM	CAN	LEO	VI	LI	SCO	SAG	CAP	AQ	PI
4°17'	Ar	Sco	Gem	Cap	Leo	Pi	Li	Tau	Sag	Can	Aq	Vi
8°34'	Tau	Sag	Can	Aq	Vi	Ar	Sco	Gem	Cap	Leo	Pi	Li
12°51'	Gem	Cap	Leo	Pi	Li	Tau	Sag	Can	Aq	Vi	Ar	Sco
17°8'	Can	Aq	Vi	Ar	Sco	Gem	Cap	Leo	Pi	Li	Tau	Sag
21°25'	Leo	Pi	Li	Tau	Sag	Can	Aq	Vi	Ar	Sco	Gem	Cap
25°42'	Vi	Ar	Sco	Gem	Cap	Leo	Pi	Li	Tau	Sag	Can	Aq
30°	Li	Tau	Sag	Can	Aq	Vi	Ar	Sco	Gem	Cap	Leo	Pi

Dashamsha Table

Long up to	AR	TAU	GEM	CAN	LEO	VI	LI	SCO	SAG	CAP	AQ	PI
3°	Ar	Cap	Gem	Pi	Leo	Tau	Li	Can	Sag	Vi	Aq	Sco
6°	Tau	Aq	Can	Ar	Vi	Gem	Sco	Leo	Cap	Li	Pi	Sag
9°	Gem	Pi	Leo	Tau	Li	Can	Sag	Vi	Aq	Sco	Ar	Cap
12°	Can	Ar	Vi	Gem	Sco	Leo	Cap	Li	Pi	Sag	Tau	Aq
15°	Leo	Tau	Li	Can	Sag	Vi	Aq	Sco	Ar	Cap	Gem	Pi
18°	Vi	Gem	Sco	Leo	Cap	Li	Pi	Sag	Tau	Aq	Can	Ar
21°	Li	Can	Sag	Vi	Aq	Sco	Ar	Cap	Gem	Pi	Leo	Tau
24°	Sco	Leo	Cap	Li	Pi	Sag	Tau	Aq	Can	Ar	Vi	Gem
27°	Sag	Vi	Aq	Sco	Ar	Cap	Gem	Pi	Leo	Tau	Li	Can
30°	Cap	Li	Pi	Sag	Tau	Aq	Can	Ar	Vi	Gem	Sco	Leo

Dwadashamsha Table

Long up to	AR	TAU	GEM	CAN	LEO	VI	LI	SCO	SAG	CAP	AQ	PI
2°30'	Ar	Tau	Gem	Can	Leo	Vi	Li	Sco	Sag	Cap	Aq	Pi
5°	Tau	Gem	Can	Leo	Vi	Li	Sco	Sag	Cap	Aq	Pi	Ar
7°30'	Gem	Can	Leo	Vi	Li	Sco	Sag	Cap	Aq	Pi	Ar	Tau
10°	Can	Leo	Vi	Li	Sco	Sag	Cap	Aq	Pi	Ar	Tau	Gem
12°30'	Leo	Vi	Li	Sco	Sag	Cap	Aq	Pi	Ar	Tau	Gem	Can
15°	Vi	Li	Sco	Sag	Cap	Aq	Pi	Ar	Tau	Gem	Can	Leo
17°30'	Li	Sco	Sag	Cap	Aq	Pi	Ar	Tau	Gem	Can	Leo	Vi
20°	Sco	Sag	Cap	Aq	Pi	Ar	Tau	Gem	Can	Leo	Vi	Li
22°30'	Sag	Cap	Aq	Pi	Ar	Tau	Gem	Can	Leo	Vi	Li	Sco
25°	Cap	Aq	Pi	Ar	Tau	Gem	Can	Leo	Vi	Li	Sco	Sag
27°30'	Aq	Pi	Ar	Tau	Gem	Can	Leo	Vi	Li	Sco	Sag	Cap
30°	Pi	Ar	Tau	Gem	Can	Leo	Vi	Li	Sco	Sag	Cap	Aq

The Gunas

According to ancient Vedic philosophy, creation is the product of the meeting of **purusha** and **prakriti** - the male and female influences. Prakriti is the main element, the female regenerative forces and it is full of desires and needs. Purusha (which also represents the soul) meets prakriti to create life. The purpose of purusha is to enjoy what prakriti has to offer, and prakriti has to fulfil the desires of purusha. When this cosmic birth takes place **ahankara** or individual ego/intellect is born. Ahankara gives birth to all the senses and the mind. In astrological terms then, purusha is represented by the Sun, prakriti by the Moon, and ahankara by Mercury. Once we start to think for ourselves we also wonder what our position is in the cosmos; and at that point, when we actually care who and what we are, the ego is born. Consciousness has a balance of the three qualities sattva, rajas and tamas. Once this universal consciousness identifies with individuality, one of the three qualities or **gunas** become out of balance and we reflect that quality in our birth. It is important to understand the impulses (gunas) of the planets that give them their unique behaviour- patterns so you can identify them in your own chart. The gunas appear in the personality as both positive and negative characteristics.

'Guna' also means 'strand', the strands of twine that make up a rope. The rope is seen here as an allegory to personality. The various strands, or gunas, entwine to produce the individuality of a person. The attribute of each guna is usually seen as mental rather than physical, but the mind has a great capacity to affect the physical side of our life.

We all have a balance of the gunas within us. They express themselves as a mental attitude that leads us to see life in a certain way and have particular priorities, and it is vital that we recognise both the gifts and the challenges that they have to offer in our lives. Looking through the descriptions below, you will probably find some aspects easier to understand than others. How does this relate to your own balance? Can you appreciate both the positive and the negative sides of your predominant guna?

Sattva is the attribute of purity. 'Sat' means being, existing, pure, true and real. 'Va' means where purity dwells. A sattvic person believes in purity of being, thought, and action. Water is pure sattva. Vegetarianism is sattvic because it rejects killing animals to satisfy the need to eat. Sattvic people have a mental attitude that emphasises purity.

Sattvic people believe in Truth and seek the good of others through their own deep spirituality. They are fearless, generous, self-controlled, tranquil, charitable and generally have an open mind. They find it hard to hurt others. They are able to rise above worldly matters and face the dramas of daily life with equilibrium; they still experience pain and unhappiness, but the way of dealing with them is different.

Whilst it might sound a wonderful, idyllic state to aim for, being sattvic and all that the image implies can present a huge challenge. The responsibilities of day-to-day existence are a necessary part of life on earth, and although sattvic people are drawn to a state of contemplation and inner quiet, they have to find a way to survive 'out there' too. The path towards enlightenment and higher consciousness is not an easy one, and the qualities of the other gunas are very much needed to bring a sense of balance into their lives.

On the negative side, sattvic people can take asceticism to extremes and be very self-righteous. They can find it impossible to understand those on a different path from themselves and to allow them their own self expression. Good examples are vegetarians not allowing others to eat meat, or the animal liberationists who use the threat of violence to further their cause; in fact here, people are only pretending to be sattvic. Their guna changes when they lose their purity. Their initial impulse may have been sattvic but the method of carrying it out becomes tamasic or rajasic. Sattva works very much on the abstract level.

Rajas is the cause of activity in mankind, and is the searching quality that as humans, we all have. It can be translated as 'pollen of the flowers', 'a particle in the sunbeams' or 'emotional, moral or mental darkness'. 'Pollen of the flowers' indicates the potential of pollen to create new flowers - humans activating more life; experiencing life and birth. 'A particle in the sunbeam' - a sunbeam is pure and the particle introduces a new element into its purity. 'Moral, emotional or mental darkness' is the inability of humans to see the answers within themselves, with the result that they seek fulfilment in the material, illusionary world. Rajasic people have a mental attitude that emphasises strong emotional impulses. They can be described as being led by passion towards achievement of their material desires, but to find true happiness they need to look within.

Rajasic people are driven by a great inner thirst; they are easily moved by their feelings. They are very active, mentally and physically, and are continually searching for new challenges. They are high-achievers, wanting recognition, respect and success.

On the more difficult side it is true that rajasic people can be so restless they can't settle into either their work or relationships. They have a tendency to cling to pleasant tasks while avoiding difficult situations. They lack peace of mind because they are unsure of what they really want; they are continually seeking answers in the outer world whereas what they are looking for is within themselves. Western culture is generally considered to be rajasic. Rajas moves between the abstract and the practical.

Tamas is the attribute of darkness. The Sanskrit word can also be translated as 'ignorance', making it plain that the darkness is a mental one. Tamasic people have a mental attitude that emphasises sensuality. They can be described either as being led by a lack of knowledge or a dearth of spiritual insight to a life focusing on human sensual desires. Vedic philosophy encourages tamasic people to dispel their darkness with the light of spiritual insight. Tamasic people revel in the everyday, material world; preferably one with lots of good food and good company. They usually view life in the here and now and allow their desires to dominate their actions. These desires keep them tied to the world of happiness and unhappiness - through their own needs they create their own problems.

It is important to stress here that all three gunas are present in the natal chart but the balance of them will be different for each of us; we can be influenced by our own desires (tamas) and at the same time be on a spiritual quest (sattva) to make this world a better place (rajas). However, **maya**, the illusionary world of self gratification and sensual living, ties tamasic people to their own desires. They tend to view the material world as the only reality and can be very greedy for all it can offer - for example, they often have weight problems! Yoga and meditation can help to strengthen their inner being and make them aware of the spiritual side of existence.

Qualities of the Planets, Signs and Houses

The lists below show the qualities of each planet, sign and house. The guna of your ascendant will be determined by the sign it occupies.

The Planets

Sattvic	Rajasic	Tamasic
The Sun	Venus	Saturn
Moon	Mercury*	Mars
Jupiter		Rahu
		Ketu

* Adaptable Mercury is generally interpreted as taking on the guna attribute of those planets it is aspecting in any chart.
Ketu can be a very sattvic planet under the right circumstances.

The Signs

Sattvic	Rajasic	Tamasic
Cancer	Aries	Virgo
Leo	Taurus	Scorpio
Sagittarius	Gemini	Capricorn
Pisces	Libra	Aquarius

Gemini is usually considered to have all three gunas; it is **Tri Guni**.

The Houses

Sattvic	Rajasic	Tamasic
4th	1st	6th
5th	2nd	8th
9th	3rd	10th
12th	7th	11th

Calculating the gunas in your chart

To study the gunas in your own natal chart you need to look at these key points:

- the ascendant

- the Moon sign

- the Sun sign

- the position of the other planets, their gunas, and the overall influence of the gunas

Rahu and Ketu are tamasic. Rahu is purely tamasic, and it affects mainly the practical areas of life. Ketu's tamas is shaded with sattva, which is to do with searching for enlightenment, but its being called tamasic indicates the issues that Ketu represents have to be faced in this world. However, these intrinsic qualities will be overridden by the guna of the planet that rules the sign they are in.

For each key point in your chart:

1) determine which guna it has in its natural state
2) look at the sign it is in; this will indicate its focus
3) its house will indicate how and where this focus is directed

Key Points
You will probably have a combination of qualities - use the section below to understand how they work together:

• **All sattvic**
Your key point will be acting at its purest level.

• **Two sattvic, one rajasic**
If a key point in your chart is sattvic and also placed in a sattvic sign it will be pure and natural in its inclinations. But if it is placed in a rajasic house, it will need to carry out its activities in an active (rajasic) manner. You may feel the drive and dissatisfaction the rajasic guna gives. These urges will need to be satisfied but the end you strive towards will be a sattvic one.

If your key point is sattvic and placed in a rajasic sign but in a sattvic house, you will experience a great deal of inner conflict. However, as sattvic gunas outnumber the rajasic, your sattvic qualities will predominate.

• **Two sattvic, one tamasic**
When a sattvic key point is placed in a sattvic sign but in a tamasic house, you will need to act out its sattvic guna in a practical, tamasic manner. There will be times when this is difficult as it contradicts your inner nature.

If you have a sattvic key point in a tamasic sign you will be pulled two ways by conflicting impulses: negative/positive, cosmic/earthly, idealism/practicality. If the key point is in a sattvic house it will enable the guna of sattva to be predominant.

- **All three rajasic**

The rajasic energy will be very strong.

- **Two rajasic, one tamasic**

If your key point is rajasic and is placed in a rajasic sign but in a tamasic house, the need to be active and to achieve can be thwarted by practical considerations.

When you have a rajasic key point in a tamasic sign, you will go back and forth between activity and stasis, ambition and laziness, changeability and stability. If the key point is in a rajasic sign your rajasic impulses will be stronger than your tamasic tendencies, which will have to follow in a rajasic direction.

- **Two rajasic, one sattvic**

A rajasic key point in a rajasic sign but in a sattvic house can make you unhappy with your spiritual direction. However, the general restlessness of rajas can make it hard for you to maintain that sattvic focus. A rajasic person with sattvic direction might be tempted to look for personal gain from their principles and actions.

- **All three tamasic**

If you have a key point which is tamasic of itself, by sign and by house, its energy will be taken up almost entirely by practical concerns. It will lead making the kind of choices which result in a build up of negative karma.

When the tamasic impulse is this strong, you will not be able to adapt to change or develop your spiritual side very easily.

- **Two tamasic, one rajasic**

A tamasic key point in a tamasic sign works in a practical but worldly way. The rajasic house makes it focus on change, activity and ambition. As tamasic people find it very difficult to adapt, you will experience inner conflict concerning the eventual direction of your ambitions. If you have a tamasic key point in a rajasic sign you will struggle between keeping things the same and making changes. If it is in a tamasic house, the balance of the two forces leans towards inactivity and your rajasic ambitions will be frustrated. It is be important to allow your rajasic side nature appropriate expression.

• **Two tamasic, one sattvic**

A tamasic key point in a tamasic sign but in a sattvic house will create great turmoil. The focus is towards purity but its inherent nature is materialistic. The conflict is that much greater if the key point is your ascendant, Moon or Sun, but you can achieve a balance through yoga and meditation.

When the tamasic key point is in a sattvic sign, it does not want to deal with the spiritual energy which is being activated. This is usually a difficult combination, but it can be rewarding if you activate the sattvic energy.

• **One of each guna**

If any key point in your chart is exposed to all three influences, its house position becomes very important - this will indicate which guna will dominate. The combination of all three gunas can create a wonderful blend of energies - but in practice, it is difficult to make that happen. Tensions are created within you as to what you really want from life. You should also see which other key points are placed within the same house, as their influence may have a bearing on the direction you eventually take.

Chart Example

To illustrate how this works in real life, let us study His Holiness the 14th Dalai Lama, focusing on the energy of the gunas in his chart (shown on the next page). The Dalai Lama was born to be the spiritual leader of an isolated kingdom deep in the Himalayas, so we would expect to see the sattvic guna dominate, but in reality he was forced from his home by the invasion of the Chinese and now lives a life of exile in India. From his travels around the world he has made an international impact with his form of philosophy and practice of Tibetan Buddhism. We would expect his chart therefore to reflect the fact that he is now regarded as a spiritual leader by people from many different religions and cultures.

The Dalai Lama's **Sun** is in Gemini, which reflects all three gunas. The Sun is a sattvic planet so Gemini will accentuate his sattvic nature and the higher thinking (Mercury) he brings in from beyond - its twelfth house position also indicates the personal sacrifices he has had to make for the sake of his beliefs.

His Holiness the 14th Dalai Lama

Birth data (not fully confirmed):
6th July 1935
6:00 (-7:00) Taktser, Amdo, Tibet.

Rasi Chart

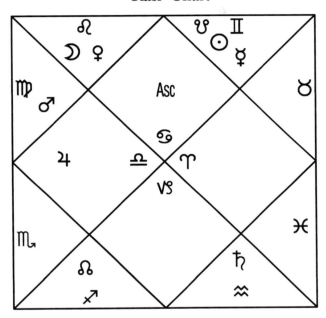

Ascendant	01° 08'	Cancer	Jupiter R	20° 30'	Libra
Sun	20° 00'	Gemini	Venus	05° 19'	Leo
Moon	17° 20'	Leo	Saturn R	17° 05'	Aquarius
Mars	25° 20'	Virgo	Rahu	29° 26'	Sagittarius
Mercury	02° 34'	Gemini	Ketu	29° 26'	Gemini

His **ascendant** is in sattvic Cancer and its ruler, the Moon, is also sattvic; together the two indicate that the Dalai Lama will be concerned with purity and spirituality in this life.

The **Moon** is coloured by Leo which is sattvic as well - but placed in a rajasic house. The Dalai Lama accepts the responsibility of his homeland and defending his people (action - rajasic), but by the exemplary use of diplomacy and a fundamental belief in the good of humanity, rather than by physical violence. The traditional Leo ambition is redirected towards guiding his people. Experiencing the rajasic guna himself makes it easier for the Dalai Lama to understand the Western mind which it is usually rajasic in nature. Leo has the ability to overcome the rajasic location (second house).

Mercury is in Gemini in the sattvic twelfth house. It is **tri guni**, taking on the energy of the planet it conjuncts. As the Dalai Lama has a Sun/Mercury conjunction, Mercury will also act in a sattvic way like the Sun. This shows clearly in his ability to both talk to, and get other people to talk about, the problem that most occupies his mind - his homeland.

Saturn is tamasic, rules his seventh house, and is placed in tamasic Aquarius in the tamasic eighth house (which it also rules). The seventh house is rajasic by nature, so there will be some conflict here; we know that the Dalai Lama would never have the option to give up his worldly responsibilities and retreat into a totally spiritual environment as reflected by the qualities of the Moon and the Sun. Saturn will keep him firmly attached to his practical considerations, but his way of dealing with them is purely sattvic.

Venus is a rajasic planet placed in the sattvic sign of Leo with the sattvic Moon - this which enable him to resist temptation and keep his desires pure. Venus is in a rajasic house - the second. There could have been temptations on his path, but the intense sattvic purity of the planet that rules Venus, the Sun, indicates that the Dalai Lama is more than able to control his desires and activate the higher energies of Venus.

Mars, a tamasic planet, is placed in Virgo, another tamasic sign and rajasic house (third). This is the house for self motivation and action, and Mars - the best planet for Cancer ascendants as it rules the fifth and tenth houses - is well-placed there. In the past the Dalai Lama would traditionally have stayed in Tibet and remained all but invisible to the rest of the world, but Mars has given him the impetus to travel widely - resulting in many converts to Buddhism and a much higher profile for Tibet. The tamasic quality of the Mars/Virgo combination gives him both the courage to speak out and the clarity of thought to ensure his message will be understood.

Jupiter is a sattvic planet, but it is placed in Libra which is a rajasic sign, in the rajasic fourth house. Jupiter represents wisdom and philosophy, whilst rajas is about ambition, activity and action; this combination gives him the ability to communicate with the West, which is usually regarded as rajasic in quality.

Rahu and Ketu are tamasic by guna, but will act like the planet which rules the house they are placed in. Ketu, the past life indicator is ruled by Mercury (acting as sattvic) and is placed in the twelfth house of enlightenment, indicating that past incarnations have prepared the Dalai Lama for his spiritual path. Rahu is ruled by the sattvic/rajasic Jupiter, but is in the tamasic sixth house of obstacles and enemies. Rahu gives the Dalai Lama the necessary drive to confront the might of China and enlist the help of the rest of the world in his attempts to regain his spiritual heritage.

The Dalai Lama's Gunas at a Glance
The **planets** - how they reflect their qualities in his chart:

Sattvic	Rajasic	Tamasic
Sun	Jupiter	Mars
Moon	Rahu	Saturn
Mercury		
Ketu		
Venus		

The table of planets suggest that the Dalai Lama's inner life is completely sattvic. The Sun (his consciousness), the Moon (his mind), and Mercury (his intellect and speech) are all influenced by the sattvic guna. His moksha (enlightenment) and spiritual realisation planet Ketu is also influenced by sattva. Venus, the potentially sensuous side of his nature, becomes sattvic, so his inner self is deeply spiritual. His outer persona has an equal influence of tamas and rajas, which keeps him very much in touch with the outside world.

The **signs** where the planets are placed:

Sattvic	Rajasic	Tamasic
Sagittarius	Gemini	Virgo
Leo	Libra	Aquarius

The balance of the planets is equally divided. This indicates the Dalai Lama's inner harmony and also his ability to work on all levels.

and finally the qualities of the **houses**:

Sattvic	Rajasic	Tamasic
(4, 5, 9, 12)	(1, 2, 3, 7)	(6, 8, 10, 11)
The Sun	Moon	Mars
Mercury	Venus	Rahu
Ketu		Saturn
Jupiter		

The Overall Planetary Indications

	Natural	Natal Sign	Natal House
Sun	S	S	S
Moon	S	S	R
Mars	T	T	R
Mercury	Tri	S	S
Jupiter	S	R	S
Venus	R	S	R
Saturn	T	T	T
Rahu	T	S	T
Ketu	T	S	S

Mercury is tri guni and will reflect the planet it conjuncts
Ketu can be sattvic under the right circumstances.

We can see that the houses occupied by the planets are predominantly sattvic, but rajas and tamas are also prominent and it is this that gives him the overall ability to work out in the real world. The experience of life is considered tamasic and our search for spirituality is essentially rajasic; if the Dalai Lama were to have followed his highly sattvic nature, he would not have been able to deal with the worldly issues which are the domain of rajas and tamas. Also, as a continously reincarnating spiritual figure, his purpose is not to find enlightenment for himself, but to guide others towards it.

The Yogas

The concept of yogas is unique to Vedic astrology and recognised by planetary combinations placed in specific relationships to each other. The important thing to realise about the yogas is that they show the maturity of the soul and, through various tests, will help it to develop and progress along the evolutionary path it has chosen. Of course you can have yogas which ease the way as well as those which seem to create difficulties for no obvious reason other than to make you grind to a halt.

There are many yogas and it would be impossible to illustrate them all, so we will concentrate on those that are usually considered in a normal consultation. The astrologer studies them first to give an indication of the special qualities of your chart; only then will they consider the other aspects. It's also important to realise that not **everybody** has a yoga in their chart. The lack does not put one at some kind of disadvantage!

The yogas can also be looked at from the Moon and Sun ascendant charts. In the divisional charts like the navamsha and drekkna they can be used identify specific areas in your life.

The Panchamahapurusha Yogas

'Panch' means 'five' and 'Mahapurusha' means 'exalted person'. The Panchamahapurusha yogas are a combination that indicate a very special individual. They are formed when Mars, Mercury, Jupiter,

Venus and Saturn are in their own sign or in exaltation in the **kendras** (first, fourth, seventh and tenth houses). The kendra houses are the foundation to life and a person with the Panchamahapurusha yoga is going to make an extraordinary impact on the environment and those he comes into contact with; this sense of 'greatness' in an individual is due to repercussions from past lives. Panchamahapurusha relates to conditions for individual success based on karma of the past. The important consideration here is that these yogas can become spoilt or reduced if they are placed with or aspected by rulers of malefic houses - third, sixth, eighth, eleventh, or twelfth. The yoga still exists but its power is reduced. If it is conjunct Rahu or Ketu, it becomes powerful in a karmic way. The results then become unpredictable.

Ruchaka Yoga

Mars in its own or exaltation sign in kendras - Mars in Aries, Scorpio or Capricorn.

When Mars produces this yoga, it indicates a very powerful person who has the ability to externalise his talents. Action and energy are the keywords here. It could be in the field of sports, adventure, defence or in an area where power, aggression and authority are required. Ruchaka yoga makes an individual very ambitious with the ability to achieve whatever they set their minds to. They will be extremely successful in gaining their worldly desires.

Bhadra Yoga

Mercury in its own or exalted sign in kendras - Mercury in Gemini or Virgo.

When Mercury produces this yoga it indicates a powerful intellect. Someone who can clearly and profoundly. They will be wise, academic, knowledgeable and be able to influence others through speech and writing.

Hamsa Yoga

Jupiter in its own or exalted sign in kendras - Jupiter in Sagittarius, Pisces or Cancer.

When Jupiter produces this yoga, it indicates a person with

great sattvic thoughts and knowledge. Hamsa yoga makes one ethical and truthful and gives the ability to influence the most powerful people of the land. This is an exalted soul who wants to impart wisdom and knowledge to others without the need for material rewards. The connection towards divinity is strong. Hamsa yoga also produces people who are highly sexed and may not be happy with one partner. Their sexuality usually does not have an adverse effect on their reputation.

Malavya Yoga
Venus in its own or exalted sign in kendras - Venus in Taurus, Libra or Pisces.

When Venus produces this yoga, the individual has the ability to be greatly successful in the material world. This shows immense attraction, beauty and charm, wealth and material success. Malavya yoga shows a person who is very popular and can be famous. Their knowledge of spiritual literature can be deep and they use this to enhance their earthly resources.

Shasha Yoga
Saturn in its own or exalted sign in kendras - Saturn in Capricorn, Aquarius or Libra.

When the placement of Saturn produces this yoga, it indicates a commanding personality; someone who is not interested in being popular or sociable but will be a strong champion for unfashionable causes. Here is a person who will shoulder great responsibility and will not be afraid of facing karmic issues in life. Sex can be enjoyed as a way of understanding the partner, not just to satisfy desire.

Any yoga dealing with kendras will play an important part in raising profile. It endows an individual with the ability to work at higher levels than others in order to fulfil special roles. The Sun and Moon are excluded from these yogas as they show the connection of the individual with the eternal; if they are in their own houses or in exaltation it creates other special situations which are more linked to the infinite.

Raja Yoga

Raja Yoga is known as a 'king-making' combination. Nowadays this indicates the ability to attain success. As in Jyotish we believe that good karma from previous lives will affect us in this one as well, Raja yoga in a birth chart will show inherent tendencies which make the person especially great. It doesn't mean that this 'greatness' will come automatically, but that extra effort will be rewarded with special results. This yoga drives a person to aim for higher things and be ambitious. The important thing to understand is that the Raja yoga does not just indicate great monetary wealth, it could indicate wealth of knowledge, respectability and status as well.

Raja yoga is an auspicious combination of the fifth and ninth house rulers with the rulers of the kendras. It can be created by aspects, **parivartana** (mutual reception) and conjunctions. The strongest Raja yogas are created by:

- Ruler of the ninth house in the tenth and the tenth house ruler in the ninth

- Rulers of the ninth and tenth houses placed in the ninth or tenth houses

- Rulers of any trikona house (fifth and ninth) linked to any kendra house (first, fourth, seventh and tenth) and if they are placed in any of the above houses.

The Raja yoga indicates good luck and success. This brings about great success during the dasha and sub dashas. Some planets create Raja yogas by themselves, like Mars for Leo and Cancer ascendants, Venus for Capricorn and Aquarius ascendants and Saturn for Taurus and Libra ascendants. The quality of the yoga depends on how well the planets are placed. There will be obvious differences if a yoga is formed when two planets are well placed in their house of friends, exaltation or mooltrikona. In the case of a Leo ascendant this might for example be Mars in Leo and the Sun in Aries. There is no aspect here but there is **Parivartana** (mutual reception) as Mars is in the sign of Leo and the Sun is in Aries. Here the rulers of the first and ninth houses are in mutual reception. Mars is very happy in his friend's house and the Sun is exalted. This yoga would differ if it was formed by the Sun and Mars conjoining in Aquarius in the seventh house. Saturn, the ruler of Aquarius, is the enemy to both the Sun and Mars, so for this Raja yoga to give result, there would first be delay or obstruction caused by Saturnian influence.

Neechabhanga RajaYoga - Cancellation of Debilitation

This is one of the most important yogas to consider when starting out on your journey as a student of Vedic astrology. 'Neech' means 'debilitated', 'Bhanga' means 'cancellation'. Many new students are concerned that debilitated planets in a chart mean some kind of weaknesses, but this is where a little learning can be dangerous. A planet which is debilitated may not act so because of other conditions in the chart. In fact these conditions enhance the planet so much that it becomes a very special planet with the ability to give results like a Raja yoga. So when is a debilitated planet not debilitated? The rules are numerous. Here are some of them :

When the planetary ruler of the sign containing the debilitated planet is in its exaltation. For example if the Sun is in Libra, Venus, the ruler is exalted.

When the ruler of the sign that the debilitated planet is placed in is in a kendra from the ascendant or the Moon ascendant. For example, Jupiter is debilitated in Capricorn for an Aries ascendant, but if Saturn, the ruler of Capricorn, was placed in a kendra house the there would be a cancellation of debilitation. If we assume that the Moon is in Cancer, then Jupiter would also be in a kendra; if we used a chart with the Moon as the ascendant it would be in the seventh house from the Moon. Jupiter here will have a proper cancellation of its debilitation and therefore will have the ability to be greatly beneficial.

When the planet which is debilitated in the rasi chart is exalted in the navamsha; for example if Venus was in Virgo on the ascendant of the rasi chart but in Pisces in the navamsha chart.

When the ruler of the sign of the debilitated planet and the ruler of its exalted planet are in kendras from each other. Take the example of Saturn in Aries, where it would usually be debilitated: if Mars (ruler of Aries) was in Capricorn, and Venus (ruler of Saturn's exaltation sign, Libra) was in Libra the two planets would be in kendras from each other and there will be a cancellation of debilitation.

When the debilitated planet is conjunct the ruler of the sign of its debilitation. The Moon placed with Mars in Cancer would create Neechbanga Rajayoga.

When the debilitated planet is aspected by the ruler of its sign. For a Moon debilitated in Scorpio, Mars in Aries for example, would have an eighth house aspect to Scorpio and create the cancellation of the debilitation.

The important thing to realise here is that a planet which appears to be debilitated will not necessarily create problems. You have to understand the subtle energies of the planets and the yogas before making that assumption.

Support Yogas to the Sun

Buddhi Aditya Yoga
This yoga is formed when the Sun and Mercury are conjunct. The Sun represents the eternal connection and our soul, whereas Mercury is the conduit through which the desires of the soul are expressed in this world. Mercury connects the subtle world with the physical world, so it gives the ability to harness the subtle powers of nature, with the main emphasis being on intellectual development.

Vasi Yoga
Vasi yoga is formed in the same way as the Anapha yoga when benefic planets, other than the Moon, are placed in the twelfth house from the Sun.

Vesi Yoga
Vesi yoga is formed when benefics (not the moon) are placed in the second house from the Sun. Both these yogas support the Sun and give strength to the chart.

Both Vasi and Vesi yogas show success, wealth and good fortune.

Obhachari Yoga
When benefics, other than the moon are present in the second and the twelfth houses from the Sun. Again this yoga shows a popular person, well-liked and successful.

Yogas to the Moon
The Moon, as the significator of the mind and the reflection of the universal soul (the Sun) on earth, is an important planet. It controls life on earth and therefore yogas to the Moon have an important bearing on day to day functioning. There are many yogas indicating support to the Moon; benefic planets on either side are considered very good as they give support, security and strength. Even a malefic planet is better than nothing.

Adhi yoga
When benefic planets are placed in the sixth, seventh and eighth houses from the Moon, the Adhi yoga is formed. This yoga's importance is again in support of the Moon. Planets placed here would aspect the houses either side of the moon and enhancing the mind as well as giving success, popularity and happiness.

Anapha Yoga
This yoga is formed by benefic planets in the twelfth house from the Moon. It shows princely appearance, strong personality, good mind, fair reputation. Anapha yoga indicates success but also giving up material aspects of life at a later date.

Sunapha Yoga
Benefic planets placed in the second house from the Moon. This indicates material success and happiness.

Dhurudhura Yoga

This is formed when benefic planets are placed on either side of the Moon or in the adjoining house - second and twelfth - from it. This gives a person success, eminence and wealth.

Gajakesari Yoga

This yoga is due to the relative positions of Jupiter and the Moon, which must be in the first, fourth, seventh or tenth house from Jupiter. Again the quality of the yoga depends on the strength of Moon and Jupiter; a yoga formed by a full or waxing Moon in Taurus and Jupiter in its friendly sign of Scorpio will generate a different quality from one formed by a waning Moon in Scorpio and Jupiter in Aquarius. In the latter situation the moon is debilitated and Jupiter is in the sign of its enemy - Saturn.

Gajakesari yoga makes you wise, attractive, skilful and learned. It helps you to develop your latent faculties and protects you from negative forces. Gajakesari is related to the Moon and Jupiter brings out the inner strength of the Moon, the significator of the mind. This allows mental capabilities to strengthen; a strong mind gives an individual the ability to overcome any difficulty.

Sakata Yoga

Sakata yoga is created when the Moon and Jupiter are placed in the sixth, eighth and twelfth houses from each other. So if the Moon is in Taurus and Jupiter in Libra (here the Moon is placed in the eighth house from Jupiter), or the Moon is in Aries and Jupiter in Pisces (here Jupiter is placed in the twelfth house from the Moon) there is a Sakata yoga. This is a difficult yoga to have. It indicates that the placement of the benefic Jupiter from the Moon in the dusthana house obstructs the free flow of fortune. People with Sakata yoga are considered very powerful souls who are made to face difficulties in their present incarnation to learn some important lessons. Sakata means a wheel and Sakata yoga makes a person evolve on a wheel of life. The wheels rotate and so can life. There can be ups and downs, with sudden endings to be faced. Sakata yoga usually leads to a person having to start all over again at various stages in life. The combination of the mind (Moon) and wisdom (Jupiter) can create problems in overall expression.

Kemadruma Yoga

Kemadruma yoga is caused when there is no planet in the second or twelfth house from the Moon, leaving it unsupported. With this yoga the mind can be difficult to discipline. The Moon as representative of the mind is usually at the root of all our problems and this particular yoga is considered by the ancient sages to be the cause of poverty and difficulties. It is also said to weaken other good yogas in the chart. The Sun is not considered here.

Kemadruma yoga is nullified if there are planets in conjunction to the Moon or in kendras (fourth, seventh and tenth houses), and if it is a full Moon the yoga is said not to exist.

Yogas from Dusthana houses

These are contrary yogas which give strength to the individual when the planets that rule dusthanas are placed in their own signs or each other's signs. These yogas give enormous success during their dasha periods and endow the individual with special attributes.

Vipireeta Raja Yoga

This is a special combination which gives great wealth. It is created when the rulers of the sixth, eighth and twelfth houses are conjunct, placed anywhere in the chart; instead of creating problems, they give great wealth and fortune. You can see this yoga from the Moon ascendant chart as well; Bill Gates, the Microsoft billionaire, has this combination

Harsha Yoga

This yoga is formed when the ruler of the sixth house is placed there. Harsha means happiness. This yoga brings good health, ability to confront obstacles, deal with difficulties, healing and service to others. It indicates power through fair means.

Sarala Yoga

This yoga is formed when the eighth house ruler is placed in the eighth house. It makes a person learned, long lived, wealthy, famous but there can be some hidden depths to the person which can lead to negative use of power.

Vimala Yoga

This yoga is formed when the twelfth house ruler is placed in the twelfth house. It shows success abroad and the ability to control expenses. As the house of isolation, it shows a strong personality who finds it difficult to mix with others.

Other important yogas

Papakartari Yoga

Papakartari yoga is created when two malefic planets are placed on either side of the planet or sign. This restricts the activity of the planet. If Mars and Saturn - two malefics - are placed in the second and the twelfth houses from Venus, they will hem it in and stop it from functioning properly.

Subhakartari Yoga

Shubhakartari yoga is formed when two benefic planets are on either side of a planet. This enhances the quality of the planet. If Jupiter and Venus are placed on either side Mars its energies will be greatly enhanced.

Dhana yogas - combinations for wealth

For **Dhana** (wealth) yogas to exist in a chart there have to be connections between the second (wealth, assets), eleventh (earnings, profits) and ninth house (good luck). If the rulers of these house are in mutual aspect or conjunction, then a Dhana yoga is formed. Some ascendant signs have one planet that rules both the second and the eleventh house: for a Leo ascendant, Mercury rules both the second and eleventh houses, so if Mercury is conjunct Mars - the ninth house ruler - then there is a Dhana yoga.

Jupiter rules the second and eleventh houses for Aquarius ascendants. Its conjunction with Venus will create a Dhana yoga for people with Aquarius ascendants. For other ascendants, a conjunction of the ninth house ruler with the eleventh house ruler will indicate a high earner. A conjunction between the rulers of the ninth and second houses can show wealth from inheritance.

A conjunction of the second and eleventh house rulers is also considered a combination for wealth but it will not be so strong as the luck factor (ninth house) is missing from it.

For the Dhana yoga to be strong it must not be placed in the dushtana houses (sixth, eighth or twelfth).

Laxmi Yoga - immense wealth

Laxmi is the goddess of wealth. This yoga indicates a seriously wealthy person. It could be from inheritance or through plain hard work. The ninth house ruler and Venus should be in their own or exaltation signs, either in a kendra (first, fourth, seventh or tenth houses) or a trikona (fifth or ninth houses). The yoga can be looked at from the relative positions of the ascendant, Moon and Sun. If it exists from all these ascendants then unimaginable wealth is indicated.

Kal Sarpa Yoga

Kala Sarpa yoga is formed when Rahu and Ketu contain between them all the planets in the natal chart. For example, where Rahu is 10 degrees Leo and Ketu 10 degrees Aquarius and all the planets are ranged between these points; either from Leo to Aquarius or Aquarius to Leo (remembering here of course that Vedic astrology does not use the outer planets Uranus, Neptune and Pluto). For this yoga to be complete, no planet should conjunct Rahu or Ketu. It contradicts completely any other indications on the chart - however capable the person, his life is impeded due to past karma.

This yoga does not suggest either success or failure, rather the picture of somebody caught up in karmic forces so great that they are forced to look at issues they have avoided in the past before they can move forward. I've noticed this can appear to divide someone's life into two distinct parts.

Nelson Mandela has it in his chart and spent many years in prison before emerging to become a political statesman. It is almost as though he had to pay a karmic debt before he could move on to fulfil his destiny.

Paul McCartney has Kal Sarpa yoga and he cannot escape the legacy of the early years of the Beatles. Whatever else he achieves, in whatever context, he will always be known as a Beatle.

In the political arena, Margaret Thatcher also has this yoga, and after being a major figure in world politics she was dramatically ousted from her position as Prime Minister of the Conservative party in the U.K., to live in relative obscurity. In complete contrast to this, a client of mine who had lived in religious orders for 36 years underwent a dramatic change of heart and realised that she wanted to return to life in the outside world.

The Wheel of Vishnu

The Sudharshan Chakra: the Wheel of Vishnu

The sudarshana chakra is a very specialised chart, assessing the integration of our physical world with the eternal. How we attempt to combine these different levels shows the depth of our personality. The Vedic astrologer will consider three charts based on different ascendants: the lagna, the chandra lagna (Moon on the ascendant) and the surya lagna (Sun on the ascendant). The Wheel of Vishnu shows the lagna, chandra and surya charts as concentric circles, demonstrating the three energies together but on different levels:

The **surya** chart describes the eternal connection which our soul brings with it into our current physical body. It shows our inner self, our soul, and how it is connected to our past, present and future. It indicates the direction in which our soul is moving.

The **chandra** chart describes the mental connection between the soul and the physical world - how we express in everyday life the knowledge we carry within.

The **lagna** chart (the natal chart) describes the outer personality that results from the blending of the eternal and mental energies. It also indicates the issues that will arise in this life.

If the rulers of the lagna, chandra and surya charts are all friends, the personality is fully integrated; if they are enemies, the tensions between them cause friction. Your life will also be easier if planets repeat their qualities, house placements and house rulerships in the two or three different types of chart. If this is not the case, a careful assessment of the relative power of the planets in each chart can reveal which ones are likely to be most influential and in what ways. The three charts also give rather different information about you. The lagna chart represents the physical body, the chandra your mind and the surya your inner consciousness and future direction; together the three represent an integrated self.

When making predictions, Vedic astrologers look at the transits of planets to the chandra ascendant, not the rasi ascendant. The Moon controls life on Earth; on the level of the individual, the mind controls all actions, so transits to the chandra chart make a stronger impact on our lives. I personally look at all three charts when assessing the likely effect of major transits: when planets are making transits to all three charts (good or bad) their effect is greatly increased.

The easiest way to understand this is to look at an example: I have chosen the chart of HRH Prince Charles as it shows some interesting characteristics. His rasi chart is shown first, followed by the sudharshan.

The innermost wheel is the surya chart with the Sun sign as the ascendant. Prince Charles' Sun is in Libra, so this becomes his ascendant at the soul level. Scorpio rules his second house, Sagittarius the third and so on.

The middle circle is the chandra chart, with the Moon on the ascendant; it represents the mental level. Prince Charles' Moon is in Aries so it reflects the way he deals with spiritual questions on a material level, and how he reconciles his physical and spiritual needs.

The outermost wheel is the rasi chart, with the Cancer ascendant reflecting the present incarnation. Prince Charles' physical body and his attitude towards daily life are thus symbolised by the attributes of Cancer.

Rasi Chart

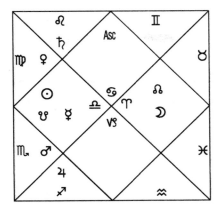

HRH Prince Charles
Born 14th November 1948 21.14
GMT London, England
(51N 0W10).

Sun	29° 16'	Libra
Moon	07° 17'	Aries
Mercury	13° 48'	Libra
Venus	23° 14'	Virgo
Mars	27° 48'	Scorpio
Jupiter	06° 44'	Sagittarius
Saturn	12° 07'	Leo
Rahu	10° 47'	Aries
Ketu	10° 47'	Libra

Sudharshan chart

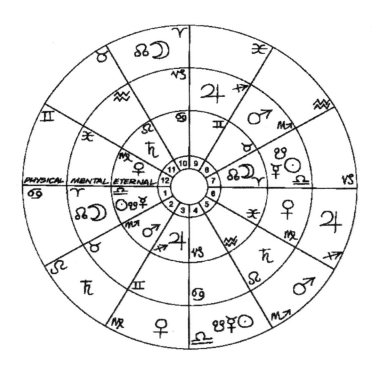

Surya Chart

On the eternal level - the Sun, Mercury and Ketu are placed in a Libra Ascendant. Prince Charles' Sun in Libra is at $29°13'$, almost the end of the sign. Libra is the sign where balance is sought between the physical and the spiritual life. The Sun is debilitated in Libra, but this Sun has moved past the debilitation degree, where involvement in the material world is total, so in Prince Charles the balance has shifted towards the spiritual side. When the Sun is located so near the end of a sign it indicates that one chapter of life is closing down and another opening. However, some issues do have to be resolved before he can move on.

Ketu, the moksha karaka, is placed with the Sun. Ketu seeks enlightenment and wants to leave mundane reality behind: it has a selfless purpose. Ketu is an enemy of the Sun and although there was not an actual solar eclipse on the day Charles was born, symbolically it will always be eclipsed by Ketu. Mercury takes on the character of any planet it conjuncts and in this chart it is within $3°$ of Ketu; Mercury is more likely to take on Ketu's persona than that of the Sun, almost $18°$ away. Ketu and Mercury combine together to eclipse Prince Charles on a soul level. This is a soul which has lost its purpose. Its direction is towards spiritual enlightenment, but it has to finish some important karmic issues before it can progress. Venus, as the dispositor of the Surya lagna is debilitated in the twelfth house, indicating loss, imprisonment of the soul, and a helplessness on that level.

Chandra Chart

On the mental level - the Moon and Rahu are placed in an Aries ascendant. As the first sign of the zodiac Aries represents a new beginning, a fresh start in life; it is impulsive, militant, adventurous and stubborn. An Aries person is not always willing to listen to others. Because Aries is working at the mental level for him, Prince Charles continually needs to push back the frontiers of conventional thought. He wants to take risks and to act first and think later, but this in itself creates obstacles in his life.

Mars, the dispositor of Aries is in its own sign of the intense and spiritual Scorpio, which usually fights between base instincts and higher aspirations. There is no halfway house here.

Rahu is closely conjunct the Moon. Rahu's influence on the mental plane suggests that the soul is guiding this mind through Ketu, the other end of the axis of the Moon's nodes. The Moon is afraid of Rahu, an inner fear which cannot be fully expressed. It could be of failure or of disappointment. The symbolic eclipse of the Sun in the soul chart is emphasised and increased by the mental chart. Rahu creates immense ambition but it also brings with it anxiety and unhappiness. Rahu will darken Prince Charles' mind until it learns to see through the darkness. The Moon is the significator of the public. The conjunction of the Moon with Rahu shows that Prince Charles has an inherent fear of his public duties as well as the power of the masses. I think he understands that his soul purpose is not on the material level but towards enlightenment. However, he has an important act to perform in his material life which he fears but will have to carry out; that act might result in the end of the monarchy as we know it.

Lagna Chart

On the physical level - no planets in the Cancer ascendant.
There are no planets in this ascendant house, but it is ruled by the Moon, which also rules his mental level. The Moon-Rahu conjunction in the tenth house shows that Prince Charles has to live out his life on the world stage, but in a way he will be eclipsed by others - for reasons which are not obvious to him.

The three levels together

All three levels of Prince Charles' chart are ruled by a cardinal sign on the ascendant, so the three second house signs are all fixed, the three third house signs are all mutable and so on. This clearly shows a channelling of similar kinds of energy on all levels. Cardinal sign ascendants are about leadership qualities; however, Prince Charles' leadership qualities will not be allowed their full expression until he succeeds to the throne, a karma which he cannot do anything about. He has, though, managed to put his tenth house Moon (in the lagna chart) to good use in other areas. Following the difficulties and upsets of recent years, Prince Charles has learnt to use his high profile to bring areas close to his heart more into the public eye. In the chandra chart, his ascendant ruler, Mars, is in the moksha eighth house, and in the surya chart, the ascendant ruler, Venus, is in the moksha twelfth house. As a champion of alternative medicine and organic gardening to name just two of his interests, he has succeeded in combining the spiritual needs reflected by these planets with the physical requirements of his lagna ascendant.

Here we have looked only at the relationship between the different ascendants. You can study the Sun and Moon charts more comprehensively to see what other insights are offered.

Putting it all Together -
A Chart Interpretation

I think the easiest way to synthesise all you've read so far is to go step-by-step through a chart interpretation. You will notice as we go through each section there is sometimes conflicting information regarding the condition of the planets and how well they work in the chart - this always happens in an interpretation, and it is only by constant practice and following the threads through to the end that we can finally draw a conclusion. You will also find that the same themes crop up in different places, and whilst I have tried not to repeat the same information endlessly, it is helpful to note which issues are becoming dominant. I have chosen Prince William because he is well-known, and has a verified time of birth; when he was born a notice was posted outside Buckingham Palace announcing the exact time of arrival. Also, the Vedic techniques we have learnt so far reveal some fascinating insights into his chart. William Arthur Philip Louis is the son of Prince Charles and the late Diana, Princess of Wales. He is the heir apparent with the title Prince William of Wales.

It is common practice to show both the rasi and navamsha charts together. Whereas Western charts show the degrees of the planets and their aspects Indian astrologers give very little detail on the chart itself, so a list of the planets' positions and their nakshatras appears alongside.

Prince William
21.6.82   21:03 BST   London 51N30 0W10

Rasi chart

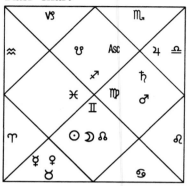

Navamsha chart

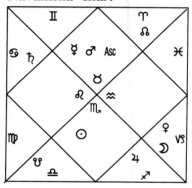

Vimsh. Dasha, Bhukti Start Dates		
Dasha Year Used:		365.25
Rahu	Sat	06/21/1982
Rahu	Merc	02/03/1984
Rahu	Ketu	08/21/1986
Rahu	Ven	09/09/1987
Rahu	Sun	09/09/1990
Rahu	Moon	08/04/1991
Rahu	Mars	02/01/1993
Jup	Jup	02/20/1994
Jup	Sat	04/10/1996
Jup	Merc	10/22/1998
Jup	Ketu	01/27/2001
Jup	Ven	01/03/2002
Jup	Sun	09/03/2004
Jup	Moon	06/22/2005
Jup	Mars	10/22/2006
Jup	Rahu	09/27/2007
Sat	Sat	02/20/2010
Sat	Merc	02/23/2013
Sat	Ketu	11/03/2015
Sat	Ven	12/12/2016
Sat	Sun	02/12/2020
Sat	Moon	01/24/2021
Sat	Mars	08/25/2022
Sat	Rahu	10/04/2023
Sat	Jup	08/10/2026
Merc	Merc	02/20/2029
Merc	Ketu	07/20/2031
Merc	Ven	07/16/2032
Merc	Sun	05/17/2035
Merc	Moon	03/23/2036
Merc	Mars	08/22/2037
Merc	Rahu	08/19/2038
Merc	Jup	03/07/2041
Merc	Sat	06/13/2043
Ketu	Ketu	02/20/2046

Rasi Chakra positions

Planet	Degree	Sign	Nakshatra
Asc	03°53'	Sagittarius	Mula
Sun	06°29'	Gemini	Mrgashira
Moon	11°21'	Gemini	Ardra
Mars	15°35'	Virgo	Hasta
Mercury	15°21'	Taurus	Rohini
Jupiter	06°52'	Libra	Swati
Venus	02°03'	Taurus	Krittika
Saturn	21°53'	Virgo	Hasta
Rahu	20°28'	Gemini	Punarvasu
Ketu	20°28'	Sagittarius	Purvashadha

Step One - The Basic Information

The first thing to do after erecting the chart is to make a Rasi Chakra grid, so you can see at a glance how the planets relate to each other.

House	Sign	Ruler	Placed in	Sign	Disp
Asc/1st	3°53' Sag	Jupiter Rx	11th	06°52' Li	Venus
2nd	Capricorn	Saturn	10th	21°53' Vi	Mercury
3rd	Aquarius	Saturn	10th	21°53' Vi	Mercury
4th	Pisces	Jupiter	11th	06°52' Li	Venus
5th	Aries	Mars	10th	15°35' Vi	Mercury
6th	Taurus	Venus	6th	02°03' Tau	Venus
7th	Gemini	Mercury	6th	15°21' Tau	Venus
8th	Cancer	Moon	7th	11°21' Gem	Mercury
9th	Leo	Sun	7th	06°29' Gem	Mercury
10th	Virgo	Mercury	6th	15°21' Tau	Venus
11th	Libra	Venus	6th	02°03' Tau	Venus
12th	Scorpio	Mars	10th	15°35' Vi	Mercury

It is immediately obvious from the rasi grid that all the planets are ruled either by Venus or Mercury; the ascendant is ruled by Jupiter, which is placed in Libra, also ruled by Venus. When planets form such a stark pattern, it shows an individual who has some important destiny to fulfil.

Here are some other features of the rasi chart:
- Sun Moon and Jupiter are in mutual trines.
- Mars, Saturn, Venus and Mercury are in mutual trines.
- All the planets are placed in four houses - sixth, seventh, tenth and eleventh.

Planetary Grid

Planet	Sign	House	Element	Mode
Sun	06°29' Gem (Mercury)	7th	Air	Mutable
Moon	11°21' Gem (Mercury)	7th	Air	Mutable
Mars	15°35' Vi (Mercury)	10th	Earth	Mutable
Mercury	15°21' Tau (Venus)	6th	Earth	Fixed
Jupiter	06°52' Li (Venus)	11th	Air	Cardinal
Venus	02°03' Tau (Venus)	6th	Earth	Fixed
Saturn	21°53' Vi (Mercury)	10th	Earth	Mutable
Rahu	20°28' Gem (Mercury)	7th	Air	Mutable
Ketu	20°28' Sag (Jupiter)	1st	Fire	Mutable

From the rasi chakra and planetary grids we can summarise:

The Sun rules the ninth house and is placed in the seventh.

The Moon rules the eighth house and is placed in the seventh.

Mars rules the fifth and twelfth houses and is placed in the tenth.

Mercury rules the seventh and tenth houses and is placed in the sixth.

Jupiter rules the first and fourth house and is placed in the eleventh.

Venus rules the sixth and eleventh houses and is placed in the sixth.

Saturn rules the second and third houses and is placed in the tenth.

The **Rahu Ketu** axis is placed in the seventh/first house axis.

We can also see that the number of planets placed in the different elements and modes are:

Elements		Modes	
Water	0	Cardinal	1
Earth	4	Fixed	2
Fire	1	Mutable	6
Air	4		

You will see that earth and air energy dominate Prince William's chart. There is a complete absence of water, which rules emotions and feelings. The modes are dominated by six planets in mutable signs, which shows a changeable personality. His ascendant degree is in a fire sign.

Now we can fill in more of the picture by looking at the **nakshatras**:

Planet	Sign	Nakshatra	Ruler
Asc	Sagittarius	Mula	Ketu
Sun	Gemini	Mrgashira	Mars
Moon	Gemini	Ardra	Rahu
Mars	Virgo	Hasta	Moon
Mercury	Taurus	Rohini	Moon
Jupiter	Libra	Swati	Rahu
Venus	Taurus	Kritika	Sun
Saturn	Virgo	Hasta	Moon
Rahu	Gemini	Punarvasu	Jupiter
Ketu	Sagittarius	Purvashadha	Venus

......and the karmic axis:

Node	House	Sign	Dispositor	Placement
Rahu	7th	Gemini	Mercury	15°21' Taurus
Ketu	1st	Sagittarius	Jupiter Rx	06°52' Libra

Planets conjuncting Rahu - Sun and Moon
Planets conjuncting Ketu - None

The Gunas

Before we move on to the next step we also need to analyse which, if any, guna is predominant in William's chart - the Sagittarius ascendant is sattvic - pure and idealistic. This quality will be strong in his chart.

The Signs

Sattvic	Rajasic		Tamasic
Sagittarius -	Libra -	Jupiter	Virgo - Mars, Saturn
Asc and Ketu	Taurus -	Venus and Mercury	
	Gemini -	Sun, Moon and Rahu	

Most of the signs are rajasic: these people are always searching - for the truths, for happiness. They move between sattvic (idealistic, spiritual) and tamasic (materialistic and practical).

The Houses

Rajasic	Tamasic
1st house - Ketu. Asc	6th house - Mercury, Venus
7th house - Sun, Moon, Rahu	10th house - Saturn, Mars
	11th house - Jupiter

You will notice there are no planets placed in sattvic houses (4, 5, 9 or 12). The houses are either tamas or rajas. Tamas indicates somebody who is caught up in the practicalities of life, while the rajasic person works in polarities - searching for meaning by immersing themselves in either the sattvic world or the tamasic, by turns. I think we must remember here that William's sattvic ascendant (Sagittarius) will lead him towards more of an idealistic approach to life, regardless of the conflict within.

Step Two - Planetary Strengths

William has no planet placed in its sign of exaltation or debilitation. Most planets are placed above the horizon, so it shows that he has new karma to create, most of which will be connected with the public aspect of his life; inevitably this means his personal life will be neglected. A more positive aspect is that whatever dilemmas he may face internally, he will be more than happy to carry out the public duties which are part of his destiny as a future king.

The Sun

The Sun rules the ninth house and is placed in Gemini in the seventh, a neutral sign and house. No planet is considered to be good in the seventh house, in terms of marriage, as it indicates multiple relationships, but as the Sun rules the ninth house it will in this case be an excellent planet for William; it rules his good luck and fortune and is reasonably strong, so all will be well.

The Sun conjuncts Rahu and the Moon, which, as ruler of the eighth house will not have an easy relationship with the Sun. Also Rahu placed with the Sun creates karmic issues which are hard to get to grips with. (see the Karmic Axis).

The Sun's aspect to the first house from its position in the seventh is very good as the Sun is also the ruler of the auspicious ninth house (which also aspects his rising sign). This usually denotes a person of high calibre.

The Moon

The Moon rules the eighth house and is placed in the seventh. As a new Moon it is considered weak and as the eighth house ruler it will create problems wherever it is placed; the conjunction with Rahu, its greatest enemy, reinforces the Moon's weakness. In Gemini there are more difficulties as the ruler, Mercury, does not like the Moon. (See Mrigshira nakshatra for details of this.) The Moon aspects the first house too, which is not especially good for William, as it is aspecting the ascendant in its role of the ruler of the eighth house; this shows that William will undergo great turmoil in his life.

Mars

Mars rules the auspicious fifth and difficult twelfth houses and is placed in the tenth.

The mooltrikona of Mars is Aries (which is ruling the fifth), so it will give good results. Mars is placed in its enemy sign of Virgo, with Saturn, which usually provides a great challenge. It is considered to be in its Dik Bala in the tenth house so it is strong by location.

Mars aspects the first house with its fourth house aspect (from its position in Virgo), fourth house with its seventh house aspect (again from Virgo), and fifth house with its eighth house aspect. Mars is an auspicious planet for the Sagittarius ascendant, so its aspect will be beneficial. Mars here aspects its own house Aries, and thus enhances the qualities of the fifth house.

The Mars energy is very complex here and as it has both strengths and weaknesses it will have a neutral impact. William will need to focus his energy on his career and responsibility, which will be a struggle. Effectively his freedom-seeking Mars is being restrained by Saturn, so in terms of the physical pursuits of any normal teenager, he will have to be more restrained than most: Mars in the tenth will make sure that any misdemeanours are immediately obvious to the rest of the world. Its aspect to the fifth house endows William with the ability to take an intelligent interest in his work; being the house of children - and its ruler being in the tenth house - it is likely that any children will follow in his footsteps. However, any activity connected to Mars will have the Saturnian influence restraining it.

Mercury

Mercury rules the seventh and tenth houses and is placed in the sixth.

Mercury is a very important planet for William as it rules the signs occupied by half his planets; its strength or weakness will have a major impact. It is placed in the dusthana sixth house so it will have problems, but there is a positive side: the sixth house is an Upachaya house so Mercury will strengthen over time. Its energy is further enhanced as it is in Taurus with its friend Venus, which also rules the sign; it will however be generally neutral.

Mercury is the karaka planet for intellect, and placed in the sixth house it shows that William will work hard and become used to his responsibilities as time goes on, but is likely to worry inwardly that it is never quite good enough.

Mercury aspects the twelfth house, suggesting that William will be interested in the hidden and less accessible areas of life, but it also shows he is tempted to give up sometimes, at the height of his struggles.

Mercury changes from benefic to malefic, ruling the seventh and tenth houses showing struggles with intellectual issues in his life. Mercury is vargotamma, which means it is placed in the same sign both in the rasi chart and the navamsha chart. Vargotamma planets become especially strong.

Something to note here is that as the ruler of the seventh house of relationships, it will create problems by being placed in the sixth house of obstacles. William may become involved with someone who is not necessarily acceptable to the royal family or perhaps a person who lets him down emotionally.

Jupiter

Jupiter rules the first and the fourth houses and is placed in the eleventh, in the neutral sign of Libra.

Planets placed in the eleventh house become very strong; the fact that Jupiter is also retrograde adds to its strength, however retrograde planets can cause a weakness in the house they rule, and there is a strong past-life connection to consider. On the whole Jupiter is generally powerful and strong in William's chart.

Jupiter's aspects to the third, fifth and seventh houses are very beneficial. The ascendant ruler is always uplifting and here it aspects the ninth house ruler in the seventh house, enhancing William's luck factor; it also shows a direct connection between himself and his father, the ninth house representing his father and the first, himself. The Sun aspects the first house and Jupiter, the planet signifying himself, aspects the Sun - which shows the close relationship between father and son.

Venus

For Sagittarius rising, Venus is the most negative planet as it rules both the sixth and the eleventh houses, both of which could signify obstacles and disease in his life. It is placed in the sixth house which gives William the ability to deal with his problems with charm and calm judgement. Although Venus is a negative planet in this situation, it is placed in its own house, creating a Harsha yoga, which generally brings success and happiness. When a negative planet controls the energies of all the others (as it does in this case) its powers are first encountered as being very restrictive. In time, and through working at understanding its subtleties, William will gain in strength and maturity. It also indicates working for others and this yoga would powerfully show William's involvement in charities and work for the good of others. Venus (which rules most of the planets) adds strength to William's chart from this position. It shows a strong work ethic as well as the willingness to face difficulties in a charming and pleasant manner. Venus aspects the twelfth house, again showing William's desire to be alone, work idealistically, and sever his links with the material world.

Saturn

Saturn rules the second and third houses and is placed in the tenth. Saturn is placed in the house of its friend Mercury and in a house which gives it strength. Saturn is placed with Mars, the auspicious fifth house ruler, so this quality of Mars will enhance Saturn, but as the two planets have an inherently difficult relationship there will be a conflict with this placement. This particular configuration highlights the importance of the astrologer being able to make judgements and evaluate conflicting information.

Saturn aspects the twelfth house by its third house aspect (from its position in Virgo), the fourth house with its seventh house aspect and the seventh house with its tenth house aspect - all of which will create difficulties for William. The aspect to the twelfth house will cause problems with his feet, the fourth house is the aspect representing his mother, which in this case shows a loss and separation from her. Two natural malefics aspect this house, which further shows the problems his mother had to face as well as William's final separation from her through death. Please be aware that all similar aspects of Saturn and Mars do not necessarily indicate identical trauma. For the timing of the events indicated by this aspect we will later consider the dasha pattern and the planetary transits.

Step Three - Special Yogas

Anapha Yoga
Benefic planets are present in the twelfth house from the Moon. Both Venus and Mercury are in the twelfth house from Gemini: Venus is in its own sign of Taurus and Mercury, the dispositor of the Moon, is in its friend's house, so this is a strong yoga. Mercury is also vargottama (in the same sign in navamsha) and Venus is placed in the ninth house in the navamsha chart. Anapha Yoga indicates success but also surrendering the material aspects of life at a later date.

Vasi Yoga
Vasi yoga is formed by aspect from the Sun in the same way that the anapha yoga is from the Moon, and the same comments are applicable.

These two yogas add strength to William's Sun and Moon - there is both success and renunciation indicated with them. William will express himself in the public arena but will crave solitude, aloneness and spiritual pathways.

Papakartari to Moon
The Moon is hemmed in between Rahu and the Sun; this creates a papkartari yoga which will result in emotional difficulties for him; the Moon's signification of the mother in William's chart also indicates the unhappiness and difficulties she faced in her own life.

Vargottamma Mercury
Mercury is very strongly placed here as the dispositor of both the Sun and Moon - it is vargottamma and so will act like an exalted planet. Mercury is unhappy in the sixth house but at least it is with its friend Venus in the friendly sign of Taurus. In the navamsha chart it is placed in the ascendant with Mars. The Mars/Mercury

combination is a difficult one but here it creates another raja yoga combination of seventh and fifth house rulers.

Parivartana Yoga

This is created between the nakshatra rulers of Jupiter (Rahu) and Rahu (Jupiter) and is an indication of the subtle energies at work on William. His ascendant ruler is placed in Swati nakshatra which is ruled by Rahu, which is placed in Punarvasu, ruled by Jupiter; this represents a mutual reception between the nakshatra lords and further indicates his connection with the karmic axis. But Rahu is about ambition, achievement and experiencing life; this mutual reception between the two planets further enhances the fact that, whatever his inner conflicts may be, William will want to leave his mark on the world. He will be stronger than either of his parents.

Step Four - The Bhava Chakra Analysis

The Ascendant

Prince William's ascendant is at 3°53' in Sagittarius and ruled by Jupiter, which is retrograde and placed at 6°53' Libra in the eleventh house.

The Sagittarius ascendant is a fire sign, mutable and sattvic. William will have loads of energy, and no doubt be very active and dynamic, but mutable Sagittarius gives him a changeable quality. The sattvic guna indicates idealism and purity of thought and action which can be misunderstood in this material world. Jupiter has a neutral relationship with Venus. They are both teacher or guru but their audiences are very different - Jupiter is the teacher to the gods and Venus to the demons. This shows an inherent conflict within William but also the ability to deal with people at different levels of spiritual growth. He will have the ability to lead, advise and teach. Jupiter, the dispositor of the ascendant ruler is in the sign of balance - between spiritual and material, negative and positive - it is also the sign for judgement and detachment. Venus and Jupiter will pull him in two directions, but the Libran influence will help William learn to balance his inner and outer needs. Jupiter's position in the eleventh puts it in an upachaya house. Any planets placed here are enhanced.

On a spiritual level the eleventh house deals with the crown chakra and on the material level with the fruits of one's achievements - usually thought of in financial terms. William will be very focused on what he wants to achieve in life and will have ambitions beyond the normal expectations. A retrograde Jupiter indicates issues from the past that he may need to deal with and this could lead to some discomfort with his very public role; there is shy person reflected here with a tendency to retreat to his inner sanctum.

Jupiter is aspected by the fifth aspect of Rahu, which creates problems and a feeling of separation from others as well as further tying his life to the karmic axis. The Rahu aspect (through Jupiter's rulership of the fourth house) also shows William's sudden separation from his mother.

Jupiter is placed in its own navamsha of Sagittarius but in the eighth house, thereby creating sarala yoga. The eighth is a dusthana house and the ascendant ruler placed there in the navamsha chart indicates that William will face major loss in his life. As Jupiter also rules the fourth house in the rasi, it is another indication that the loss would be connected to himself and his mother.

A quick review shows that the negative planets for William are the Moon and Venus. Jupiter will always work well for him as it rules the ascendant. The positive planets are Mars, the Sun, Mercury and Saturn

The subtle energies of Prince William's ascendant nakshatra
Mula nakshatra is ruled by Ketu, the shadow planet, which indicates past-life knowledge. Mula is the nakshatra which shows the soul's final direction when it moves towards fulfilling its dharma or duty. It is a difficult nakshatra to be born into; it is here that the soul struggles to come to terms with its final journey towards spiritual realisation, and where it breaks away slowly from its earthly shackles. For William this shows the powerful experiences he will face during his life. The exact degree of his ascendant is a crucial degree of Mula which again shows loss or separation from mother.

Ketu is placed in the sign of the ascendant, Sagittarius. The rising nakshatra is ruled by Ketu and Jupiter; the ruler of his rising sign is placed in Swati, ruled by Rahu. You can see that William's

295

chart shows Rahu Ketu dominating - so the Law of Karma will be powerfully operational. Sagittarius is the sign which rules dharma or duty and I feel that William will have a strong sense of duty which may be at odds with his personal needs. He may be more willing to accept his personal duty than either of his parents were able to.

The Sudarshana chart - the Sun and Moon as the ascendant
It is interesting - and indeed necessary - at this point to compare the ascendant in William's Sun and Moon ascendant chart with that of his rasi chart. (In his case the Sun and Moon ascendant charts will be the same, as the luminaries are in the same sign).

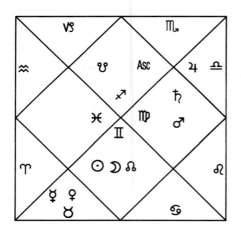

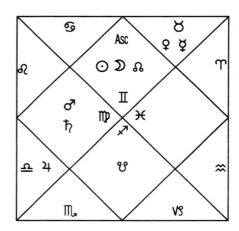

Rasi Chart   Sun and Moon Asc. Chart

The physical body, represented by the ascendant - is Sagittarius
The mental self, represented by the Moon - is Gemini
The eternal self, represented by the Sun - is Gemini

When we compare this and the rasi chart, we see that the Sun and Moon are both in Gemini, which is directly opposite his ascendant. It shows that William's physical and mental inclinations are directly opposite to each other. Again like his father, all the planets are in similar modes for similar houses. His rasi ascendant, and the Sun and Moon chart ascendants are all mutable, the second houses all cardinal and so on. This chakra shows that his physical needs conflict with the desires of his mind and soul. His surya and chandra lagna are ruled by Mercury, which is placed in the twelfth house from them; as we know, the twelfth house is concerned with loss and energies that are obscured from us (see the similarity of this with his father's Sudharshan Chakra). Again the Rahu Ketu axis plays an important part in William's life.

The second house - Capricorn, ruled by Saturn

The second house is ruled by Saturn which is placed in the tenth house of career, but the second is the house of childhood and family ties. With its ruler placed in the house of career and future life-direction, the pressure will be on William to adapt to this duty and responsibility. Capricorn is directly identified with duty and responsibility and facing one's karma however hard. Capricorn ruling the second house usually indicates accepting responsibility from an early age. Saturn is placed in its friend's sign of Virgo and in the tenth house where it is strong; the responsibility will be easier to deal with and from this point of view William will not resist the duties he has to carry out. Saturn is conjunct Mars (fifth and twelfth house ruler), a potentially difficult situation as we've already discussed. Saturn is placed in the third house of Cancer in the navamsha chart, which shows an indirect link to his brother - Saturn is well placed in the third house but not so in Cancer, which indicates the problems he has had in childhood.

The second house is also the house of wealth and its ruler being strongly placed with the ruler of the fifth house represents the heritage into which William was born.

Third house - Aquarius, ruled by Saturn

Aquarius on the third house cusp shows the qualities of William's brother. When Saturn rules a house it usually restricts the energy of the house, and here it suggests just one sibling, and as Aquarius is a male sign, a brother. Aquarius is the sign of strong, unusual people who want to make the world a better place for others. Watch out for Prince Harry's environmental agenda as he grows older. Saturn is also placed in the tenth house - again showing William's connection to his public life. Saturn is placed in the third house in the navamsha chart, again indicating the closeness of the brothers. As Saturn rules the house of brothers and siblings, it suggests that they will move away from each other as they grow older. Jupiter as the ascendant ruler aspects the third house with its fifth aspect, showing the love that William feels for Harry.

Fourth house - Pisces, ruled by Jupiter

Jupiter also rules the ascendant as well as the fourth house, Pisces. The fourth house indicates William's mother; when the same planet rules the ascendant and the fourth house it means that child and mother will be very similar in appearance. Looking at William now, you can see that he is the spitting image of his mother.

Unfortunately, when a benefic planet rules a cardinal house it becomes malefic, so William might find it difficult to deal with Jupiter's expansive energy. Jupiter is placed in the eleventh house, which is eighth from the fourth (representing his mother) as well as in the eighth house in the navamsha chart; this again emphasises the separation between them. The Moon, as significator of the mother, is also involved in an eclipse - showing a weakness in the relationship with her. This would usually just show separation or difficult relationship with your mother; only in extreme cases would it show early death. The fourth house is also aspected by two malefics, Saturn and Mars (seventh aspect from its position in Virgo), and Rahu, which aspects the fourth house ruler (by the fifth house aspect from itself). There is no benefic aspect to the fourth house. Mars is the significator of accidents, Rahu of sudden events and karmic issues, and Saturn of separation - receiving the aspect of these three planets is much worse than if they were placed in aspect with each other. When we examine the dashas and the transits to William's chart at the time of Diana's death, we will see how all this came to its sad conclusion. The difficult aspects also indicate his mother's unhappiness at this point in her life.

Pisces, as ruler of the fourth house, shows a mother who is mystical, emotional and changeable, and has a strong spiritual connection - all the factors which reflect Diana.

Fifth house - Aries, ruled by Mars

The fifth house of children is ruled by a male planet, Mars, which also aspects it. There is a further aspect by Jupiter as well as by Ketu. These aspects show the birth of two male children; Ketu's aspect is not considered good - so it may show a miscarriage for William's partner. (This would be virtually certain in a female chart.) The conjunction of Saturn with Mars can show either a delay in conceiving, or a separation from children - the separation may be due to them being sent to a boarding school. Mars is placed in a Taurus ascendant in the navamsha chart, which shows a strong link between William and his future children; he will want to be closely involved in their upbringing.

Sixth house - Taurus ruled by Venus

The sixth house is the most important area for William as it contains the two planets, Mercury and Venus, which control all the others in the chart. The sixth house is concerned with obstacles, healing, work, service to others - not a house usually connected with princes, but Prince William will surprise people. It is a very strong house: it has a harsha yoga (sixth house ruler in the sixth) which gives a strong personality and success, and Mercury, (which is vargottamma) the ruler of his seventh and tenth houses, is placed here with Venus, the karaka of relationships. This could indicate William becoming involved with either a foreign person (as discussed earlier) or a commoner, which could be very difficult for him considering the amount of media attention he has to put up with - and of course the reaction of the royal family - but William's strong sixth house shows his ability to deal with detractors using a mixture of charm and strength. Also his attitude towards others will be one of equality despite his royal birth. He will be the prince with the common touch.

Seventh house - Gemini, ruled by Mercury

If a mutable sign rules the seventh house, it usually indicates multiple relationships or the inability to settle in one relationship; this area could turn out to be at the root of William's problems. He has both the Sun and Moon, the significator of mother and father, placed here so the difficulties of his parents' marriage overshadow his own relationships. This is further highlighted by Rahu's presence. Its connection with foreigners also suggests that Prince William will surprise everyone by falling in love with someone from a another country - maybe black or Asian - which will cause an uproar or scandal.

The Sun as the ruler of the ninth house should enhance the seventh, but as we've already discovered, no planet is well placed here; the Sun's intense focus of heat and brightness can overwhelm a relationship and cause it to overheat. The Moon's connection as the ruler of the eighth house will bring further difficulties.

One good point about the seventh house is Jupiter's aspect to it, which will give him the ability to deal with difficult situations in this area, and may help to balance the seventh house aspect of Saturn which usually creates separation.

Mercury's position in the same sign in both the rasi and navamsha charts indicates its strength which likewise can suggest a strong relationship. It is placed in the first house in the navamsha, again showing William's need for a relationship.

Eighth house - Cancer, ruled by the Moon
The planet that rules the eighth house can create difficulties wherever it is placed. In a way it highlights the issues that we are born to learn from and overcome. Usually the difficulties are represented on a physical, material level. As we've already seen, Prince William's eighth house is ruled by the Moon, and placed in the seventh house of relationships it represents great challenges for him. On a spiritual level, these relationship issues will lead him to think deeply about life and its mysteries. The Moon is also conjunct the Rahu Ketu axis, further highlighting his connection to karma.

The Moon is placed in the ninth house in the navamsha chart, indicating the problems his father faces. When difficulties for the parents are highlighted in a chart, it doesn't necessarily mean that the person whose chart is being analysed is facing problems; in William's case it suggests that his father is having to deal with turbulence and unforeseen situations. Also the Moon is in Capricorn, an enemy sign.

The eighth house connection with longevity
I don't feel it would be appropriate here to anticipate the length of Prince William's life. This is a beginner's book and the key to judging longevity is complex and carries a lot of responsibility. It's

not that we are avoiding the issue - it is probably of great interest to most of us - but it is extremely important to explore the techniques fully and look at many, many charts before coming to a conclusion. The ancient sages in India felt that this deep knowledge should not be imparted without care and consideration; one needs the necessary wisdom and spiritual strength to deal with such a sensitive area. I would encourage you to explore this technique for yourselves.

Ninth house - Leo, ruled by the Sun

The ninth house and its ruler are the best house and planet for William. Here, the house is Leo and the ruling planet, the Sun: both indicate royalty, and show that William's royal birth is part of his good karma. We know that the placement of the ninth house ruler will highlight the house involved and, from its position in the seventh house, it indicates partnership with royalty or at the very least somebody who is powerful in his or her own right.

But here there is a contradiction - planets placed in the seventh house create problems for relationships regardless of the house they rule. It is considered that the seventh house should be without planets as their presence focuses the attention away from relationship issues. Apart from this, the Sun will help William; it aspects the ascendant (seventh house from itself) so it will enhance the good qualities of the ascendant and so of William himself. Here the ninth house and the Sun, both representing the father, show Prince Charles' careful nurturing and deep love for his son. The ninth house ruler of dharma is placed with the karmic axis Rahu Ketu, involved in an eclipse on the day of William's birth. This again indicates destiny playing an important part in his life; it is obvious that he has a role to play that is beyond that of the ordinary individual. (Read the sixth house details.)

Tenth house - Virgo, ruled by Mercury

When Virgo rules the tenth house it shows that intellectual stimulation is important in the pursuit of the career. Virgo aspires for the highest ideals but it is essentially a practical sign. Mercury rules the tenth and the seventh houses in William's chart, so it is responsible for the two houses we look at for career as well as relationships. This also shows that good relationships will naturally enhance the energy of the career. Mercury is vargottamma and placed in the sixth - an upachaya house of its friend Venus. It is a powerful Mercury. William's outward expression of his public life will be connected with service to others, and in the course of his duties he will not lose touch with ordinary people. In the navamsha chart Mercury is placed in the first house, so the ultimate responsibility for his public life will rest with himself.

William has both Mars, ruling the fifth and twelfth houses, and Saturn, the ruler of the second and third placed here, which makes for a highly energised house. There is no other aspect here. Mars as the ruler of the fifth house of children, placed in the tenth shows how William's children will be connected with his career. (Prince Charles also has a similar connection in his birth chart). Mars, as the ruler of the twelfth house in the tenth, shows a foreign connection in William's career, and also the desire to relinquish his public responsibilities. The mooltrikona for Mars is Aries, so it will behave more like a fifth than a twelfth house in William's life. Saturn rules the second house - childhood, speech and inherited wealth - all connected with his career.

Eleventh house - Libra, ruled by Venus

This is a very important house for William. It is also the house where his ascendant ruler is placed. The eleventh house connection is with profit from the fruits of our labour. This is essentially a house for material gains - and it indicates how we will earn our money. All planets are considered well placed here and become planets of gain, so Jupiter works well for William. In this position its dispositor, Venus, is also placed in its own house (sixth). This makes for a very interesting point in Prince William's chart: although he is of royal birth and doesn't work in the same way that you and I consider it, William's chart has strong connections with the two houses of hard work - the sixth and eleventh. I feel William will be very drawn to the ordinary way of life and will no doubt express himself in ways that are unconnected to his royal background. Libra ruling the eleventh house indicates social success for William.

Twelfth house - Scorpio, ruled by Mars

The twelfth house is the most difficult house to understand as it represents the last act of life where we merge the individual consciousness with the eternal. Here the loss is not purely physical but concerned with the consequences of giving up our individual identity; learning about physical isolation, working with astral energy. Scorpio is a very intense sign when it rules the twelfth house and its ruler is placed in the tenth house of outward expression and ambition. William is likely to have ambivalent feelings towards his royal duties and there will be times when he just wants to be left alone. Mars in Virgo shows the redirection of the active energy into an intellectual one. William will be very open about the deep insights gained from the Scorpio energy (the tenth house connection), possibly in a similar way to the manner in which his father has raised awareness for alternative medicine.

The placement of the twelfth house ruler also represents loss, which for William may be regarding his chosen ambition. This can be by giving up his royal duties or most probably letting go of his personal ambitions for his more public role as a prince. Also from its position in the tenth house, the twelfth house ruler aspects the fourth house of mother - further highlighting William's loss.

Step Five - The Navamsha Chart

The navamsha chart is studied alongside, and in the context of, the rasi chart; we start off by comparing the two. The navamsha ascendant ruler (Venus) is strongly placed in the rasi chart in its own sign (Taurus) but it is in the sixth house - the rasi ascendant ruler (Jupiter) is placed strongly in its own sign (Sagittarius) and in the eighth house in the navamsha chart. This connection between the sixth and eighth house energies show a deep conflict between William's outward duty (rasi) and his inner self (navamsha). But in a strange way there is a harmony as both these planets are placed in their own houses activating sarala and harsha yogas - suggesting ultimate happiness.

Yogas in the navamsha chart:

Parivatana yoga - Moon/Saturn in mutual reception between the third and ninth houses. This combination usually indicates people who follow in their father's footsteps.

Raja yoga - aspect Venus (first) and Saturn (ninth and tenth)

Raja yoga - aspect between Mercury (fifth) and Sun (fourth)

Raja yoga - conjunction between Mercury (fifth) and Mars (seventh) in the first house

Sarala yoga - Jupiter in Sagittarius in the eighth house

Sakata yoga - Jupiter and Moon in first/twelfth to each other.

Anapha yoga - Jupiter in the twelfth house from the Moon

Vesi yoga - Jupiter in the second house from the Sun

The qualities in William's navamsha chart further strength to his rasi chart.

Step Six - The Subtle Influence of the Nakshatras

By examining the nakshatras we can pick out the finer points that may well be missed in the rasi chart; they represent the soul factor in the chart. Here's a summary:

- Three nakshatras are ruled by the Moon - contributing the water element which is missing in his outer planetary placement. It brings an emotional intensity that is not obvious in the rasi chart.

- Three nakshatras are ruled by fire energy - Ketu, Mars and the Sun; the nakshatra rulers of the ascendant, Sun and Venus show a fire energy on the subtle level almost absent in the rasi chart.

- The ascendant nakshatra, Mula, is where the soul moves on the final part of its journey towards enlightenment. It is connected with the Muladhara chakra (the base chakra) where kundalini becomes activated.

- The Moon in Ardra, a nakshatra ruled by Rahu, shows a karmic aspect for William. Ardra shows a brilliant mind which looks deeply into esoteric aspects of life. The first dasha was Rahu, when he experienced the breakdown of his parents' marriage.

Step Seven - The Karmic Axis

Prince William has a notable karmic axis. The meaning of the trials and tribulations he faces will become clearer as he matures.

The first/seventh house axis shows that many aspects of himself (first house) and relationships both personal and public (seventh house) are ruled by the shadow planets.

Ketu in the first house often suggests a lack of self-confidence and the inability to accept yourself as you are. There is a very strong link with past lives which can show itself as a feeling of guilt - but for no obvious reason. Prince William can feel it as a restriction in his present life: the loss of his mother at a young age; the responsibility of being the second in line to the throne; the media interest in his every move, to name but a few reasons. Ketu in the first house also shows a tendency to retain feelings that should have been released. William will need to have an emotional 'clear-out' periodically otherwise he may find himself suffering physically or psychologically. Rahu is in the seventh house of relationships - already discussed in some depth and it also indicates the wider platform for his activities. Relationships are vital, but the same time a dissatisfaction with them makes him feel lonely - even when he appears to be with someone compatible.

William was born on the day of an eclipse. (The eclipse of the Sun took place at 12:07pm GMT). This would have a powerful prenatal influence on him. As the Moon is close to both the Sun and Rahu on his chart the new Moon shadow was obscuring the sunlight from the earth. People born during the eclipses usually have a powerful destiny to fulfil, and William's karmic issues will be played out in the first/seventh house axis. Whenever Ketu is placed in the ascendant, it indicates blocks brought forward from a past life which need to be worked out.

The Sun, as significator of the father, and the Moon as significator of the mother, are close to Rahu and Ketu, showing that William's karmic issues are connected to his parents. The Moon is afraid of Rahu, which causes fear, anxiety and distrust - any conjunction between them brings detachment, separation from, or loss of one's mother. The fact that the Moon eclipses the Sun gives some indication of his parents' problems. Diana, here represented by the Moon, was always considered to have eclipsed Prince Charles. The Moon is in a papakartari yoga - hemmed in by malefics (the Sun and Rahu), which shows the great unhappiness Diana suffered due to the Sun - the ninth house ruler (Prince Charles) and Rahu - the lord of karma. In hindsight we can see that the loss of his mother was indicated in William's chart. All three of them were entwined in the karmic axis here, and it is the most important aspect of William's chart. Also the Sun signifies the monarchy and the Moon the public - so William's destiny is linked to both.

Ketu will aspect the fifth, seventh, and ninth houses, and Rahu will aspect the eleventh, first and third houses. Rahu's aspect shows separation and Ketu's aspect shows accident and injury.

Rahu's aspect to the eleventh, first and third houses can show a separation from, or problems with his brother Harry, but again there is the positive aspect of Jupiter which smooths over any sibling rivalry when or if it happens.

Step Eight - How the Dashas Indicate Key Timings

We'll study the dashas for William to find out when the events indicated in his chart should occur. I only ever look at the first few dashas from the date of birth as I've found in my consultations that clients are more interested in what is happening now, rather than many years hence.

William's Dasha Periods

No	Maha-dashas	From	R/ship	Hse	Aspects	Conj
1	Rahu	21/6/1982	None	7th	11th, 1st, 3rd	S,M
2	Jupiter	20/2/1994	1st & 4th	11th	3rd, 5th, 7th	
3	Saturn	20/2/2010	2nd & 3rd	10th	12th, 4th, 7th	Mar
4	Mercury	20/2/2029	7th & 10th	6th	12th	Ve
5	Ketu	20/2/2046	None	1st	5th, 7th, 9th	
6	Venus	20/2/2053	6th & 11th	6th	12th	Me
7	Sun	20/2/2073	9th	7th	1st	M,R

The nakshatras of the dasha rulers:

Rahu	**Punarvasu** ruled by Jupiter, first and fourth house ruler	
Jupiter	**Swati** ruled by Rahu, placed in the seventh house	
Saturn	**Hasta** ruled by the Moon - the eighth house ruler	
Mercury	**Rohini** ruled by the Moon - the eighth house ruler	
Ketu	**Purvashadha** ruled by Venus - sixth and eleventh house ruler	
Venus	**Krittika** ruled by the Sun - ninth house ruler	
Sun	**Mrigsira** ruled by Mars - fifth and twelfth house ruler	

Looking further at William's dasha pattern, we can see the nakshatra influences at work. A study of the planets that rule them, and then the houses they rule gives us an idea of what the soul really desires during the dasha. There are two distinct patterns emerging:

The Rahu nakshatra is Purnavasu ruled by Jupiter (self) and the Jupiter nakshatra Swati is ruled by Rahu (seventh house). This influence will affect William very strongly in his first 25 years. Rahu is conjunct the Sun and Moon and Jupiter's nakshatra dispositor is also conjunct the Sun and Moon. The issues of his parents dominate his life.

In the second pattern, the next two dashas are dominated by nakshatras that are ruled by the Moon.

Saturn is in Hasta, ruled by the Moon. Its symbol is the palm of the hand, where the complete destiny of an individual is given. Hasta's guna is tamas and its motivation is moksha. Tamas is about intense involvement in materialism and moksha is concerned with giving up the self to merge with universal consciousness. Mercury is in Rohini - a nakshatra of desires, passion and comfort. The symbol of Rohini - the chariot - is the transport of royalty. The Moon rules the eighth house of power and intrigue and is placed in the seventh house of re-lationships. Saturn is in the tenth house, ruled by Mercury. The two dashas again show similarities on the inner and outer level. The issues likely to confront William will be of an intellectual nature as both the planets connected with the mind - the Moon and Mercury - are involved.

The First Dasha - Rahu from birth until 20/2/94

William's first dasha was Rahu, which eclipses both the Sun and the Moon on his chart. When we consider his parents' situation, this dasha clearly indicates that his parents were caught up in circumstances which were beyond their power to resolve. The eclipse of the Sun also suggests during this dasha his father would have felt somewhat overshadowed himself. The Rahu dasha with its karmic factors is usually difficult to face, especially as the first one. It highlights the seventh house as one of the main areas where William will have difficulties.

If you refer back to the dasha grid at the beginning of the chapter, you can see that William was born into a Rahu-Saturn bhukti. Rahu is said to act like Saturn: Saturn represents the physical restrictions and Rahu the psychological. Placed in the tenth house Saturn links the relationship aspects with William's career, ambition and public duties. Both the planets are related to karma which will have to be dealt with in this life. Quite a difficult start to life really, despite being born into material wealth.

The nakshatra of the ruling dasha is Punarvasu - which is ruled by Jupiter. The nakshatra indicates the soul connections at birth. Punarvasu deals with the transfer of knowledge from the spiritual to the earthly, and Jupiter as the true teacher has the responsibility to guide this process. The deep meaning of Punarvasu is the ability to live at different levels of astral consciousness; it gives great insight in William's chart into the two polarities - the royal and the common connections. Rahu will focus these two needs so that William uses the knowledge he has brought into this life. It will give him the ability to deal with all types of people, moving amongst them with ease.

We'll now look at other events in William's life so far, to see how they fit in with the dasha pattern:

The birth of Prince Harry, 15th September 1984 - Rahu dasha
From its position in the seventh house, Rahu has a ninth house aspect to the third house, so during Rahu's dasha, William would have gained a brother. Rahu is in the house ruled by Mercury, which is placed with the karaka of brothers, Mars, in the navamsha chart. There is an aspect of Jupiter on the third house as well, so we would have to look at the transit of Jupiter when it aspects the third house or Rahu. In September 1984 transiting Jupiter was at 10° Sagittarius, so it was making a seventh house aspect to the dasha ruler Rahu. Transiting Saturn, the third house ruler, was at 19° Libra - almost the degree of its exaltation and conjuncting natal Jupiter. Transiting Mars was in Scorpio casting its fourth house aspect on the third house (brothers), sixth house (Mercury - Rahu's dispositor), and seventh house Rahu - the dasha ruler.

His parents' troubled marriage:
In William's Rahu dasha both the Sun and Moon are conjunct the karmic axis. Signs of a troubled marriage.

9th December 1992 - The Prince and Princess of Wales' official separation was announced by the Prime Minister, John Major, in the House of Commons - Rahu dasha, Moon bhukti.

Charles and Diana were going through a very public break up. Although their separation was announced in 1992, the Rahu dasha and Moon Bhukti would have created immense fear in Diana as well as William, taking a huge emotional toll on him. The dasha suggests that at this time there was some kind of emotional separation from his mother as well. William could have suffered a real fear of loss and his way of dealing with it may have been by emotionally detaching himself.

The present dasha 20/2/94 - 20/2/2010
William is now going through his Jupiter dasha. To analyse the dasha properly you should consider:

- **The strength of the dasha ruler** - Jupiter is fairly strong. See Step Two - Planetary Strengths.

- **The relationship of the dasha ruler with the ascendant** - the dasha ruler is also the ascendant ruler. The main focus of this dasha will be on William himself - his needs, relationships, creativity, ideas, and higher learning.

- **The karaka of the dasha ruler** - Jupiter is the karaka for gurus, teachers and children. This is a good dasha for learning. William is too young as yet to have children, but when the Jupiter/Mars bhukti starts on 22/10/2006, expect the arrival of a male child - a male planet Jupiter aspects the fifth house, ruled by Mars.

- **The houses ruled by the main dasha ruler** - the first (self) and the fourth (mother).

- **The placement of the dasha ruler** - it is placed in the eleventh house from Sagittarius, the planet of the self, and the eighth house from Pisces - the sign ruling his fourth house and signifying his mother. So Jupiter is badly placed from its own sign, Pisces. It was during the Jupiter period that William lost his mother. It is also placed in the eighth house in the navamsha chart - a negative placement.

- **The houses the dasha ruler aspects** - it aspects the third (courage, siblings), fifth (children, creativity) and seventh (relationships).

- **The houses ruled by the bhukti ruler** - the bhukti at time of writing is Ketu, which began on 27/1/2001. Ketu rules no houses so it is analysed by its house position. It is placed in the Ascendant, so William's focus will be on himself. Ketu wants to move from the material side of life towards self-knowledge.

- **The relationship of the dasha with the bhukti ruler** - Jupiter is an enemy sign to Ketu and stands for tradition, while Ketu is eccentric and rejects tradition. Prince William has so far expressed his Ketu bhukti very well by taking a gap year from his studies at Edinburgh University to work as a volunteer in many unusual countries.

- **The placement of the bhukti ruler** - in the first house, which creates a conflict between his inner needs and his outer duties. Ketu is often described as a mendicant in classical texts, which is appropriate to Prince William's volunteer work in deprived areas.

- **The relative placement of the dasha/bhukti rulers** For Ketu we study the placement of Jupiter, its dispositor. Jupiter is well placed in the 11th house from Ketu, which will allow him to find an answer to his inner conflicts.

Bhuktis in the Jupiter dasha

In analysing the other bhuktis in Jupiter we have to look at the planets which have a difficult relationship with Jupiter, or rule difficult houses to see which will cause problems for him.

Bhukti Periods for William's Jupiter Dasha
Dasha Bhukti From Jupiter Jupiter 20/02/1994

Dasha	Bhukti	From	
Jupiter	Saturn	10/04/1996	Saturn is placed in the twelfth house from Jupiter
Jupiter	Mercury	22/10/1998	Mercury is placed in the eighth house from Jupiter
Jupiter	Ketu	27/01/2001	Ketu is placed in the third house from Jupiter
Jupiter	Venus	03/01/2002	Venus is placed in the eighth house from Jupiter
Jupiter	Sun	03/09/2004	The Sun is placed in the ninth house from Jupiter
Jupiter	Moon	22/06/2005	The Moon is placed in the ninth house from Jupiter
Jupiter	Mars	22/10/2006	Mars is placed in the twelfth house from Jupiter
Jupiter	Rahu	27/09/2007	Rahu is placed in the ninth house from Jupiter.

William's Jupiter dasha ends on 20/02/2010

From this table we can see that Saturn, Mercury and Venus bhuktis will be difficult for William as the planets are placed negatively from Jupiter in the natal chart. In Saturn bhukti he lost his mother. Mercury bhukti was a good time for studying at Eton College. Mercury being vargottama helped him to achieve good A-Level results (an unusual fact among royalty). Mercury's placement in the 6th house of service and democracy made Prince William decide not to be called by his royal title until he has finished his education. The Ketu bhukti enabled him to work as a volunteer and this period will be the most soul searching for him as well as the most satisfying emotionally. He will be working with issues that concern him and will learn to express himself in a novel way. He began his study at St. Andrews in September 2001 and appears to have temporarily rejected the royal way of life for that of an ordinary student.

The Venus Bhukti begins just as William is leaving his teens, so this period will be given great focus. Through Jupiter and Venus as the ruling planets of the dasha and bhukti (and their connection to different polarities of life), William will become aware of the duality of his purpose. The freedom of university life and his future role as heir apparent will cause conflict. He should be able to deal with it. I think what William wants to achieve is so idealistic that it will take time before the Royal Family (and the press), are ready for it.

The two bhuktis which will be very special for William are the Sun (the ninth house ruler) and Mars (the fifth house ruler). Both the planets are friends of Jupiter as well as being the best planets for a Sagittarius ascendant. The Jupiter-Sun dasha from 2/9/2004 will focus on a serious relationship, marriage, and his father. This could also be the time when William assumes responsibility of his duties. Jupiter-Mars can see the birth of a child for William - a male child - but the inter-relationship between Jupiter and Mars (Mars being placed in the twelfth house from Jupiter) also shows he will experience some kind of loss; he may have to give up his creative ambitions for the sake of his official duties.

The dashas need to be analysed with the help of the transits. It is always important to note the transits of the dasha ruler as it will enhance or detract from the quality of the dasha.

The decree absolute finalising his parents' divorce was given on 28th August 1996 - Jupiter dasha/Saturn bhukti

Saturn is a maraka planet for William, so during its bhukti William faced a deathlike situation, where he faced a new way of life. It showed serious separation issues for his parents, as Saturn is placed in the twelfth house from Jupiter, the dasha ruler the fourth house representing his mother is the eighth house (sudden transformations) from the ninth (his father).

The death of his mother - 31st August 1997 - Jupiter dasha/ Saturn bhukti

First let's examine the Jupiter dasha in relationship to William's mother. Jupiter rules Pisces in the fourth house - it is placed in Libra, which is the eighth house from its sign ruler. This is troublesome. Jupiter is placed in the eighth house of death and transformation in the navamsha chart. The beginning of Jupiter dasha/Saturn bhukti were going to be difficult for his mother. Pisces is aspected by Mars and Saturn, both great malefics - Saturn rules the twelfth house (loss, endings) from Pisces and Mars rules the second (maraka). They are placed in another maraka house - the seventh. Saturn is placed in the twelfth house from the dasha ruler Jupiter. Also Jupiter and Saturn do not have a good relationship with each other. The karaka of the mother - the Moon - is weak, as well as it being a new Moon involved in an eclipse. Transiting Saturn was in Pisces, also creating problems, and transiting Jupiter was in Capricorn in debilitation - Jupiter ruled both mother and son; transiting Mars was in Libra, again the eighth house from Pisces. There was an eclipse of the Sun the next day.

The Jupiter dasha/Saturn bhukti was undoubtedly the most difficult period in William's life.

Step Nine - Gochara (Transits)

The Lunar Transits
As we've discussed in the Nakshatra Chapter, we use a tarabala chart to indicate how the transits of the Moon affect us on a daily basis. The Moon's natal nakshatra in William's chart is Ardra. The nakshatras falling in columns 1, 3, 5, and 7 do not vibrate well with his birth nakshatra, . During the course of the lunar cycle these will not be particularly good for him. If other planetary conditions are difficult, a weak tarabala can aggravate it.

William's Tarabala grid is shown on the next page. If he wanted to plan his days for optimum effect, he would avoid the nakshatras ruled by Saturn, Ketu and the Sun.

William's Tarabala Grid

	1st Pariyaya	2nd Pariyaya	3rd Pariyaya
1. Janma	Ardra	Swati	Shatabishak
2. Sampat	Punarvasu	Vishakha	Purva Bhadrapada
3. Vipat	Pushya	Anuradha	Uttara Bhadrapada
4. Kshema	Ashlesha	Jyeshtha	Revati
5. Prayatak	Magha	Mula	Ashwini
6. Sadhana	Purva Phalguni	Purva Ashadha	Bharani
7. Naidhana	Uttara Phalguni	Uttara Ashadha	Krittika
8. Mitra	Hasta	Shravana	Rohini
9. Param Mitra	Chitra	Dhanishta	Mrigsira

The Time to Face Karma - William's difficult transits

It is usually the transits of Saturn that show the difficult periods in life. This period does not have to be negative if the role of Saturn and its nature of teaching lessons for personal growth is understood; the intention is, that in the process of overcoming the trials and tribulations strewn along the way we should (hopefully!) mature into better, deeper people.

Saturn was transiting Pisces, the fourth house in William's chart, during the divorce of his parents and the death of his mother. It was also aspecting the first house with its tenth aspect, and the tenth house (mother's maraka house) with its seventh aspect. Saturn's aspect is said to give more pain than its actual position.

Sade Sati is the most important of Saturn's transits. This happens when Saturn transits the twelfth, first and second houses from the Moon. It is impossible to over-emphasise the importance of this transit. The 7½ year cycle is at its most powerful when Saturn is directly over the Moon, but the beginning of it will indicate the issues that will become important. William has not faced Sade Sati so far. He will experience it from 6/6/2000. It is important not to be afraid of Sade Sati; it is a period that forms part of your life experience and everyone has to face it sometime. You need to accept that there will be difficult periods and be prepared to deal with the issues as they arise - there is absolutely no point in trying to avoid them!

1st Sade Sati period

Dasha during Sade Sati

Starts:

(Saturn enters Taurus) 6/6/2000	Jupiter/ Mercury
Saturn conjuncts Moon in Gemini 23/7/2002	Jupiter/Venus
End (Saturn enters Cancer) 5/9/2004	Jupiter/Venus

William will experience his first Sade Sati between 6th June 2000 and 5th September 2004, and it is focused on his seventh house as that is where the Moon is placed. The main issue will involve partners and marriage issues, but during this transit Saturn will also conjunct the Sun, so there will be some redefining of his relationship with his father. The Moon is the karaka for the public and William may feel disenchanted with them; Sade Sati always increases stress. It will seem for a while that there is always some obstacle between William's ambitions and the achieving of them; it is a time of stress and tension, but by the end of Sade Sati he will have gained in wisdom, maturity and experience. After this he enters his Jupiter-Sun dasha, which will be very good for him; it shows success and happiness gained from facing up to the struggles of Sade Sati. Most of the bhuktis of the Sade Sati are difficult ones, so during this time he will also face most of the problems young people have to contend with on their way to maturity.

The Happy Transits

Jupiter's transits herald happier times for Prince William, promising romance, marriage, birth of children, with achievement of desires and ambitions.

Romance will definitely be in the air when William experiences the first dasha or bhukti of the seventh house ruler, or the planets placed there; also when Jupiter aspects the seventh house ruler, seventh house, or Venus, the karaka for relationships.

Another happy phase in terms of relationships is likely to be when Jupiter moves into Taurus on 3/6/2000 it will conjoin the seventh house ruler (Mercury) and its karaka (Venus). Here the dasha is still Jupiter-Mercury. This indicates a more serious relationship and it may be the first time the public are allowed to meet his girlfriend. Jupiter then transits through the seventh house, further strengthening relationships.

Sometimes a happy transit overlaps with a difficult one, as in William's case. In 2000 both Jupiter and Saturn will be in Taurus, creating both restrictions and opportunities. It is the astrologer's job to weigh up the effects.

Eclipses and Prince William

Prince William has a strong connection with eclipses: there was a solar eclipse at 12.07 GMT on the day of his birth and there was also a lunar eclipse (sixth July) and a solar eclipse (20th July) in the month after his birth. In her Panorama interview (BBC Television 20th November 1995), Diana said that the seeds of her unhappiness were sown in the depression which followed Prince William's birth. This is shown in his chart by the three eclipses taking place on the karmic axis. The eclipse connection doesn't end here. William has since experienced many eclipses closely conjunct his planets; they serve to highlight the influence of these mysterious forces as agents for the laws of karma.

You will notice that the eclipses regularly contacted William's planets to the exact degree; this is a most unusual pattern. The contact and the influence on various planets was further highlighted as the dashas he experienced from birth are also connected to the nodal axis - Rahu dasha until 20/02/94, followed by Jupiter, which is placed in Swati, a Rahu nakshatra.

Here are some of the important eclipse dates:

Date	Type	Degree	Planet conj/opp
30/12/1982	Solar	14° Gem 49'	Moon/Rahu
25/06/1983	Lunar	09° Sag 36'	Conj. asc
			opp Sun/Moon
20/12/1983	Lunar	03° Gem 58'	Sun
30/05/1984	Solar	15° Tau 48'	Mercury
24/4/1986	Lunar	10° Lib 23'	Jupiter
03/10/1986	Solar	16° Vir 36'	Mars
29/03/1987	Solar	14° Pi 37'	opposite Mars
07/10/1987	Lunar	19° Pi 40'	opposite Saturn
21/12/1991	Lunar	05° Gem 18'	Sun
30/06/1992	Lunar	15° Gem 11'	Moon/Rahu
09/12/1992	**Solar**	**24° Tau 25'**	**in the 6th house**
29/11/1993	Lunar	13° Tau 16'	Mercury
18/11/1994	Lunar	01° Tau 54'	Venus
24/10/1995	**Solar**	**06° Lib 25'**	**Jupiter**
04/04/1996	Lunar	20° Vir 42'	Saturn
17/04/1996	Solar	04° Ar 23'	Opposite Jupiter
24/03/1997	Lunar	09° Vir 46'	Mars
02/09/1997	**Solar**	**15° Leo 45'**	**in the 9th house**
			trine Mercury

I've picked out some of the more obvious ones, as an example of just how important the eclipses are in a chart:

9th December 1992 - Prime Minister John Major announced the separation of The Prince and Princess of Wales.

24th October 1995 - about a month before Diana's famous interview for the BBC, there was a solar eclipse on the exact degree of William's moon indicating far-reaching changes were in store for him. The BBC interview directly led to the Queen writing to the Prince and Princess asking them to consider divorce.

There was a solar eclipse on the **2nd September 1997** at 00:03 GMT, two days after Diana's death - in the ninth house of his future dharma, again underlining the changes that were happening in his life.

Conclusion

You can see from William's chart how important themes show up time and time again, especially when considered using the wide range of techniques we have at our disposal - each adds its subtle hue to the overall picture. William's birth on the day of the eclipse shows that he is an important factor in the changing face of the Royal Family, and the strength of the sixth house lends dedication to his work and the ability to communicate at all levels - this will be of vital importance as the monarchy faces an uncertain future. The strongly intellectual influence of Mercury will ensure that William takes an active interest in planning his future role, adapting to both his own needs and those of the public. It will be interesting to see how he develops in the coming years.

Everybody has some drama in their chart. I chose somebody well-known for the chart interpretation, but as you do more charts for yourselves you will see that each one has a complex story, regardless of fame or wealth. I am constantly humbled by the problems my clients bring to discuss, and even more so when, having allowed astrology to give some insight, they leave with the feeling that they can cope. It is indeed a privilege to be able to help. Go forth and do as many charts as you can!

The Final Word

'Hari Om. Here in this city of Brahma is an abode, a lotus flower: within it is a small space. What is within this space should be sought, for that is what we want to understand.'

'So far the space extends within the heart. Within it are both heaven and earth, fire and air, sun and moon, lightning and the stars. Whatever is there of him in this cosmos and whatever is not, all that is contained within us.'

A few shlokas from Chandogva Upanishad VIII 1.2

These profound shlokas - hymns - from the Chandogva Upanishad sum up our search as human beings for answers that lie within us, rather than in the outer world. It is this search that has brought you to the science of Jyotish. As with all knowledge, there is no easy route to understanding, and those of you who really want to learn will have to study hard and with great persistence. This book is meant as a beginners guide to inspire you and to encourage you to continue the search within.

On a practical level the only way you can progress is by looking at many, many charts, and using the precious information gained to unravel the language of the stars. A word of caution: you are privy to knowledge that can have a real impact on another's life - use it wisely and kindly.

Finally, this book is my gift to you, all those who are aspiring to learn more. I was at a crossroads in life when I discovered Vedic astrology, and it has helped me greatly. Hopefully this book will also help you towards a better understanding of yourself, and true happiness. The information contained here is gathered from the ancient texts of India; the knowledge is very profound and deep. If there are any mistakes in presenting this material of my forefathers, then it is entirely mine.

Peace and Happiness

Komilla Sutton
January 1999

Appendix

Schools and Organisations

American Council of Vedic Astrology (ACVA)
PO Box 2149
Sedona, AZ 86339
Tel: (520) 282 6595   Email acva@sedona.net
The Institute of Vedic Astrology also operates from this address. For
course information contact Dennis Harness at DMHarness@aol.com

British Association for Vedic Astrology (BAVA)
1 Greenwood Close
Romsey
Hants
SO51 7QT
Tel: + 44 (0)1794 524178   Website www.bava.org

Dirah Academie
Brunostraat 64B
NL 5042 JA Tilburg
The Netherlands
Tel: + 31 13 463 5468

Indian Council of Astrological Sciences
64 Gowdiamutt Road
Royapeeta
Madras 600 014
India

Northeast Institute of Vedic Astrology and Studies
854 Brock Avenue
New Bedford MA 02744
Tel 1 508 990 7898   Email crystalx@ici.net

NW Institute of Vedic Sciences
7212 Woodlawn Avenue NE
Seattle, WA 98115
Tel: (206) 525 2229

Computer Software

Shri Jyoti Star Software
Shri Source, Barn Cottage
Brooklands Farm Close
Kilmington, Devon
EX13 7SZ
England

Email   Andrew@vedicsoftware.com
Website   www.vedicsoftware.com

Goravani Jyotish
211 Crest Drive
Eugene, OR 97405 USA
Tel 1 541 485 8453

Email vrajesvari@aol.com
www.Goravani.com

Further Reading

Ancient Hindu Astrology for the Modern Western Astrologer, by James Braha. Miami: Hermetician Press 1986.

Astrology of Death by Richard Houck. Gaithersburg, MD: Groundswell Press 1997.

The Astrology of the Seers by David Frawley. Salt Lake City: Passage Press, 1990.

Eastern Systems for Western Astrologers by Armstrong, Braha, DeFouw, Erlewine, Flaherty, Houck, Grasse and Watson. York Beach: Samuel Weiser 1997.

Esoteric Principle of Vedic Astrology by Bepin Behari, Salt Lake City: Passage Press, 1992

Fundamentals of Vedic Astrology by Bepin Behari. Salt Lake City: Passage Press, 1992

Hindu Astrology Lessons - 36 Teachers Share their Wisdom, ed. by Richard Houck. Gaithersburg, MD: Groundswell Press 1997.

How to Judge a Horoscope, by B.V. Raman. Bangalore, India: IBH Prakashana 1981.

Light on Life - An Introduction to the Astrology of India, by Hart DeFouw and Robert Svoboda. London: Penguin Arkana 1996.
Myths and Symbols of Vedic Astrology, by Bepin Bihari. Salt Lake City:

Passage Press, 1990. Now out of print but worth searching for.

Vedic Astrology - A Guide to the Fundamentals of Jyotish, by Ronnie Gale Dreyer. York Beach, Maine: Samuel Weiser 1997.

Reference Texts

Brihat Parasara Hora Sastra, translated by G.C. Sharma. New Delhi, India: Sagar Publications, 1991. All students of vedic astrology should have a copy of this.

How to Study Divisional Charts* (illustrated) by V.K. Choudhry. New Delhi: Sagar Publications 1992.

Kalprakshika: Translated by N.P. Subramania Iyer. Asian Educational Services (no date given).

Lahiri's Indian Ephemeris of Planets' Positions* (published yearly). Calcutta: Astro-Research Bureau 1997.

Phaladeepika by Manteshwara. Translated by Dr. G.S. Kapoor Ranjan Publications, 1991.

Varaha Mihira's Brihat Jataka translated by Swami Vijnananda. Oriental Books Reprint Organisation, 1985.

* These books were used as reference guides to produce the tables shown in the Varga and Dasha chapters.

Good translations of the Bhagawat Gita, Rig Veda, and the Upanishads are all available from the Penguin Classics series.

Glossary

Aditi   Eternal space.

Agni   Fire.

Antar dasha   Also known as a bhukti. It is a sub-period of a dasha.

Artha   Purpose, objective; material goals.

Atma   The soul and self.

Atmakaraka   The astrological indicator of the soul and the self.

Ayanamsha   The difference in degrees between the sidereal and tropical zodiacs.

Ayurveda   The Vedic science of medicine.

Benefic   A planet which naturally brings good results.

Bhava   The houses of the astrological chart.

Bhukti   A planetary sub-period within a dasha (also known as antar dasha).

Brahaspati   Jupiter.

Brahma   The creator, the cosmos.

Buddha   Mercury.

Buddhi   The intellect.

Chakra   Wheel, also a name for the natal chart.

Chakras   Energy centres.

Chandra   The Moon.

Chandra lagna   The chart showing the Moon as the ascendant.

Dasha   Directions, planetary periods.

Dhanus   Sagittarius.

Dharma   One's way of life, or duty as seen in the four functions of life described in Hindu philosophy.

Dik bala   Directional strength of the planets.

Dosha   Body type or humour - used in ayurveda.

Dusthana house   6th, 8th or 12th house, considered unlucky or inauspicious.

Ganesh   The Hindu god of astrology.

Gochara   Transits of the planets.

Graha   Planet.

Guna   Mental quality.

Guru   Jupiter.

Jyotish   The Sanskrit name for Vedic astrology, the science of light.

Kama   Passion, desire, one of the four functions of life according to Hindu philosophy.

Kanya   Virgo.

Kapha   The water humour - ayurvedic body type.

Karaka   Significator.

Kartaka   Cancer.

Kartika   Another name for Mars.

Karma   Action. On a more subtle level it represents the actions of our past lives.

Kendra   The cardinal houses.

Kumbha   Aquarius.

Kundalini   The latent power within us - represented by the coiled snake.

Lagna   The ascendant.

Malefic   A naturally inauspicious planet.

Mahadasha   A major planetary period.

Makara   Capricorn.

Manas   The mind.

Mangal   Mars.

Mantra   A combination of sacred sounds used for meditation.

Mesha   Aries.

Mina   Pisces.

Mithun   Gemini.

Moksha   Liberation, the soul breaking away from the cycle of life and death to find eternal happiness.

Mooltrikona   Special degrees where planets become strong.

Nakshatra   The name given to a group of stars. Vedic astrology uses 27 of them.

Navamsha   The 9th divisional chart.

Nirvana   Another name for moksha. Spiritual liberation.

Om   Sacred mantra.

Pitta   The fire humour - ayurvedic body type.

Prakriti   Nature, the female principle.

Purusha   The male principle, Atman.

Rajas   Action, search and agitation. Quality of one of the gunas.

Sattva   Purity, truth. Another quality of the gunas.

Shani   Saturn.

Shukra   Venus.

Simha   Leo.

Surya   The Sun.

Surya lagna   A chart showing the sun as the ascendant.

Tamas   Darkness, laziness, earthly attachments. One of the qualities of the gunas.

Triguna   Containing all three gunas.

Trikona   The trinal houses, 1st, 5th and 9th.

Tula   Libra.

Upachaya   The growth houses.

Vargas   Divisions, also used for the 16 divisional charts used in Vedic astrology.

Vargottamma   When planets are in the same sign in the natal and navamsha chart.

Vata   Body humour related to air - used in ayurveda.

Vrishabha   Taurus.

Vrishchika   Scorpio.

Yoga   In astrology it refers to a planetary combination. It is also a physical discipline which combines mental and physical exercises. Spiritual practices.

Index

K

kalpurusha 74
Kama 2
Kamadeva 38
Kantaka Shani 232
kapha 76
Karakas 95
Karma 4
Karma Phal 10, 188
Karmic Axis 55
karmic relationship 68
karmic restriction 183
karmic retribution 48
kendras 94, 266
Ketu 51, 52, 174, 186, 198
  and Jupiter 68
  and Mars 67
  and Mercury 68
  and Saturn 69
  and the Moon 67
  and the Sun 66
  and Venus 69
  conjunctions 66
  past life connection 66
Krishna 88, 204
Krishna paksha 36
Krittika 30
Krittikas 38
kriyamana karma 5, 124, 152
Kshema 229
Kumbha Mela 235
kumbhaka 90
kundalini 55, 62, 141

L

lagna 96
Lagna Chart 281
lagna ruler 97, 105
  in the eighth house 107
  in the eleventh house 108
  in the fifth house 106
  in the first house 105
  in the fourth house 106
  in the ninth house 107
  in the second house 105
  in the seventh house 106
  in the sixth house 106
  in the tenth house 107
  in the third house 105
  in the twelfth house 108
Lahiri 11
Leo 30, 82
Libra 84
longevity 141
lotus 196
luminaries 17

M

maha dasha 217
Mahurata 169
male signs 75
malefic 16, 24, 29
Mandara 53
maraka 95
marriage 48, 73
Mars 38, 78, 81, 82, 86, 90,
177, 179, 191, 196, 204
meditation 163
Mercury 80, 83, 92, 184, 197, 209
millionaires 193
Mitra 197, 229
moksha 2, 163, 167, 174
moksha karaka 80
mooltrikona 20
Mrigsira 38
mrityusthana 3
mutable signs 75
mutual reception 268

N

Naga Vasuki 53
Nagas 184
Naidhana 229
nakshatra
  Anuradha 196
  Ardra 180
  Ashlesha 184
  Ashwini 174
  Bharani 175
  Chitra 191